Divine LANDSCAPES

A Pilgrimage through Britain's Sacred Places

✠

RONALD BLYTHE

Photograph opposite the title page is of Durham Cathedral. Photograph on
page 8 is of St Govan's Chapel, Pembrokeshire (Janet and Colin Bord)

By the same author

A Treasonable Growth	*Akenfield*
Immediate Possession	*Aldeburgh Anthology*
The Age of Illusion	*The View in Winter*
Writing in a War (ed.)	*From the Headlands*
William Hazlitt: Selected Writings (ed.)	*Collected Short Stories*
Word from Wormingford	*Private Words* (ed.)

Text © Ronald Blythe 1986 and 1998

Photographs © Olive Cook

First published in hardback in 1986 by Viking,
a division of Penguin Books Ltd.

First published in paperback in 1998 by the Canterbury Press Norwich
(a publishing imprint of Hymns Ancient & Modern Limited
a registered charity)
St Mary's Works, St Mary's Plain
Norwich, Norfolk, NR3 3BH

British Library Cataloguing in Publication Data

A catalogue record for this book is available
from the British Library

ISBN 1-85311-194-5

Printed in Great Britain by Biddles Ltd, Guildford and King's Lynn

For Alan Cudmore

Contents

Introduction

Essentially, this is my walk-book. These walks began during boyhood and have wandered on somewhat haphazardly ever since, the only difference being that the youthful excursions were informed by local legends and historical novels, and the later ones by poetry, natural history and history proper. Also, it is is only fair to add, that many of my early wanderings involved a heavy Rudge bicycle as well as long hikes in East Anglia.

Like many children I was often drawn to the morbidity of certain places, one of which was marked by an obelisk on Aldham Common. Without knowing exactly why it stood there a mile or so outside Hadleigh, I did know that it rose on the spot of a terrible bonfire long ago when they burned the rector. When I put my hand through the rusty railings to touch the stone, it would sometimes feel warm where the sun had caught it. It was ages before I was interested enough to become properly informed about what happened here. The obelisk had actually been erected during the early nineteenth century by Father Hugh Rose who had convened the Hadleigh Conference which in turn had begun the Oxford Movement. Nor could I have possibly imagined that a descendent of the burnt man, Rowland Taylor, would have been the organist of the little church just below my farmhouse before he was killed in the Western Desert, aged twenty-four. During my early explorations, what I needed was a kind of exuding of the emotion of a particular spot, not its facts. What I went to Aldham Common to experience was something akin to what I felt where we, my brothers and sisters and myself, had buried a swallow. Quite the most evocative site for these feelings was the grave by the side of the Newmarket road which to this day is never without wild flowers or tinselly offerings. It is that of a shepherd boy, or a gipsy boy and when I was a child it was protected by bent willow branches. It was then said that he had been wrongly hanged for theft. How I mourned him! I suppose because at that time I had no one else to mourn. The smart Newmarket traffic sped past him and the local roadman kept a fatherly eye on him.

Walking confirms all sorts of facts as one begins to grow up and gets the hang of landscape, although it would be many years before it occurred to me that, among so much else, we in this country live in an ancient gazetteer of prayer and worship. Most societies do, of course, though with varying degrees of recognition. Britain's natural contours are drawn all over with religious symbols and references, most of them Christian, though many from earlier faiths. There is hardly a field or hill, let alone a village or town, which cannot be read in religious terms. Architecture and plants, weather and views, creatures and stones, seasons and roads, rivers and soils, gardens and forests, skies and shores, 'all that is', as Julian of Norwich summed it up, are doubly immersed in the sacred and in the scientific. In an old country where everything from a hut to the kingdom itself was once placed under divine protection, a complex underlying 'holy land' is only to be expected. It was to visit this holy land, if only peripherally — for it is extensive country — that these walks were made.

Having pointed the reader in this direction, he is at liberty to branch out where he likes. Take any turning. Many find their own parish so rewarding in this respect that they do this walk intensively and give no more than a glance to what lies further afield. Yet, as does Rowland Taylor's martyrdom site on Aldham Common, Suffolk, a parochial 'holy land' often ignores local boundaries and has the widest connections. All the same, an ancient parish church or a more recent chapel, meeting house or citadel, and one may now add mosque, are the home base for most of us of a divine cosmos.

Turned out of Paradise, the safe garden, for preferring a God-inspired intelligence to mindless bliss, Man and Woman, in John Milton's sublime ending to his great allegory, though wretched at having disobeyed their Creator, are far from defeated.

Som natural tears they drop'd, but wip'd them soon;
The World was all before them, where to choose
Their place of rest, and Providence their guide:
They hand in hand with wandring steps and slow,
Through Eden *took their solitary way.*

They were setting out to found the first village. Their God, though no longer easy and intimate, but protective, would lead them to its site. Their son would build the first city in the land of Nod, east of Eden and call it Enoch after his own son. This story and that of the Redemption have made fascinating marks on our landscape. By writing out of their ethos, poets from Caedmon to Seamus Heaney and R S Thomas have reasserted the sacred in our local scene.

Alan Ecclestone in his book *Yes to God* deplores the Church's long refusal to count certain Christian writers of genius among the saints — unless they happen to have been executed, of course. He writes

> William Blake, artist and poet, finds no place as yet among those commemorated in our churches as prophets and teachers and lights of the world in their several generations. But neither do Shakespeare and Milton, Keats and Wordsworth; nor are the great novelists remembered for glorifying God or helping mankind. Our notion of saints and confessors is strangely narrow. Our spiritual life is the poorer for it. The absence of any such names points to a disastrous split in our thinking about our life towards God . . . Our spirituality has hardly yet touched upon exploration of the way we call Christ.

I had long shared these views and have been equally depressed by the near-meaninglessness of some of the names which revolve through the Church's year. But since Ecclestone's protest I have noticed a change. In my 1998 lectionary I see the dates for remembering George Herbert, Julian, William Tyndale, Nicholas Ferrar, John of the Cross — sparse enough saints within literature, but they make a beginning. The omissions remain great. Quite early on in my walks to

Christ-marked places I was including the territory of botanists, the homes of writers and artists and composers, the visionary heights such as George Fox's Pendle Hill in Lancashire, and the countryside of the English mystics Rolle and Hilton, and the unknown author of that strange master-piece *The Cloud of Unknowing*. When, for the purpose of this book, a friend and myself set out to explore the flat fields near Bedford to discover where John Bunyan lost — and found — himself in *Grace Abounding*, arguably the finest English Christian autobiography, we were amazed to discover that they could be found as easily as the track down to my old house, once we had found the initial direction. This and the landscape of *Pilgrim's Progress* which Vera Brittain had mapped out just before the last war.

And so it has often been with some poet or storyteller in hand that I have arrived at a consecrated scene. In *Divine Landscapes* I have limited my walks to my most personally understood territories, those of men and women who have sought for God with a pen in their hands. In so doing I have journeyed very little into what is virtually a limitless land. Ever since I was a child I have sensed my impermanency in scenes which, compared with human transience, are, as the psalmist said, everlasting. Here and there, now and then, a poet, a liturgist, a novelist, a hymn-writer, an allegorist, makes a few miles of often quite ordinary countryside his, and it is towards these that I have over the years often directed my steps. Once I have decided on a 'way' I have been surprised by the lavishness of a particular writer's map references.

RB
January 1998

ACKNOWLEDGEMENTS

Many friends have assisted me in these wanderings and writings but I owe a particular debt to Cherida Campion, Librarian of the Julian Library, Norwich, Libertad Cabielles, Olive Cook, Alan Cudmore, Allan Freer, Jane Garrett and Alan Webster, Dean of St Paul's. I am also most grateful to three friends who helped me with extra photographs, Charles Hall, Ursula Hamilton-Paterson, and the late Kurt Hutten, and to the Francis Frith Collection.

The author would like to thank the following for granting permission to quote from copyright material:

For Kevin Crossley-Holland's translation of 'The Husband's Message', Deborah Rogers Ltd; for extracts from 'Four Quartets' and 'The Waste Land' from T.S. Eliot's *Collected Poems 1909–1962*, Faber & Faber Ltd, and in the USA Harcourt Brace Jovanovich, Inc.; for 'Tinder' from Seamus Heaney's *Wintering Out*, Faber & Faber Ltd, and in the USA Farrar, Straus & Giroux, Inc.; for 'The Priest' from R.S. Thomas's *Selected Poems 1946–1968*, Granada Publishing Ltd; for an extract from Andrew Young's 'A Traveller in Time' from *The Poetical Works of Andrew Young*, Martin Secker & Warburg Ltd.

1

*W*here Priests in Black Gowns were Walking Their Rounds

The parish as a unit of landscape is the most associative, contentious and distinctive personal region. It is venerated as the landscape of nativity and cursed as the landscape of limitation. Parish scenery pulls us this way and that. It is in control of us. Even the twist and turns of a city parish's streets have their special private direction for the born parishioner. In the country, where one can often see an entire parish from boundary to boundary, one can also often see one's entire life. It is comforting – and painful. For those who have remained in the same place a parish is not an address, it is somewhere you don't need one. But if one moves away after only a few formative years there is no severing the umbilical link that feeds one with its particular parochialism. One of the great difficulties experienced by a priest is that his flock never really understands that their parish can never be his – not in anything like the sense in which they possess it. Unless, as frequently happened at either end of Christian parish history, he happened to be a son of the village. Medieval farmer's son, Victorian squire's son, there is a broken tradition of the local holy man taking charge of the local holy ground.

It used to be thought that Archbishop Theodore invented England's parochial system, laying out its honeycomb of small loyalties. But now we know that there was a pagan pattern of grouped agriculturalists with their holy hill, stream or sacred wood a thousand years before he came. Much of it must have been as faint as temple tracings on an aerial photograph when he arrived. Where it existed, he renewed it. Thanks to the Ordnance Survey and to the meticulous attention we give to the property deal, and to its role in law and administration, the

Celtic–Theodoran parish boundary was never in better shape. Up until the fourth century a parish was a diocese, but then it became just a fraction of a bishop's jurisdiction, to be cared for by his deputy, the priest. The lists of these priests often hang at the west end of churches and are, to me, as absorbing as the architecture. The enigmatic names have a compelling quality. All the way from Adam de Stacey 1302–42 to Canon Michael Parmenter, 1968– there is ample space for the parochial imagination. First, there are just names, then names and doctrines, names and ambitions, names and politics, then, gradually, names with faces. I am looking into the features of one of the latter now. It is 1898 and he stands smiling under the copper beech in the vicarage garden with thirty ladies in big hats. Contrary to most nineteenth-century photographs, there are a lot of smiles. They are now all dead but the garden, begun in the seventeenth century, still flourishes. It is a comparatively simple matter to enter an incumbent's scene from the Reformation onwards, but a theoretical one earlier.

Where did they live? Which, probably still existent, lanes and tracks did they plod to their ploughs between offices? The parish boundary below our church is the Stour, from whose rushes it takes its name. There would have been much carting of these up from the mill-race and the ford for lights and carpets, much fishing for the fasts, much willow-stripping for frails and other baskets, much humping of corn and flour, and much eyeing of what was taking place over the river in the water-meadows of the neighbouring village, which was as autonomous in its way as a city state. Miscreants, vagabonds and unmarried women about to give birth were hustled across such boundaries. Overseers saw to it that as few were 'on the parish' as legally possible. In the eighteenth century groups of parishes formed unions and built union houses to cope with the human debris, which was set to work for its keep. Society went to incredible lengths to make these shelters shameful and to be dreaded so that even those in the utmost want of a roof and assistance struggled frantically to avoid entering them. Many killed themselves rather than go to the 'house'. The identification of so much interference and control at the parish level from Saxon times to within living memory has blackened the name of charity. Almost the worst place an erring, or even a nonconforming, man or woman could

The Pre-Reformation Priest's House at Muchelney, Somerset

be was in their native parish. The pressures on them there were intolerable.

Alternatively – if rarely – such pressures created the saint, the artist and the poet. John Clare and Helpston, in which, for him, the going was as rough and finally tragic as any parish could make it, have become the ultimate triumph of the basic parochial experience. For Clare, the place which injured him most nourished him most. Not even Hardy has been able to reveal the spiritual primacy of the home patch as Clare did at Helpston. When Clare left his parish the universe tilted and his equilibrium with it. When they straightened it all out under an Enclosure Act he lost his way. His poetry is parish joy and grief, at its most articulate. He is the master of the vernacular of the individual village, able to put into language what the locals often feel or smell or hear or see but have no words for. A total taking-in of a parish's land by its more powerful residents shocked him. A village had always had its wastes; they were where men breathed. How could an Act of Parliament snatch his 'mores'?

> *Far spread the moorey ground a level scene*
> *Bespread with rush and one eternal green*
> *That never felt the rage of blundering plough*
> *Though centurys wreathed springs blossoms on its brow*
> *Still meeting plains that stretched them far away*
> *In uncheckt shadows of green brown and grey*
> *Unbounded freedom ruled the wandering scene*
> *Nor fence of ownership crept in between*
> *To hide the prospect of the following eye*
> *Its only bondage was the circling sky*
> *One mighty flat undwarfed by bush and tree*
> *Spread its faint shadow of immensity*
> *And lost itself which seemed to eke its bounds*
> *In the blue mist the orisons edge surrounds*
>
> *Now . . . Fence now meets fence in owners little bounds*
> *Of field and meadow large as garden grounds*
> *In little parcels little minds to please*
> *With men and flocks imprisoned ill at ease . . .*
> *These paths are stopt – the rude philistines thrall*
> *Is laid upon them and destroyed them all*
> *Each little tyrant with his little sign*

Shows where man claims earth glows no more divine
But paths to freedom and to childhood dear
A board sticks up to notice 'no road here'.

Forty years earlier George Crabbe was seeing off the false pastoral in a series of stunning attacks in its own couplet form. Its charming amorous pains were likely to be 'the only pains, alas' that a young shepherd never felt. So soon to be 'O'ercome by labour and bowed by time', men such as he might well be spared 'the barren flattery of a rhyme'. Crabbe's parish wilds, though botanically exquisite, are a disaster. They are the sterile fields of a Suffolk coastal village from which beer-sodden labourers are pressganged for the navy, and across which a sporting parson

A jovial youth, who thinks his Sunday task
As much as God or man can fairly ask

hunts the fox. The scene is the commonplace of a thousand sporting prints. The poor who inhabit Crabbe's parish are 'lost to life'.

Can poets soothe you, when you pine for bread,
By winding myrtles round your ruin'd shed?

He was still in his twenties when he wrote *The Village* and perilously close to the time when he too could have been lost in the parochial no-man's-land. Yet, the region glimmers for him with a grim beauty.

Lo! where the heath, with withering brake grown o'er,
Lends the light turf that warms the neighb'ring poor;
From thence a length of burning sand appears,
Where the thin harvest waves its wither'd ears;
Rank weeds, that every art and care defy,
Reign o'er the land and rob the blighted rye:
There thistles stretch their prickly arms afar,
And to the ragged infant threaten war;
There poppies nodding, mock the hope of toil;
There the blue bugloss paints the sterile soil,
Hardy and high, above the slender sheaf,
The slimy mallow waves her silky leaf;
O'er the young shoot the charlock throws a shade,
And clasping tares cling round the sickly blade.

Crabbe is the philosopher of the ecological dilemma, the adorer of wild flowers and the supporter of clean fields. The same might be said of him where people were concerned, for no one, not even now, has written about the toilers of the parish with such a tender strength and accuracy while, at the same time, indignantly longing for those social improvements which would eventually take them away from his gloomy interest and pity. His second book was to be *The Parish Register, Baptisms, Marriages and Burials*, a perfect format for his purpose, taken from the records locked up in the chest of every parish church. His late-eighteenth-century parishioners are a revelation: gardeners, readers – 'Learning we lack, not books' – gunshot bridegrooms, the rich, the destitute, an 'author rector' too busy writing to do much else, and his successor, an impressively saintly young clergyman to begin with, but soon to become a fundamentalist fanatic. Dibble the gravedigger buries them all. Thomas Hardy would take identical material and fill it out. In a Hardy novel the parishioners answer back in a way which disconcerts the reader, and makes him feel uncomfortable. Like Jane Austen, he uses a parish as a contained space in which, as in life, a group of people who know each other very well, and who are unconsciously conditioned by a shared background, are forced to cross and recross the same ground. Both novelists enjoy stirring things up by causing a 'foreigner' to arrive. If you live in a city a foreigner comes from another country, if you live in a village, he comes from five miles down the road. Jane Austen and Hardy intrude upsetting characters into the parish, sexually and socially enthralling men, like Mr Bingley, Frank Churchill and Sergeant Troy, and thrusting women who consider themselves above having to learn the local ways, such as Mrs Elton.

Jane Austen's parish pivots on a coolly amused Anglicanism in which Christianity is little more than a moral requisite, Hardy's on a sad and beautifully fragmented Bible and Prayer Book tradition in which the statements on salvation are worn to shreds. Their parishes are full of dance music. For Jane Austen the most spiritual destination a parishioner can head for is a gentleman's grounds, for Thomas Hardy the graveyard. Neither balk village frustration, boredom and longueurs. I once found myself writing about Jane Austen's parochial defensiveness. However dull a village in one of her novels was, every other place had to be inferior to it, London most of all. 'In London it is always the sickly season', declared old Mr Woodhouse in *Emma*. When that parish paradigm, Mr Knightley, is emotionally disturbed he has to go to London 'to learn to be indifferent'. For Mr Elton, on his way there to get Harriet's portrait framed, London is the destination of fools. To leave Highbury is to leave paradise. Hardy had mixed feelings about parish abandonment. Sometimes he sardonically encouraged his village-stuck characters to pull themselves out of the local rut and flee, sometimes he liked to see them as the last bastions of sanity and happiness.

While English literature abounds in every kind of work written in rectories and vicarages, manses and presbyteries, a range of poetry, fiction, science, history and philosophy so magnificent that one has only to remind oneself of a fraction of it to have one's general notion of their inhabitants sharply revised, and while clergymen such as Francis Kilvert and R.S. Thomas have shown their hand, so to speak, we possess nothing equivalent to Georges Bernanos's *The Diary of a Country Priest*, in which the novelist (or poet) investigates this separated figure. In film, play and novel he appears as the necessarily stock character for certain situations, or for fun. No effort is made to realize him, the obvious outline is all that is called for. Although in some slight defence of the writers who treat them thus it could be said that there is more than enough clerical behaviour and claims to warrant such treatment, it does not absolve today's writer from his general ignoring of what, in its best serious sense, is a very interesting subject, that of the ordained stranger being required to enter the parish limits of a community and to be of them as much as his parishioners are of them. Even more so, they usually insist, most parishes aren't all that anxious to be shown paths to God; they are far keener that their priest should go in their particular direction. In place of the wearying stereotypes and grotesques, the eccentrics and simpletons, how good it would be for a novel to begin on this parochial level.

My parish is bored stiff; no other word for it. Like so many others! We can see them being eaten up by boredom, and we can't do anything about it. Someday perhaps we shall catch it ourselves - become aware of the cancerous growth within us. You can keep going a long time with that in you.

This thought struck me yesterday on my rounds. It was drizzling. The kind of thin, steady rain which gets sucked in every breath, which seeps down through the lungs into your belly. Suddenly I looked out over the village, from the road to St Vaast, along the hillside - miserable little houses huddled together under the desolate, ugly November sky. On all sides damp came steaming up, and it seemed to sprawl there in the soaking grass like a wretched worn-out horse or cow. What an insignificant thing a village is. And this particular village was my parish! My parish, yes, but what could I do? I stood there glumly watching it sink into the dusk, disappear ... In a few minutes I should lose sight of it. I had never been so horribly aware both of my people's loneliness and mine. I thought of the cattle which I could hear coughing somewhere in the mist, and of the little lad on his way back from school clutching his satchel, who would soon be leading them over sodden fields to a warm sweet-smelling byre ... And my parish, my village seemed to be waiting too - without much hope after so many nights in the mud - for a master to follow towards some undreamed-of, improbable shelter.★

Only the Welsh poet-clergyman R.H. Thomas touches the current parochial nerve with similar dead accuracy. Put the

Southrop, Gloucestershire: the Vestry

Many vestries are, like Charles Spencerlayh paintings, a touching muddle. John Keble was curate here from 1823 to 1825 and lived in the vicarage, where he and Hurrell Froude and other friends, plus reading parties from Oxford, discussed the ideas which created the Anglo-Catholic Movement. Nearby Southrop Manor was the home of Dorothy Wadham, founder of Wadham College. Keble was in his early thirties when he was at Southrop and from here he eventually went to Hursley, the Hampshire parish with which he was to be so closely associated, and whose church he restored with the royalties of his bestseller *The Christian Year* and the proceeds from his hymns. Although he was Professor of Poetry at Oxford for over thirty years and could have gone in almost any direction he wished in the Church, Keble could only rarely be persuaded to leave a country parish once its individual spell took him over. As he said,

The trivial round, the common task,
Would furnish all we ought to ask,-
Room to deny ourselves, a road
To bring us daily nearer God.

The Christian Year is an 1827 version of a medieval Book of Hours in which a cycle of devotions and (word) pictures of the English countryside support each other.

★ Georges Bernanos, *The Diary of a Country Priest*, 1936, translated by Pamela Morris.

Chewton Mendip, Somerset

West Country towers are
elaborately pinnacled and
sumptuous, the parish marker on
the landscape in all its finery.
This one rises 126 feet above old
lead-mines and is among the
loveliest in Britain. Lead from the
mines roofed many other towers
and churches generally, and was
also in demand for fonts. The
village still possesses its statutory
1611 Authorized Version of the
Bible.

*Footpath, Ampney St Mary,
Gloucestershire*

The Ampneys – Crucis, St Mary
and St Peter – are close to the
Fosse Way, that archetypal path.
The significance of footpaths and
the social and spiritual role they
have played is most originally
assessed in Kim Taplin's *The
English Path*, which draws
together countless mainly very
small routes by which local
people came to more than just
their destinations. Visitors to a
village or even to a city will
often have a thorough look
round, as they think, but by not
seeing the pattern made by
human feet they will have missed
a vital piece of local information.
Geoffrey Grigson said, 'Roads,
lanes, paths, we use them without
reflecting how they are some of
man's oldest inscriptions upon the
landscape, how they are evidence
of the wedding between men and
their environment.'
    A millennium of brides and
grooms, as well as corpses – and
worshippers – assisted in making
the path to many a church door.

following truths in an urban setting and they would be the same.
This is only one of a whole sequence of hard reflections on the
man-apart's landscape.

> *The priest picks his way*
> *Through the parish. Eyes watch him*
> *From windows, from the farms;*
> *Hearts wanting him to come near.*
> *The flesh rejects him.*
>
> *Women, pouring from the black kettle,*
> *Stir up the whirling tea-grounds*
> *Of their thoughts; offer him a dark*
> *Filling in their smiling sandwich.*
>
> *Priests have a long way to go.*
> *The people wait for them to come*
> *To them over the broken glass*
> *Of their vows, making them pay*
> *With their sweat's coinage for their correction.*

Field-work on the Font, Great Walsingham, Norfolk

In the seventeenth century, in a field in this village, were discovered the Roman pots containing incinerated bodies which inspired Sir Thomas Browne's *Urn-Burial* (1658). Although he himself was to receive burial within St Peter Mancroft, Norwich – 'Christians have handsomely glossed the deformity of death by careful consideration of the body, and civil rites which take off brutal terminations' – he half-admired the way in which earlier religions banned graves from their temples. He mused on these Romans who lived on the then 'thinly-filled' map of England and their many processions to the Walsingham field 'with rich flames and hired tears', as they carried burnt bones to the isolated sandy cemetery. Over fifty were excavated 'in a field of Old Walsingham, not many months past', and one was sent to Browne by his friend Dr Witherley, who lived there. Since to live in terms of Christian immortality, 'is to be again ourselves,' Brown concludes, ''tis all one to lie in St Innocent's church-yard, as in the sands of Egypt'. St Innocent's was a Paris graveyard where flesh rotted speedily.

He goes up a green lane
Through growing birches; lambs cushion
His vision. He comes slowly down
In the dark, feeling the cross warp
In his hands; hanging on it his thought's icicles.

'Crippled soul', do you say? looking at him
From the mind's height; 'limping through life
On his prayers. There are other people
In the world, sitting at table
Contented, though the broken body
And the shed blood are not on the menu.'

'Let it be so,' I say. 'Amen and amen.'

So little has been said of this aspect of the parish. The records are all of comings and goings, of legal fights and organization, of building and quarrelling, of how they coped locally with the Reformation and the Poor Law, of those who came to grief but never of those who came to their own conclusions about the place, the village priests. I imagine this long line of minuscule spiritual rulers passing one by one through the lanes, taking the same twists as the car takes now, calling out to all the generations who have occupied the farmhouses and planted fields called Alder Car, Bloody Hill, Commolions (grinding toil?), Black

Cotterdale, Yorkshire

Remote farms could be brutalizing or, as they frequently were, stimulators of strongly held convictions which had often been arrived at through the interplay of a hill-farmer's loneliness and contemplation. To be of a community but to live outside sight and sound of it has always been the lot of the few.

Madown and Arrans Land, and I think of their equivalents from Zennor to Mey, a vast concourse of parsons, each confined to a few souls and their strictly ditched domain. Given the odds, it is unlikely that any village escaped being a very sacred Christ-filled place at some moment in its history, or a dark prison for many a clergyman who could not adapt to its dull habits. It has been the tradition for centuries to give priest and parish a bad press and today's ideal would be to have a kind of cheerful local master of the revels, whose chief task it is to put on concerts in the church, run fêtes, etc., and identify himself with a conservation

area. Betjeman said that if a clergyman is prepared to have a breezy word for everybody he will be tolerated, but if he teaches the Gospel he will be despised and rejected, when not actually mocked. Contrary to all that has been said and written of them the unassessable collective spirituality of some thirteen centuries of now unknowable parish priests must have left its own culture wherever we look or walk.

Anstey, Hertfordshire

There is a tradition that the Elizabethan poet and musician Thomas Campion was born here.

2

*T*he Sacred Shore

St Cedd christianized Essex from its flood-line, one of Britain's most deluge-prone shores, where the topographer John Norden rightly said that the county 'encountreth the mayne Ocean, an infallable bounde', for here as late as February 1953 such an infallible encounter drowned 119 people. Since then Essex has been walled in all the way from Judas Gap on the Stour estuary to the Port of London. Wild walking can be done along these defences, with the sea slapping the blockwork on one side and birds crying up from the delf on the other. The saint's own walking level lies a few feet below under the salt and peat. Sabine Baring-Gould, rector of East Mersea, wrote, in his novel *Mehalah: A Story of the Salt Marshes* (1880),

A more desolate region can scarce be conceived, and yet it is not without beauty. In summer, the thrift mantles the marches with shot satin, passing through all gradations of tint from maiden's blush to lily white. Thereafter a purple glow steals over the waste, as the sea lavender bursts into flower, and simultaneously every creek and pool is royally fringed with sea aster. A little later the grasswort, that shot up green and transparent in the early spring, turns to every tinge of carmine.

When all vegetation ceases to live, and goes to sleep, the marshes are alive and wakeful with countless wild fowl. At all times they are haunted with sea mews and Royston crows;★ in winter they teem with wild duck and grey geese.

St Cedd's diocese, from Stour to Thames, is bordered with 'ripe' pastures. The tides heaped up the mud until they could no longer flow over it, the mud dried out and grew the grass full

★ Hooded crows.

of salt and iodine which sheep thrive on, and it was then 'inned' by the marshland shepherds. Soon rain washed away all the excess salinity of the little embanked meadow and its soil became fertile. The marshlanders judged when it was ripe to act. Every now and then the sea overturned their judgement and the history of the county is one of sudden drenchings and immersions. 'Much a doe,' said William Camden in the sixteenth century, 'have the inhabitants to defend their grounds with forced banks or walls against the violence of the Ocean, ready to inrush upon them.' The boy king Edward VI, writing to a friend in France in 1552, said, 'Of late here hath bene such a tide heire as hath overflowen al meadowes and marshes. All the' Isle of Dogges, al Plumsted marshe, al Sheppey, Foulnes in Essex, and al the sea cost was quite drowned.'

Othona, the Roman fort from which Cedd was to draw building material for his spiritual headquarters, was very much undrowned in his day, though now most of it is silted from sight. Less affected by periodic inundations are the strange piles of Bronze Age industrial waste known as the Red Hills. Tracks still called peatways entangle them. Many of his converts would have been the descendants of the makers of the Red Hills, and of the Othona garrison, and the new people from Denmark and Saxony who were filling the vacuum left by the Roman colon-ists when they withdrew in 407. The Red Hills are thick on the briny ground from Mersea to Maldon, and scatterings of them lie along the Blackwater estuary and around Walton-on-the-Naze. They are the briquetage of red-soil leavings of the salt-makers. Many of them would have been all of half a millennium old when Cedd arrived from Lindisfarne, but would have presented no mystery to him, as salt was then still part of the economy of his new diocese, its preservative, rather than its *condimentum*. Did Christ refer to it in both senses when he told his followers that they were the salt of the earth? Were they to be the world's essential additional ingredient which would both prevent what existed from decaying and also bring out its fla-vour? But in the Old Testament salt was conflictingly associated with lifelessness because it reminded men of the sterile shores of the Dead Sea. In the Middle Ages, fortunes were salted away, and so were herrings for fast-days. Privately, the taste of blood, semen and sweat, of war, work and love-making, identified salt

St Cedd's Shore: the Swale near Teynham, Kent

'Swale' means turbulent water and shares its root with 'swallow', the bird of swooping motion. Essex is waterily glimpsed across the mouth of the Thames and the Isle of Sheppey. Recalling how an outbreak of the yellow plague panicked Cedd's converts back to heathenism, the nearby village of Iwade offers a strange link, for it was there that the one and only lazaretto in England was built, in 1801.

with both life and death. Cedd walked along the marsh causeways through salt basins to his gaunt church at Bradwell. King Sigebert of the East Saxons, having himself just been converted, had commissioned the saint, an Angle brought up in the Celtic Church, to do the same for his nation. However, just as from time immemorial Essex people had 'inned' their saltings and turned them into pastures, and used the word 'marsh' sparingly, Cedd would not have thought that this was the case at first; another need grew from it. This was the need for the noise which the shore makes. Sea-sounds had become the concomitant of Celtic prayer. It sounded thin without sea-cadence. For some of them, like St Cuthbert, the sea's call was as imperative as the office bell. Bede describes such a call in his *Life of Cuthbert*.

He was in the habit of rising at the dead of night, while everyone else was sleeping, to go out and pray, returning just in time for morning prayers. One night one of the monks watched him creep out, then followed him steadily to see where he was going and what he was about. Down he went towards the beach beneath the monastery and out into the sea until he was up to his arms and neck in deep water. The splash of the waves accompanied his vigil throughout the dark hours of the night. At daybreak he came out, knelt down on the sand, and prayed. Then two otters bounded out of the water, stretched themselves out before him, warmed his feet with their breath, and tried to dry him on their fur. They finished, received his blessing, and slipped back to their watery home.★

Ironically, Matthew Arnold remains the major English poet of sea-induced reflection, and not only in *Dover Beach* but throughout his work. In *Carnac*, written in 1859, the year when Darwin's *The Origin of Species* was published, Arnold waits by a sea from which 'no soul, no boat, no hail' will ever come. In *Saint Brandon* (Brendan) he makes the celebrated navigator-monk, sailing north to find an angelic land, encounter Judas on an iceberg. It is Christmas night and the poor traitor is journeying to the 'healing snows'. Brandon realizes that the twinkling lights of Iona are now far behind him and that 'the hurtling Polar lights' are near. Arnold's 'sea without a human shore', as it appears in poem after poem, is a 'swallowing sea' that has gulped down, along with every other hopeful thing, the sea of faith itself. And so,

> *I only hear*
> *Its melancholy, long, withdrawing roar,*
> *Retreating to the breath*
> *Of the night-wind, down the vast edges drear*
> *And naked shingles of the world.*

It was just above Dover beach that the Count of the Saxon Shore – *Comes litoris Saxonica per Britanniam* – built the sixth of his nine forts, Dubris, to repel seaborne threats to an ordered society. Three hundred years later Christian missionaries were to take over these old garrisons and build churches in them, or out of them. The Irish Fursa, who helped the Burgundian Felix to convert East Anglia, turned his fort at Burgh into a monastery.

Dover Beach

The scene of Matthew Arnold's famous elegy (1867) mourning the new uncertainties which science was introducing into the old Christian culture. No matching Celtic prayer-rhythm now, only

> *The grating roar*
> *Of pebbles which the waves draw*
> *   back, and fling,*
> *At their return, up the high strand,*
> *Begin, and cease, and then again*
> *   begin,*
> *With tremulous cadence slow, and*
> *   bring*
> *The eternal note of sadness in.*

★ *Lives of the Saints*, translated by J.F. Webb, 1965.

St Peter's Chapel, Bradwell-juxta-Mare, Essex

Cedd's sea-edged base on the Dengie penisula, which he built from the stones of the Roman fortress station Othona. 'Between St Peter's chappell and Crowche Creeke . . . upon the verie shore', wrote John Norden, the great Tudor mapmaker and topographer, 'was erected a wall for the preservation of the lande. And thereof St Peter's on the wall. And all the sea shore which beateth on that wall is called the Walfleet.' Cedd and his companions sang in this windy, holy barn to the accompaniment of the Walfleet. Not far away was 'the Promontory of Fowles' (Foulness) which for centuries was reached by a path known as the Broomway as it was marked by hundreds of poles shaped like upturned besoms to guide travellers across the Maplin sands at low tide.

At Reculver, Kent, the fort contains the remains of the large, fine church founded by King Egbert in 669, and at Richborough in the same county, in what is now accepted as the most important Roman monument in Britain, only a few steps from the superb marble memorial to commemorate the Roman conquest, lie the foundations of a chapel dedicated to St Augustine, who was said to have first stepped ashore here in 597. Such massive, deserted architecture would have been known to the peripatetic Celtic Church with its bee-like habit of ceaselessly journeying from and back to base, although in its case sweetness and strength were taken out from the industrious hive, as well as created within it. The count's nine forts, stretching from Norfolk to Hampshire, Brancaster, Burgh Castle, Bradwell, Reculver, Richborough, Dover, Lympne, Pevensey and Portchester, were to prove a windfall for the proto-Church of England. Each was built for sea-access and was difficult to get to by road, a situation which ensured perfect prayer conditions.

Cedd and his party most likely walked from Lindisfarne to Bradwell unless the saint came straight on from his mission-field success with the Middle Angles. Walking was Christian, riding less so. Just as Lindisfarne had reproduced Iona, so Cedd intended that Bradwell would reproduce elements of Lindisfarne, for no monastery, in Britain at least, could totally repeat the sublime religious and cultural life of that divine Northumbrian island, with its scriptorium, music, sculpture yards, artists, poets, scholars and craftsmen. Their missionary zeal apart, men like Cedd, with their Iona-Lindisfarne credentials, must have filled even the kings of the Saxons with awe, let alone their rough subjects. They seem to have moved around with a natural prelacy. Cedd and his three brothers were among the twelve English boys trained at Lindisfarne to carry the Gospel to the Saxons, who distrusted Celts. Like St Paul at Troas, he appears to have worked intensively and then moved on, leaving a strong local church behind him. The blunt eloquence of his material presence also lingers. Cedd is no filmy legend on the saltings and in the Essex woods but a solid figure in the county's early history. One of the first acts of the present diocese after it had been created in 1914 was to mend and re-sanctify Cedd's cathedral which, save for the holes made in it for farm-carts, stood as firmly as when he had built it with stones taken from the Count's fort in the 650s. Cedd dedicated this tall and uncompromising church to St Peter, the fisherman of souls, and built one similar to it on the banks of the Thames at West Tilbury, but this has vanished. Between these two churches lies the watery ground of the Homeric *Battle of Maldon*, in which an old man brought up on King Alfred's ideals led a small, improvised defence force to disaster against a Norwegian army of 3,000 men, rather than pay the traditional danegeld fee for being left alone.

In landscape terms Maldon is for me perpetually identified with an early disappointment, a minor let-down which obstinately refuses to be mollified. It has all to do with the static nature of my childhood, of virtually never going anywhere for year after year. Nowhere beyond walking or biking distance, that is. Which made visits to the coast intensely exciting events. And they were always to the Suffolk, not the Essex, coast, for some reason. Hence the sensation when a day at Maldon was proposed. Nobody said that Maldon wasn't by the sea, and at eight or nine it was beyond my comprehension that we should travel fifty miles to anywhere which was not by the sea. So when we clambered from the bus with our food and swimming costumes, and were told to *enjoy* ourselves by the glittering mud currents of the Blackwater, nothing that Cedd's and Byrhtnoth's country could offer could even begin to compensate me for what I believed had been promised me – the sea. I sulked and was what they called 'quiet', which I knew was hurtful. But this grief did have its positive side for it fixed the Blackwater geography in my memory as accurately as a snapshot, right down to the litter bobbing about under the landing-stages and the texture of the earth on which we sat. It all seemed messy, empty and impoverished, yet, as the day drew on, absorbing in the most private sense. When I got home my pockets were full of things to remind me of it, flowers, sticks, stones and the Swan Vestas matchbox boat I had made and sailed across a salty pool. I missed Maldon as one always does miss places where one has been perfectly sad. This self-indulgent day remains isolated from all the other Essex days.

Cedd, I have constantly to remind myself, was not a Celt but an Anglo-Saxon. He and the east coast understood each other. But Lindisfarne and Iona motivated him, and so many Essex islands, Mersea, Havengore, Wallasea, Osea, Canvey, Foulness

Northumbrian Coast

'*Who gathered the bitter sea of humanity into one society? All men are united by one purpose, temporal happiness on earth, and all that they do is aimed at this goal, although in the endless variety of their struggles to attain it they pitch and toss like the waves of the sea. None but you, O Lord, gathered them together, you who ordained that the waters should collect in one place to make dry land appear, land dry and parched with thirst for you. For yours is the ocean; who but you could create it? what other power fashioned the dry land? By the "sea" is meant all the waters, gathered into one, not the bitter brine of man's ill will.*'

St Augustine, *Confessions*

Iona

The Hebridian island which could lay claim to being Britain's most inspirational Christian site. Here in 563 St Columba, an aristocratic Irish scholar, founded an abbey, choosing the spot because it lay on the boundary between the formally Christian Scots and the pagan Picts. He was forty-two years old and behind him stretched an immense missionary achievement in Ireland, though darkened in his own estimation because he had started a war. The fact that it was a 'just war' did not comfort him. At Iona he aimed to restore himself in his own and God's eyes, and inaugurated a commual life so intelligent, spiritual and attractive that it permeates Christianity to this day. A near-contemporary, Adamnan, left a comparatively legendless biography of the saint which gives an authentic picture of the Celtic Church at its zenith. Aidan reproduced Iona on Lindisfarne and from then onwards priests, writers and artists trained at both centres carried something of their perfection into British prayer and culture everywhere.

Walberswick, Suffolk

Part of the shore from which St Felix from Burgundy, first bishop of the now sea-claimed city of Dunwich, christianized East Anglia. The area has become submerged in a darkly luminous history of watery encroachment, soil erosion, Saxon art (Sutton Hoo), Saxon holiness (the saints Fursey, Edmund and Botolph among many others), and scholarship. Cornelian and amber can be found in the shingle, also the yellow horned poppy, sea holly and the rare sea pea (*Lathyrus maritimus*) which the poor looked on as famine food. An immense church dedicated to St Andrew was built here in the fifteenth century – but in 1695 was reduced to the church within a church which exists now, because of the collapse of the local economy.

– the 'headland of the birds' – Salcott, where they stored the salt and Potton, where they made the salt pots, must have pleased him. A few miles up land was Colchester, the capital of Cymbeline during the zenith of the salt trade. A melancholy destination it could have been for Cedd when he walked to it over peatway and Roman road, entering it through toppling classical cemeteries and cracked gates. But as the Celtic Church had such a minimal interest in architecture he may not have noticed anything very extraordinary. Mostly he walked to preaching places marked by oak trees, and if into Suffolk, where they were

The Gospel Oak at Ravensworth, North Yorkshire

It was not far from here that St Cedd, having accomplished his mission to the East Saxons, obeyed the request of Prince Aethelwald to build a Lindisfarne-like church where he might worship. St Cedd chose a wild, lonely site called Laestingaeu on Spaunton Moor – the present Lastingham. Here he died of the yellow plague on 26 October 664. The following year this epidemic so frightened his Essex converts that they rushed back to their nature gods.

especially venerated, by ash groves. Two Ceddian oaks remain, the one at Yeldham, still held upright in its iron corset, and one at Polstead, now in fragments, but which as a child I saw in leaf. Polstead was our cherry village and it was while visiting it to see the cherry blossom that I first heard of Cedd. The Polstead cherry-men used to shout, 'Polstead cherries! Polstead cherries! Red as Maria Martin's blood!' They sold them by the pint. My first notion of St Cedd was of a clergyman preaching in a cherry orchard. His actual appearance for those waiting to hear him under the oak and ash trees could only have been astonishing, for in common with all St Columba's followers his front hair was shaved off across his brow from ear to ear and his back hair flowed across his shoulders in the dramatic Celtic tonsure. Had there been any stone in Essex he would have marked the places for Christian assembly with great carved crosses; instead he had to make do with already sacred trees. But this was quite in order. 'Do not pull down the fanes,' Pope Gregory told St Augustine before he set off for Britain. 'Destroy the idols; purify the temples with holy water, set relics there and let them become temples of the true God. So the people will have no need to change their places of concourse.' Beasts were not to be sacrificed but might still be slaughtered, where they were once offered, to provide 'a social meal'. Some believe that this is the origin of church ales or festivals, and it might be.

The beginning of the old English poem called 'The Husband's Message', here quoted in Kevin Crossley-Holland's translation, might almost be describing St Cedd's mission to the East Saxons.

> *Now that we're alone I can explain*
> *The secret meaning of this stave. I was once a child.*
> *But now one of the sons of men, living far from here,*
> *Sends me on errands over the salt-streams,*
> *Commands me to carry a cunningly carved letter.*
> *At my master's command I have often crossed the sea,*
> *Sailed in the ship's hold to strange destinations.*
> *And this time I have come especially*
> *To sow assurance in your mind*
> *About my lord's great love of you.*

The bringing of the Celtic Church's severe and exquisite Christianity to the East Saxons must have resulted in an astounding clash of cultures. In essence it propounded hope in place of resignation to one's fate, and it was deeply involved in poetry, music and disciplines which gave pleasant access to the inner life. 'Iona did for England what the Roman Augustine failed to do,' maintained Helen Waddell. 'Not Augustine but Aidan is the true apostle of England,' said Lightfoot. Bede's account of Irish scholarship pouring across the sea like the most precious of cargoes on their way to eager ports is one of Christianity's most thrilling passages. A subsequent accretion of folk-tales refuses to obscure the brilliant reality of Patrick, Columbanus, Fursa, Columba, Aidan, Cuthbert, Cedd and his brothers, and many more. Mercia and Northumberland were transformed by these oceanic evangelists, and so, interruptedly, for it is said that after St Cedd had retired to Lastingham in the North Riding disease obliged its inhabitants to placate the old deities, was Essex. Yet his sea prayer and his sea imagery drawn neat, as it were, from the Gospels hung about the marshes and in the memories of those that lived in them. And in Colchester too, whose flag was the black raven, the same as that flown from the mast by the northern invaders and whose emblem forms the borough's seal to this day, the stern magic of his personality would still have been felt in the squalid Saxon streets. And nobody standing under the trees near the village clearings could have failed to have heard a voice, partly Latin, partly their own, and partly something not easy to define in language terms, which was a voice speaking the holy tongue of the Celtic coastline.

There are few references to Christ being on the Palestinian coast. His sea is Galilee, an inland lake, and until St Paul involved the Mediterranean in the faith, Christ's sea associations are with Galilee. His followers have to leave this little sea to become fishermen who will catch humanity in their net. The Old Testament Jews seem to have dreaded the sea and have scarcely a good word for it. It was full of monsters. Jesus evidently loved the Galilean sea and was clearly at home with its fishing community and its boats, although only one of his parables concerns the sea, that of the fishing-net. But he chose for his first four followers two pairs of brothers who, as the sons of fishermen, had been born with the sea in their ears. Although Galilee had its notorious panic-making squalls, there was never anything

St Botolph's Priory, Colchester (founded c.1150)

St Botolph died in 680, and was therefore a near-contemporary of St Cedd. He might be called the saint of destinations and arrivals. Over fifty churches in England are dedicated to him, many of them near city gates. The three in London are at Aldgate, Aldersgate and Bishopsgate, all at places which East Anglians would pass through when they came to the capital.

The Priory at Colchester is built almost entirely of bricks made by the Romans and taken from buildings which Cedd could have seen. The Roman road from his watery headquarters entered Colchester close to where St Botolph's Priory now stands.

St Botolph's rallying point was in Lincolnshire. Boston – 'St Botolph's Stone' – was a town name which was to have consequences which Saxon Christians could never have imagined, for in the seventeenth century shiploads of their descendants from eastern England, led by John Winthrop, a man who lived only a few miles from Colchester, were to found their destination of destinations in Massachusetts and call it Boston. But it is unlikely that Winthrop or his Puritan society had any notion that the name of their new ideal city commemorated the preaching-stone of an ancient open-air church.

comparable to the terrors which St Paul suffered in the Mediterranean, where such sea prayer as there was became just implorings for survival. St Luke's account of what St Paul had to put up with on his voyage to Rome in the Acts runs the whole gamut of sea disaster.

Since Iona, Lindisfarne and what is now Bradwell-juxta-Mare were regularly battered by thunderous water, the Celtic saints must also have decided upon their attitude to uproar, as their lives reveal little concern or fear at the sea's disturbance. Yet they dwelt in gales and were bitterly cold, and were lashed by northern rains. Always, after strenuous missionary forays inland, they returned to where tides and their own bloodstreams harmonized. It was all to end by the sea, at Whitby, the white town. Separatist Irish and Northumbrian Christians were to be drawn back into official Catholicism with, at the Synod of Whitby, Cedd himself acting as interpreter and go-between. All the same, for years afterwards, many members of the Celtic Church went their own divine way on lonely seashores. In 669, five years after the Celts had submitted to the Romans in Hild's clifftop abbey at Whitby, the new Archbishop of Canterbury, an old man named Theodore from Tarsus, St Paul's birthplace, probably the greatest organizational genius the Church of England was ever to know, set about laying down the episcopal and state order which remains the basis of Britain's national pattern to this day. His chief assistant in this heroic task was an African called Hadrian. One could speculate indefinitely on what might have happened if there had been no such administrative genius and no Synod of Whitby. It was only thirty years between the day when Aidan left Iona for Lindisfarne to christianize Northumbria for King Oswald according to the Celtic tradition, and the day when his pupil Cedd assisted in the plan of the Synod to submerge this tradition in that of Rome.

While there is no denying Archbishop Theodore's immense achievement, that of the Celtic Church remains the greater one. As Bishop Lightfoot of Durham remarked, in the fullest spiritual sense the Celtic Christians had laid the foundations of the English Church without realizing it. I have always thought that Cuthbert personified the Celtic ideal. An eloquent Scottish shepherd turned missionary - he gave his name to Kirkcudbrightshire,

Whitby Abbey, Yorkshire

Here in 664 what must be the most remarkable and beautiful sect to have emerged in western Christianity, the Celtic Church, returned to the Roman jurisdiction, with St Cedd acting as interpreter. The founder of the Abbey, Hild, had also been a pupil of Aidan. She was a royal woman whose sister was Queen of East Anglia. During their childhood both girls had to seek shelter in the little Yorkshire kingdom of Elmet, recently the subject of a poem sequence by Ted Hughes. Hild's monastery was unusual in that it was for both sexes. She ruled it with common sense, scholarship and exquisite taste, all in the Lindisfarne manner. Everyone in it practised Christian communism and equality, herself claiming the only title used - 'Mother'. Among her children in Christ were St Wilfrid, St John of Beverley and the poet Caedmon. Her monastery was a garden, a law-court, a hospital, a university and a prayer-house extraordinary. She built it on a headland called Streaneshalch but later the Danes called it Whitby - the white town - probably because of the way its buildings gleamed on the cliff as they sailed past them.

Lindisfarne, Northumberland

Between AD 635 and 1082 such was the reputation of this little scrap of land off the vast Northumbrian beaches in the realms of prayer, missionary genius and art that it was renamed Holy Island. Its sacred history began in 635 when the King of Northumbria, Oswald, commissioned Aidan, a monk from Iona, to convert his people to Christianity. Aidan chose to live on Lindisfarne partly because it reminded him of Iona and partly because it was in sight of his friend Oswald's palace on the great rock of Bamburgh. Aidan became Bishop of Lindisfarne and inaugurated one of the most brilliant cultures in the history of the Church. He attracted so much fame in his lifetime that he had to move out to the more difficult-to-reach Farne Island to get some peace. When he died, a Scottish boy minding sheep on the Lammermuir hills was said to have seen stars falling from the sky. The boy's name was Cuthbert and he succeeded Aidan on Lindisfarne. It was Aidan who trained Cedd for the Lindisfarne life he was to imitate at Bradwell on the Essex marshes.

the church of Cuthbert's shire – he liked to pray while actually standing in the sea, and especially in the company of birds and beasts, gulls, seals, otters and eagles. He was sane and practical – 'To comfort and advise the weak is equivalent to an act of prayer' – and all his life he put up a struggle against religious fantasy. Walking in Lindisfarne at harvest time, the island women brushing up the scraps of petal, leaf and stalk from a sanctuary carpet based on a 'carpet-page' from the Gospel book written and painted here only a few years after Cuthbert's death, recovering from the wind and drizzle, I see him everywhere. His concept of Christ as love in action, wise and unadorned, seems to have soaked into the very rocks. Bede says that he 'watched, prayed, worked and read harder than anyone else'. Saintliness and healing skills drew the crowds and Cuthbert was eventually obliged to forsake Lindisfarne for Farne, the other island, and to build a wattle and thatch wall round himself. There he listened to God and the sea for almost a decade, viewing nothing but a circle of sky, and there his body would have lain until the Resurrection, had not it been claimed as the usual ecclesiastical treasure, to be carried about and variously enshrined until, at last, it reached its present stripped-down tomb in Durham Cathedral. A long journey from one bareness to another, and with the sound of a river instead of a sea in his skull. The name of this river, 'Wear', means simply 'water'.

Before crossing the causeway to Holy Island I had wandered up that vast bow of a coastline in torrential rain. No kippers at Craster, no rooms at most of the small hotels and boarding-houses; they had all been locked away for the winter. Being wet to the skin is an interesting, even sensuous, experience once one has given up every effort to stay dry. The more or less unhoused Celtic Church, its ordinary members waiting in crowds for Cuthbert and his portable altar to arrive, would have been equally drenched many times. Beadnell Bay leads up to North Sunderland and Seahouses, hard, workaday towns, then Bamburgh Castle, one of the great shoreline dramas of Britain. Aidan, watching with horror from Farne Island, had seen King Penda of Mercia attempting to set fire to Bamburgh when the wind suddenly changed and set the incendiarists alight instead.

Then Budle Bay and Ross Back Sands, and finally the sands and flats announcing Holy Island itself, a minimally altered scene. From it via Saltpan Rocks the beaches speed up to the Tweed and to Eyemouth, with the railway sticking close all the way. What the Celtic Church possessed here was landscape magnificence, that unique Northumbrian spanning of the ground. The sea country of the East Saxons between the Stour and Thames covers the distance in a quite different fashion, and Cedd would have felt the contrast. If Northumbria is a mite brutal, Essex is a mite sinister.

The most unsettling description of how certain elements will go on pushing their way into a particular area, no matter what progress has done to it, is in Conrad's picture of Thames-side Essex, when he lets the county's old Adam, as it were, seep through its mercantile prosperity. The narrator in *The Heart of Darkness* and his companions are lazing by the mizzen mast of a yawl when one of the latter, Marlow, surprisingly observes, 'And this also has been one of the dark places of the earth.' It is Marlow's opening gambit as seaman-storyteller as he begins to describe a river scene which no one doubts is a dark place – the Congo. Marlow's quest up the Congo to find the ivory trader Kurtz, a black version of the Livingstone–Stanley legend, leads him to unspeakable corruption. As the tale unfolds it soon becomes evident that Conrad is looking at any great trading river.

We felt meditative, and fit for nothing but placid staring. The day was ending in a serenity of still and exquisite brilliance. The water shone pacifically; the sky, without a speck, was a benign immensity of unstained light; the very mist on the Essex marshes was like a gauzy and radiant fabric, hung from the wooded rises inland, and draping the low shores in diaphanous folds ... The old river in its broad reach rested unruffled at the decline of the day, after ages of good service done to the race that peopled its banks, spread out in the tranquil dignity of a waterway leading to the uttermost parts of the earth.

Marlow then imagines a Roman commander sailing up the Thames into Essex for the first time. 'Sandbanks, marshes, forests, savages – precious little to eat fit for a civilized man, nothing but Thames water to drink. No Falerian wine here, no going ashore. Here and there a military camp lost in the wilderness ... cold, fog, tempests, disease, exile and death – death

Bamburgh beach, Northumberland

The sand once trodden by Aidan, Cuthbert, Hild, Cedd and their pupils. Iona's first mission to the Northumbrians, an 'uncivilized people of obstinate and barbarous temperament', was a failure. When its leader confessed this back on Iona a quiet voice asked, 'Were you not too severe to unlearned hearers?' It was Aidan, who was never to be surprised that men without refinement and hope should be brutal. The geography of the central Northumberland coast attracted him almost as much as its inhabitants, for here was a sequence both of access and of inaccessibility. There were hours when the world could walk to Lindisfarne and hours when the tides closed it for prayer. The house of his protector-king rode high above the water. Here he founded a see, a worship pattern, a university and an art centre. Birds, fish, quadrupeds and all creatures other than man were also welcome.

'The Lord sitteth above the water-flood and the Lord remaineth a King forever.'

King Oswald's folk, taking a hard look at the community, agreed that 'they lived as they preached'.

skulking in the air, in the water, in the bush. They must have been dying like flies here ...' He then shockingly aligns the Romans with the Europeans in Africa. 'The conquest of the earth, which mostly means the taking it away from those who have a different complexion or slightly flatter noses than ourselves, is not a pretty thing when you look at it too much.' Marlow's friends then knew that they were fated to hear one of his 'inconclusive experiences'.

3

*T*he Black Map

During the reigns of the half-sisters Mary and Elizabeth, some six hundred profoundly believing Christian people were slaughtered by the state on official execution grounds and wastes, mainly in south-east England. Although there were a few such deaths in the north and west, the main concentration was in and around London, and within a terrible arc of investigation stretching from Lynn to Oxford. The victims were fairly evenly divided between Protestant and Roman Catholic, and in rank represented the whole of English society. Men and women, boys and girls, weavers, farmworkers, aristocrats, an archbishop and newly ordained young priests, the semi-literate and great scholars, artists and poets, all suffered the most atrocious deaths which the law allowed, burnt for heresy under Mary if they stuck to the 'new' religion, hanged, drawn and quartered under Elizabeth for treason if they propagated the 'old'.

These killings continue to disturb every part of the Church in Britain today in a way in which the religious massacres which occurred before and after them, those of the Lollards and the witches, do not. At the same time, and in spite of the genius of Foxe's martyrology and the grave and gradual gathering up of its saints on to the Calendar by the Church of Rome, the places where so many ordinary and brilliant people died for their convictions remain somehow 'unseen'. Even where mainly nineteenth-century monuments mark the spot, the earth fails to cry out. It could be because its witness to such violations is mercifully stifled by our disgust, mercifully for ourselves, that is, for not even the deepest understanding of the Tudor dilemma makes what happened at Smithfield, Tyburn, on Aldham Common, in Balliol ditch and scores of other sites, remotely tolerable.

Truth to tell, these locations, where Campion, Margaret Clith-
erow, Cranmer, Alexander Lane the wheelwright, Rowland
Taylor, Anne Askew, 'James Abbes, a youth' and all the rest of
them were given their carefully agonized ends, reflect our revulsion, not their ability to die for Christ. This, unless given
their circumstances, we can no longer comprehend. To be burnt
alive or to have one's entrails drawn and thrown on a brazier
before one's just-living eyes! The seat of wickedness was the
viscera and, one way or the other, cleansing fire had to reach it.

Guy Fawkes Night, Lewes, Sussex

*'Mounds of human heads are
wandering in the distance. I dwindle
among them. Nobody sees me. But
in books much loved, and in
children's games I shall rise from the
dead to say the sun is shining.'*

Osip Mandelstam

Some of the Marian and Elizabethan martyrs had actually watched such executions, and one or two had even assisted in sentencing others to them. Yet when their time came, and they were shown the brand or the knife, few recanted to stagger home amid mockery with a faggot tied round their necks. It was both the Reformers' and the anti-Reformers' big mistake not to have taken into consideration the power which operates when faith exceeds fear. Their misjudgement was doubly incomprehensible because spiritual strength overcoming natural terror had been a staple of the Church's teaching from the beginning. Countless pictures and tales witnessed to 'overcoming'; now huge crowds witnessed to it as unspeakable things were done to some poor body. Lawyer-politicians (some of them priests) acted for the present moment. So keen were they to dispatch trouble-makers and silence voices, or to save souls, as they maintained, that they turned a blind eye to the obvious, which is that today's saints are selected from yesterday's dissidents. Considering the Church's instruction, and its iconography, how could *not* a twenty-year-old ploughman blazing in the market-square of his local town because he could not believe in transubstantiation be compared with St Stephen? How could *not* Robert Southwell the Jesuit priest-poet, hanged and beheaded after torture unprecedented, they said, even for the Tower of London, because he could not disbelieve the Christ of the unreformed religion and would not betray his friends, be compared with his Lord?

Predictably, the result of these disgusting murders was the immediate ennobling of both versions of the faith. Aspects of the Reformation were given a glory like that of the early Church. The flaccid, half-worn-away professionalism of late-medieval Catholicism was dismissed by the authority of those who sang the *Te Deum* in Westminster Hall when they heard their sentence. It was all a repetition of what had happened at the start but neither prosecuting agency recognized the comparison. Also, some of the death-dealers on both sides of the Europe-shaking argument were interested in cruelty for its own sake. This is a factor in revolutions and counter-revolutions which gets overlooked for evident reasons. Few writers have been able to take an understanding look at the personality of the delighted giver of pain, although the poet Sidney Keyes attempted to in his *Gilles de Retz*.

> *Nor will you ever feel God's finger*
> *Probing you soul's anatomy, as I*
> *Have been dissected these five years; for never*
> *Since Christ has any man made pain so glorious*
> *As I, nor dared to seek salvation*
> *Through love with such long diligence as I through pain.*
>
> *Have mercy, Lord, on misdirected worship.*

Norton, rack-master at the Tower, who promised the heroic Fr Alexander Briant, aged twenty-eight, that he would stretch him a foot longer than God made him, and Lord Chancellor Wriothesley, who had with his own hands turned the screws of the rack in a vain try to make Anne Askew confess to heresy, would have been flattered. Anne was an intellectual who had first drawn attention to herself by reading the translated Bible in Lincoln Cathedral. A twenty-five-year-old married woman of good family, with two children, she had 'offended the priests' by asking questions, and by study. Wriothesley and the frightful Sir Richard Rich tortured her to such an extent that she had to be carried to her bonfire at Smithfield in a chair. They sat on a bench near St Bartholomew's to watch her burn. With Gilles de Retz it was boys, not young wives. The unsuitability of nearly everyone involved in the legal processes of rooting-out 'heresy' or 'treason' during the Reformation was apparent to many at the time, and is manifestly plain now. Their religion and their excitements, their politics and their fantasies, boiled muddily inside them. Below the surface, beneath any formulation allowed by Christian language, they recognized that there can be no sacrifice without the sacrificer. Writing of the burning of Joan of Arc Lamartine said, 'God decreed for her a complete fate. There is none without the wickedness of men, without martyrdom for one's country.' The sacrificers of the Protestant martyrs could not have avoided a picture of Isaac's burning going ahead without divine intervention, just as the sacrificers of the Catholic martyrs could not have failed to see Judas, a suicide hanging from a tree with his bowels falling out. Ecclesiastical and civil judge, examiner and executioner, each was condemned to play a part he could not refuse, and which occasionally turned out to be a part to his liking, that of the dispatching-man, without whom there can be no blameless offering.

From the earliest times, and particularly during the Middle Ages, Christians had worshipped without revulsion in buildings filled with pictures and carvings of hideous cruelties. The figures depicted were usually beautiful, and the males frequently nude, with their flesh showing little or no physically accurate response to its violation. Agony had been extracted, and all the filthiness of their deaths left far behind in some long-since bramble-smothered amphitheatre. The ferocities of the painted glass and the sculptures, and the ferocities of the field at Colchester, where five men and five women were all burned on a single bonfire, or of the Tyburn stage when the genitals were sliced from a living man before a mob, did not match. The Reformation and Counter-Reformation martyrs died in brutal squalor. The smell of roast meat would have drifted into St Bartholomew's Church. For weeks after the quarters of some butchered Catholic had been hooked above a city gate those passing through it would have held their noses. Had what they had been sentenced to not been so dreadful, it would have been ridiculous – the notion that mind and spirit can be corrected, or anathematized, by some form of total physical destruction. The martyrs knew this and, incredibly to us, also knew that they had nothing to fear.

Describing the death of Joan of Arc at Rouen in 1431, the historian Marina Warner tells of her ashes being thrown into the Seine estuary immediately after her burning so that her 'very body was freed from the bonds tied by information and was released to inhabit that wider universe where imagination is mistress of knowledge. She passed from the condition of the knowable to the condition of the all-imaginable ...' So did the martyrs of the English Reformation, although John Foxe's unsparing detail, gleaned from eyewitnesses, kept the bonfire scenes themselves from fading. They were there, seemingly for all time, for a very different kind of imagination to sate itself on, and his *Book of Martyrs* remains one of the most powerful accounts of religious pathology ever written, an uplifting-downcasting, thrilling-nauseating history drenched equally in pity and sensation. Between them, Mary Tudor and John Foxe created such a lurid view of Catholicism as to have biased Protestant thinking right up to the present. There were 232 burnings during her short reign, 18 in Suffolk, 14 in Norfolk, 39 in Essex, 58 in Kent, 23 in Sussex, 11 in Middlesex and 69 in London itself,

Smithfield: St Bartholomew's

The 1702 gatehouse to St Bartholomew's, London's oldest hospital, founded by Rahere, a courtier of Henry I, in 1123. It was re-founded by Henry VIII in 1546, which is why his statue fills the niche. Behind the gatehouse is the church of St Bartholomew the Less, in which Inigo Jones was christened. Belated memorials to the great numbers who were executed on this level field just above the bank of the now vanished Fleet River are fixed to the hospital wall. This was London's healing – and killing – place.

these chiefly at Smithfield, the 'smooth field' a mile or so away from the courts and prison, once used for jousts and later as a fairground. They included over fifty women and many teenage boys. Bishop Bonner's first taste of popular hatred came when he insisted on burning the fifteen-year-old Richard Mekin for saying that another victim had 'died holy'. Eighty-one people had been burned during the reign of Henry VIII and five only during that of Elizabeth. This was no advance in humanity; the close-on 300 devout Christians who fell foul of her treason laws would have found little to weigh up between the horrors of Tyburn and those of Smithfield. The strangely unforeseen result for a faith founded on martyrdom, on dying in order to live, a

London, Marble Arch (Charles Hall)

The one-way destination for so many for six hundred years. The permanent gallows stood by a little river whose name, Tyburn, derives from 'boundary stream'. To the north was a large wood through the midst of which ran Watling Street. The area was approached through fields and meadows watered by other streams, the Western-bourne, Kill-bourne and Mary-bourne. Ty-bourne supplied Cheapside conduit with drinking-water.

The executions provided London's most popular and frightful sideshow. Victims were drawn the five miles from Newgate, sometimes on hurdles, sometimes in carts. The route from the Tower of London was via Tower Lane, St Sepulche's, Newgate, Holborn (Hole-brook, where the horses were watered), Oxford Road (High Holborn) and then through the farmland of today's Oxford Street. Those sentenced to hanging, drawing and quartering were half-hanged on greased ropes, cut down, stripped naked, deprived of their genitals (which were stuffed in their mouths), and gutted. They were then decapitated and their heads par-boiled. Their bodies were then cut-up, par-boiled, covered in pitch if they were to be exhibited on city gates, or collected and buried by the charitable, or by friends and relations. The ritual cruelties and indecencies practised here thrilled and corrupted every class. Saints and martyrs were butchered here, like poor Elizabeth Barton, the twenty-eight-year-old 'Holy Maid of Kent', executed in 1534.

faith said to possess a love which can bear and endure all things, as St Paul put it, was the immediate strengthening and enrichment of both the old and new religions. The half-worn-away customs and orthodoxies of late medieval Catholicism were revitalized by the witness which poured from the scaffold as it had not done from the pulpit for many a long year; the brashness of the new Protestantism was turned to profound experience in the flames. Neither Mary's nor Elizabeth's prosecuting agents had allowed for this, the most persuasive teaching of all, the screams of a body undergoing torment for what it knew to be the truth.

But who now walks down Oxford Street to Marble Arch as to a most sacred place? Or who now leaving the Old Bailey and

The Old Bailey

The Central Criminal Court stands at the corner of Newgate Street and opposite Giltspur Street along which the martyrs passed to Smithfield. The City's 'New Gate', after which its chief prison was named, was demolished in 1767. Masonry from Newgate Prison was incorporated into the Old Bailey when it replaced the notorious building in 1902. Wide-eyed, unblindfolded Justice brandishes her sword and scales above the blood-soaked area in which saints and monsters, heroes and children have been executed from 1250 to 1901. Public hangings in the street before the prison only ceased in 1867, after Charles Dickens described the indecency of the mobs which attended them. Before the abolition of the death penalty it was common to see long crocodiles of spectators, chiefly women, waiting to get into the public galleries of the Old Bailey whenever there was a murder trial. In the early 1550s they would have ringed the bonfires.

following Giltspur Street through to West Smithfield is aware that he is taking the death route of the saints? Oxford Street and the streets leading from Newgate and the Tower towards St Bartholomew's are England's *via dolorosa*, its thoroughfares of pain, its paths to Christian glory. Discreet plaques say so, but little else. We are far less conscious of the landscape of martyrdom than of the landscapes of poetry, novels, art or a particular ecology. I found that I had to both dream and educate myself into Marble Arch–Tyburn and into Smithfield. A sightseeing insouciance now covers these places like turf over tesserae, hiding the pattern. A plate let in the road, an obelisk set up on a common, a pinnacle of Victorian gothic at Oxford, and in Bury St Edmund's, etc., only faintly suggest their enormity. The hard facts are extensive and easy to come by, but in a mega-massacring twentieth century we can do without them. Below the surface lies the blackest of maps, but don't consult it. Pass to a less messy sheet. T.S. Eliot knew it all too well yet he advised, 'move on'.

> *We cannot revive old factions*
> *We cannot restore old policies*
> *Or follow an antique drum.*
> *These men, and those who opposed them*
> *And those whom they opposed*
> *Accept the constitution of silence*
> *And are folded in a single party.*

Wilfred Owen said much the same thing in 'Strange Meeting'.

Getting away from the Reformation, allowing its factions to lapse into a constitution of silence, has turned out to be easier said than done for many modern Christians. Not even today's liturgical changes, the language of the New English Bible, the transformed thinking created by the Second Vatican Council and post-nuclear theology generally can stop the sixteenth century forever tugging at our sleeve. It haunts me as it haunts others. Reformation would have happened in Britain even if Henry and Catherine had produced a family of strong sons, and there had been no divorce. No worrying about what Leviticus said about marrying a brother's widow then. But the king's having three children, and two of them girls at that, by three different mothers in his desperate need to establish a dynasty, guaranteed that any reform of the Church would be attended by bizarre national difficulties. From the minute Henry died his children became rallying points for a pattern of progression-reaction-progression, although the chief group to get hurt during the reign of the boy Edward VI was that which got in the way of his government and its supporters as they loaded themselves with church property and grabbed titles. The clever child observed the looting with cold eyes as these men of a New Age seized monastic acres and buildings, and even knocked down churches to get stone for their mansions. It was not a matter of making hay while the sun shone. They expected Edward to be on the throne for many years, perhaps until the end of the century, and to consolidate their new wealth and position under stable Protestant circumstances. But Edward died, probably from tuberculosis, when he was sixteen. It was unbelievable and it threw everybody who had profited materially from the reforms into a panic. When they had held the sick boy up at the window to prove to the people that he was still breathing, it was also to dispel their own disbelief at what was happening. Frantic at the prospect of the succession of his half-sister Mary and her sombre, unshakeable Spanish religion, they persuaded the sinking Edward to name his cousin Jane Grey as queen. She was the granddaughter of Henry VIII's sister Mary, and the daughter of the Duke of Suffolk. She too was sixteen and had just been married to the Duke of Northumberland's son, Guildford Dudley.

It appeared for a day or two that the Counter-Reformation had been stalled by a union of the great Protestant families, but the people – even those who were Protestant – were appalled. Mary was not only Henry's daughter but the child of his only true marriage, as they privately maintained, to Queen Catherine of Aragon, and his rightful heir. For over a year or more after her succession Mary was able to unpick the work of Thomas Cromwell and return her country to Catholicism without doing over-much injury, but then the resistance began. It was centred upon the Bible seen as an authority above that of pope, monarch, priest or custom. For those who were reading it for the first time in Miles Coverdale's masterly translation into the vernacular, it brought about a devastating personal reappraisal of everything which the Church taught. It was the first complete Bible to be printed in English, Tyndale having published only translations of the New Testament, the Book of Job, and the Pentateuch – the first five books of the law with which the Old Testament opens. It allowed Coverdale to present the poetry of the Psalms in the exquisite version still to be found in the Book of Common Prayer. Although not quite accurate, as Professor Dickens says, 'Even in their obscure moments they have the mellow beauty of some ancient, familiar window with slightly jumbled glass; one would scarcely have the imperfections set right.' Coverdale's 'Great Bible' was published in April 1539 and ran into seven editions in eighteen months. Cranmer was to add a famous preface but the real launcher of the project, the single most influential event that was to happen to the English as a nation, was Thomas Cromwell. Having delivered this dynamite, Coverdale is said to have lain low during the worst of the troubles, leaving 'the crown of martyrdom to be earned by men of tougher fibre'. He died aged eighty-one, and was dust when the Great Fire of London raged round his tomb in St Bartholomew's church just behind the Royal Exchange. When Sir William Tite built the present Exchange, they carried Coverdale's bones to Wren's St Magnus Martyr. T.S. Eliot, sheltering from the City's noise during his lunch-hour, would have seen this second tomb

> *where the walls*
> *Of Magnus Martyr hold*
> *Inexplicable splendour of Ionian white and gold*

as he described the interior in his 'Fire Sermon'.

Thus the terrible scene was set for the English martyrs. Mary's victims died with Coverdale's language on their lips, Elizabeth's with St Jerome's. The Protestants saw themselves as a people taken back to Christian essentials by the New Testament. For the first time they had in their hands, and in their heads, everything which Jesus had said, everything he had done. They possessed too his disciples' and St Paul's groundplan for the Church. It was all much simpler and at the same time far grander than anything previously offered them by the professional priesthood. Two major issues made it impossible for them to remain with the 'old' religion. One was the belief in faith alone being the requirement for entry to Christ's eternal kingdom, the other was, after the reading the Gospel accounts of the Last Supper, doubt that a priest could, or needed to, turn bread and wine into flesh and blood. For these two principles, particularly the last, they allowed themselves to be burnt alive. The 'old' Christians died as terribly for their universal Church, the fifteen-centuries-old edifice which Christ himself had founded, and which Peter and his heirs had administered, as they believed, without break. Previous crises and splits seemed to have been little known. The enormity precipitated by Wycliffe, Luther, and now the English government, alone concerned them. For the Catholic martyrs there could be no Christendom outside their own beloved historic Christendom. To be without its saving limits was to be in a non-place, spiritually speaking. And so, in spite of knowing what would happen to them if they were captured, those who had fled the country now crept back as a secret missionary force to lay trails for the time when England would need to find its way back to Christendom. They were nearly all caught, given show trials, monstrously tortured and put to death with the utmost suffering. Even for a country with a popular devotion to executions, those during the years immediately following the secession from Rome outdid themselves in legalized obscenities.

Whether one was a common murderer, a village nuisance or some poor mother unable to believe in transubstantiation, it was the custom to die gallantly. Both the crowds and the officials were prepared for courage and eloquence at the stake and on the scaffold, and were rarely disappointed. But no blame was attached to how people behaved when fire and knife got to work. Execution literature is full of the incredible control and nobility of the penultimate moments of a nervous system fully conscious of the manner of its impending destruction. There are records of bodies shouting and shifting half an hour or more after the flames had been lit. Humane concessions such as being stood in a tar-barrel, or having a bag of gunpowder tied under the chin, were far from effective. Cremation techniques, as practised in the East, were unknown and people were burnt not dissimilarly to the roasting of the carcases of sheep and oxen on a holiday.

Scarcely less horrible than the executions was most of the so-called theology of both sides. Volumes of foul-mouthed abuse, superstition, legalisms and sheer religious fantasy poured from university pundits and politicians alike. Yet through it ran a stream of the purest Christian language, Cranmer's liturgy, Marian poetry, the newly translated Bible. Extremes prevailed. The twin Catholic and Protestant accounts of the English Reformation are of polarities; what happened on the less-caring ground which spread between these poles is still a matter of speculation.

While everybody generally believed in God, many appeared to have done so with little interest in religion. To them God was only important when it came to politics, to the crown.

In Queen Mary's reign it was Bishop Stephen Gardiner, the clothier's son from Bury St Edmund's, who had got the dread statute *De Heretico Comburendo* re-enacted, and in Queen Elizabeth's it had been Sir Francis Walsingham who had seen fit to apply the treason law to its limits. Zealous sentencing reflected patriotism. The nation was asked to see the heresies and treasons

The Church of St Magnus the Martyr, London

Near by is the Monument with its flaming ball and, until 1831, its inflammatory inscription accusing the 'Papish faction' of burning down London in 1666. The Church of St Magnus (an Orcadian?) was familiar to T. S. Eliot during his bank-clerk years and the reference to it in 'The Fire Sermon' in *The Waste Land* blazes up in the City's post First World War sleaziness. The 'Ionian' of its 'Inexplicable splendour of Ionian white and gold' meant for Eliot the last of the genuine modes of ecclesiastical music. The white and gold interior shelters the bones of Miles Coverdale of whom it was said, 'it was he more than any other single translator whose sense of rhythm produced that musical quality which is particularly evident in the Authorized Version of 1611'. Wren's City churches were to be classical phoenixes soaring from the ashes of gothic. Lost in the burning of the earlier St Magnus was the tomb of Henry Yevele, the architect of the nave of Westminster Abbey and the great master of the gothic style. Twenty years after writing *The Waste Land* Eliot was to watch Wren's phoenix churches, themselves on fire, providing pentecostal imagery for his *Four Quartets*.

which afflicted and endangered it cast into flames, ripped from its own flesh, whatever the agony. Both sentences left appalling religious scars on the landscape itself, so why don't we see them? Even if we no longer wander around with John Foxe's remorseless guidebook, or lack information about the Jesuits and their itinerary of blood, how is it possible for us now to feel nothing at all about the places where such things happened? Jesus said that if his friends failed to witness to what they had seen and heard, the very stones would cry out. But few now hear the stones of Smithfield, Marble Arch, or the flints of Aldham Common saying very much, if anything. The landscape of pain has a deadly reticence.

I sensed it at Hadleigh, that unwillingness to say more. Early teens and first wanderings in any geographical depth. Pressing through knapweed, nettles and waist-high grass to the enticing memorial. It is fiercely protected with Regency fencing, and its inscription races on and on, line after carved line, with measured accusation.

> *Mark this rude stone where Taylor dauntless stood,*
> *Where Zeal infuriate drank the Martyr's blood*
> *Hadleigh! That day how many a tearful eye*
> *Saw thy lov'd Pastor dragg'd a Victim by ...*

And very much more. Also safe within the pale, an earlier mark-stone, chipped and gnomic. I visit it every now and then, partly for the view, partly for the jolt, my own significant bonfire site. I would come straight from it to Cedric Morris's garden, within whose walls history wasn't allowed. Only today's plants and yesterday's art talk. Nothing as parochial as Rowland Taylor's burning. Its fumes never drifted through the great beds of Benton End irises. The territory of flowers and birds was what was holy to Morris, not that of ancient barbarities. He went out of his way to have nothing whatever to do with the Church, never to let his thoughts so much as brush against it. Constable had sat just down the road and painted St Mary's, with its sprawling aisles and lovely medieval lead broached spire but Morris vehemently told me that it made him feel physically sick just to go inside it. Or in any church. He was a passionate rejector. All the same, we carried him into it when he died at over ninety as it was the best way of getting a body from a bed to a grave. For all his contrariness, he would have understood.

Outside rise the towers of the Tudor gatehouse in which, they said, Dr Rowland Taylor awaited arrest, and in which, in July 1833, Father Hugh Rose certainly convened the Hadleigh Conference and thus inaugurated the Oxford Movement. During my twenties, grumpy Kensitites, followers of John Kensit, the Protestant agitator, had rented a little shop nearby and filled its window with 'no popery' posters. Hadleigh made the Reformation last, like a child with a multi-centred sweet, anxious not to see the back of it. Somehow it could not stop itself from toying with the issues for which Taylor died. At Benton End good care seemed to be taken not to know too much, or indeed anything, about such matters, so in that garden one was temporarily free of the whole thing. It was a delectable state. Yet the high ground and the monument are no more than a good long town walk away. The latter is like the tinder in the Seamus Heaney poem:

> *What did we know then*
> *Of tinder, charred linen and iron,*
>
> *Huddled at dusk in a ring,*
> *Our fists shut, our hope shrunken?*
>
> *What could strike a blaze*
> *From our dead igneous days?*
>
> *Now we squat on cold cinder,*
> *Red-eyed, after the flames' soft thunder*
>
> *And our thoughts settle like ash.*

The trouble with martyrs is the way in which every bit of their lives becomes encapsulated in their deaths. Rowland Taylor, it has always struck me, did not require such an encapsulation for him to be venerated and has been distorted by it. He perished superbly, that vast bulk incinerated speedily after Soyce, the local drunkard to whom Taylor had given his boots before stepping into a pitch-barrel, had knocked his brains out with a halberd. Soyce would have been later reviled in the Suffolk pubs for spoiling the sport. The fat old scholar (he was probably still in his fifties but physical and intellectual weight had lent him the attributes of agedness) had clambered off his horse, tugged the Ku-Klux-Klan hood from his head on which the hair had been clownishly cut to make him look ridiculous, sat on the Common and said, 'Soyce, I pray thee come and pull off my boots, and take them for your labour. Thou has long looked for them, now take them.' How long did Soyce reel round Hadleigh in dead man's boots? More pertinently, had he walked up from town specially 'to put the Doctor out of his misery'? The Doctor was saying the fifty-first psalm in the translation which is still in the 1662 Prayer Book when Soyce struck. For not saying it in Latin, the justice Sir John Shelton hit him in the mouth. The psalm contains the lines, 'Thou shalt open my lips, O Lord: and my mouth shall show thy praise. For thou desirest no sacrifice, else would I give it thee; but thou delightest not in burnt-offerings.' The Doctor was tied to an eight-foot post by horse-chains and the kindling was set alight. 'Merciful father of heaven,' he shouted, 'for Jesus Christ's my Saviour's sake receive my soul into thy hands!' It was then that Soyce moved in. The Doctor died looking down Angel Street to the broached spire on 2 February 1555, a short-light bitter day.

When poor, quarrelsome Robert Barnes had been burnt at Smithfield fifteen years earlier, he had spoken words about witnessing to truth by landscape which had greatly appealed to Wordsworth.

To burn me, or to destroy me, cannot so greatly profit them. For when I am dead, the Sunne and the Moone, the Stones and the Elements, Water and Fire, yes and also the Stones shall defend this cause against them, rather than that veritie should perish.

Rowland Taylor was too big a man in every sense for the comfort of neighbours who did not share his views and no sooner was the moment ripe when one of them, the priest of Aldham, 'one Averth', hired by a local papist lawyer named Foster, descended on his extraordinary parish, where it was said that the encouragement of learning among even the clothworkers and farmhands and their wives had turned Hadleigh into a little university. Given an armed guard by the lawyer, Fr Averth got into Dr Taylor's church, set up a Catholic altar and announced that a Mass would be celebrated the following day, Palm Sunday. When Taylor remonstrated, Foster adroitly fixed matters which could only lead to the Doctor's death. Almost a year passed before it happened, a year when he was as philosophical as Job, if cheerfuller

Hadleigh, Suffolk: the parish church and Deanery Tower

The scene from which Rowland Taylor went to his trial and death, which is also one of the crucial scenes in the life of the English Church. Hadleigh, the 'head place', was a Saxon capital whose early connections with Canterbury made it a 'Peculiar', a living which was not in the control of local administrators. Its rectors were no ordinary priests, but men of distinction and learning. Dr Taylor was Cranmer's chaplain. An earlier rector had become Lord Chancellor and Archbishop of York. In 1495 another had built himself a palace next to the church, the present 'Tower' being its magnificent gateway.

These two buildings, the big sprawling church and the brick tower, now possess associations, not only with martyrdom, but with those once-conflicting beliefs for which Catholics and Protestants alike suffered death in the sixteenth century. For in the church worshipped two boys from Hadleigh Grammar School, John Overall and John Blois, who were eventually to become translators of the Authorized Version, and in the Tower there took place, in 1833, the Conference which agreed to issue the momentous 'Tracts for the Times', thus inaugurating the Oxford Movement. The seeds of today's evangelical and sacramental dualism began to shoot in this spot.

66

I will tell you how I have been deceived, as I think, I shall deceive a great many. I am, as you see, a man that has a very great carcase, which I thought should have been buried in Hadleigh churchyard, if I had died in my bed, as I hoped I should have done; but however I see I was deceived; and there are a great number of worms in Hadleigh churchyard, which would have jolly feeding upon this carrion, which they have looked for many a day. But now I know we are deceived, both I and they; for this carcase must be burned to ashes, and so shall they lose their bait and feeding, that they looked to have had of it.

He was executed on the rough ground between his parish and Averth's, with Kersey tower clear in the distance. The tower was then almost new, being completed only seventy years before, its knapped flint distantly sparkling when the western sun caught it. Taylor had passed near it on the way back from his London trial, glimpsing the affluent little wool town before trailing on to Hadleigh, where the whole population turned out to meet him, crying and upset, but at the same time exalted. The huge, hooded figure on the horse crossed the bridge over the Brett and was then guided along Angel Street. 'I have preached to you God's word and truth, and am come this day to seal it with my blood.' The hood was supposed to stifle this sort of thing. It was the fifth week after the Epiphany and his flock, back once more to the Mass, would have heard, in Latin, the parable of the tares. 'I will say to the reapers, Gather ye together first the tares, and bind them in bundles to burn them: but gather the wheat into my barn.' What was tares and what was wheat had become an official matter and had nothing to do with Christ's understanding of the difference.

It was uphill all the way to the bonfire, and a fine view all round when he reached the spot. This was far off down the field until recently but the straightening of the A1071 to Ipswich has destroyed its earlier isolation. Similarly, Angel Street, while scattered with a few timbered houses which could have belonged to his parishioners, and leading off to right and left with Threadneedle Street, Pilgrim Cottage, Lady Lane and Magdalen Street, has become as late twentieth century as garages, fish-and-chip shops, small industries and even St Joseph's Roman Catholic Church with its modern concessional spirelet can make it. Yet it is still the Doctor's route. This is the way he came. From a mountain of flesh and a good brain to ashes all in a few hours.

Aldham Common: where Rowland Taylor was burnt at the stake in 1535 (Charles Hall)

Inscription (Charles Hall)

Mark this rude stone where Taylor dauntlefs stood,
Where Zeal infuriate drank the Martyrs blood
Hadleigh! That day how many a tearful eye
Saw thy lov'd Pastor dragg'd a Victim by:
Still scattering gifts and blefsings as He past.
To the Blind Pair "his farewell alms were cast:
His clinging Flock e'en here around him pray'd
As thou hast aided us. Be God thine Aid".
Nor taunts, nor bribe of mitred rank, nor stake.
Nor blows, nor flames, his heart of firmnefs shake:
Serene   his folded hands his upward eyes
Like holy Stephen's. seek the opening skies:
There fix'd in rapture, his prophetic sight
,Views Truth dawn clear on England's Bigot night:
Triumphant Saint! He bow'd and kifs'd the rod.
And soar'd on Seraph wing to meet his God.

The faggots had been cut from the hedgerows and copses he had passed on his walks. The greasy smoke could have drifted down into his own rectory garden, although, knowing that height in winter, the fumes would most likely have been torn along the dead fields by icy winds. There is no mention of whether it rained, shone or snowed. The Doctor stripped to his shirt; the crowd too could have unwrapped itself a little given the great heat of his fire. The hard-drinking Soyce had brought modification to the terrible scene. After his blow it had changed from execution to funeral, and to prayer-meeting.

The footpath to Aldham, 'one Averth's' parish, skirts Taylor's martyrdom site and is tangled in undergrowth, and pressed by what looks like an Enclosure hedge of hawthorn and sloe. The common has all vanished under corn and if the monument was not there, what would one see? The testimony of the elements, as Robert Barnes insisted? Only if one were a visionary, not a man taking a short-cut. But indulging in the associative game brings one close to what happened. There was lucerne by the track, and not surprisingly, for this was one of the old rotation crops. It is the 'horned clover' which William Turner is said to have introduced to England, and Turner was Taylor's close friend. They had been boys together in Northumberland and had met up again at Cambridge where Ridley, another Northumbrian, had taught Turner Greek and played tennis with him. Turner, Ridley and Rowland were among the crowd of young reformers who met at the White Horse Inn, known as 'Germany' by critics because it was where Lutheran notions were aired and where banned books were read. It was while he was at Cambridge that Turner wrote a herbal because, he said, he could 'learn never a Greek, nor Latin, nor English name' of any plant, and so became the first Englishman to study botany scientifically. He also became a plant-collector, and made a garden at Kew – and everywhere he went – and wrote on taking baths and drinking wine. It was Turner who had managed to get for Taylor the severely proscribed Protestant manual *Unio Dissidentium*, and who took him to Latimer's revolutionary sermons. It was Turner the flower searcher from Morpeth who, more than any other man, set his large friend on the path to Aldham Common.

Reading martyrologies, one would never gather how happy

so many of the Protestant victims had been before various government agents caught up with them. Black-letter type, ferocious woodcuts, Foxe's dark artistry as a superb propagandist, and the unquenchable drama of their deaths have morbidly obscured their lively characters. At Cambridge, their headquarters, they took Christianity out of its official premises and aired it in walking debates on 'Heretics' Hill' and in the White Horse Inn. On the whole, they were strong young men from the countryside, the future Marian victims among them nearly all of an age. The face of their Christ had been wiped of the murky accretions which centuries of devotion and ecclesiastical habits had deposited upon it. Wycliffe, Tyndale, Erasmus, Coverdale and Luther had lifted intelligent hands to it and removed its candle-soot. Its new brightness and reality entranced them as it had the Apostles.

Thomas Bilney, 'little Bilney' from Norfolk, burnt in the Lollards' Pit at Norwich in 1531, was one of the first victims. No heretic, even by the standards of his day, he was nudged into the flames by lawyers. His life was full of strange linkings. Only twelve years before he had been ordained on the title of St Bartholomew's, Smithfield, London's Golgotha, and one of the things held against him just before his arrest was that he had given 'the anchoress of Norwich' a copy of Tyndale's New Testament. Dame Julian's successor was an inquiring woman. Bilney's martyrdom also preshadows Cranmer, for he too recanted after fear and confusion had forced him to deny his beliefs. Bilney's daring preaching of them through East Anglia after his first trial, and a subsequent two years of nervous illness brought on by self-hatred, was an act of crazy courage. Master Bilney died holy, declared a London child, and was burnt for contempt of court as much as anything. Bilney gave himself a rough time as a Christian until he came across Erasmus's Latin version of St Paul's *Letters* when 'my bruised bones leapt for joy'.

A decade or two later the young Marian martyrs showed less painful tussles with themselves. Bilney was a penultimate medieval battering his slight self towards the modern universe of which they were a natural part. This was their tragedy. But, like Wordsworth in 1795, for a while it was bliss to be in at the beginning, and their early days reflected it. They talked, laughed and lived Christ at Cambridge, and on the long journeys up and down Britain which they had to make, for as up-and-coming leaders of the reformed Church they were given huge tasks. They were extremely good writers and speakers, with a brilliant literary and colloquial emphasis created by having the Bible and liturgy in English. Their stakes leafed in the coppices all unknown, Nicholas Ridley from Unthank Hall near Willimoteswick, Northumberland, Hugh Latimer the farmer's son from Leicestershire and Cranmer himself heading a small army destined for the blazing furze. How little the landscape has been permitted to say about them! How minimal too is the death geography of the Catholic saints. It is as if place had managed to dissociate itself from what had happened in it.

The only loss when they ban stubble-burning will be its primordial imagery. A fired field by the coast and a figure crossing it brought to mind Milton's beautiful Satan walking 'over the burning marle' to the beach of an inflamed sea to call his legions,

> *Angel forms, who lay intrans't*
> *Thick as autumnal leaves that strow the brooks*
> *In Vallombrosa ...*

Countless creatures perish when stubble is fired but seeds often escape. The Bible is full of fire and God's first appearance to the monotheist Moses is from the heart of a burning bush. Ezekiel, the fire-poet prophet, had to face a terrifying firework display of cherubims, their likeness that of wheeling lamps and lightning flashes, bright coals and rings of eyes, before 'I saw what might have been brass glowing like fire in a furnace from the waist upwards; and from the waist downwards I saw what looked like fire with encircling radiance. Like a rainbow in the clouds on a rainy day was the sight of that encircling radiance; it was like the appearance of the glory of the Lord ... "Man", he said, "stand up, and let me talk with you."'

It is only latterly that Christians have lived when a naked flame did not provide the only illumination, the only heat, the only means of utter destruction. The religious symbolism of fire is universal. 'All things, O priests, are on fire,' the Buddha tells his followers in his fire sermon. 'Our God is a devouring fire,' St Paul tells his own countrymen. St James shakes his head – 'How great a matter a little fire kindleth!' In the unreformed churches there was pentecostal fire on the altar and hell-fire over the chancel arch. Around the villages and little towns, while they did not burn stubble, they ritually burnt ling and gorse, and roused the nation during times of peril by ringing it with headland and promontorial bonfires. Pain was the body's own fire. Sunsets were pictures of torment, of the universe bleeding. One way or another, physically and spiritually, men had to brave fire to return to God. When Latimer began to hasten on his way to the stake, and when he solaced Ridley with his famous, 'Be of good comfort, and play the man. We shall this day light such a candle by God's grace in England, as (I trust) shall never be put out', he was one who was hurrying to an appointment with Christ through the fire-gate.

Poetry reaches furthest towards the psychology of those slaughtered for the faith during its years of transition. It presents a landscape which sometimes smokes, like Sinai, and a scene in which love burns. The Jesuit Robert Southwell had the misfortune to have the fiendish Richard Topcliffe as usher when he reached the fire-gate, beyond which waited his Saviour. Topcliffe chased recusants as most men chased hares. Their palpitations when on the rack to beat all racks, which he'd fixed up in his own house, thrilled him. A bonfire was considered a merciful end in comparison with that which Topcliffe could devise. Robert Southwell's end was awful. His agony, his poetry and his prayer should fissure the tarmac at Marble Arch and hang in the Park Lane trees. Oxford Street in December should no more than glimmer when compared with the light of his 'Burning Babe'.

> *As I in hoary winter's night*
> *Stood shivering in the snow,*
> *Surprised I was with sudden heat*
> *Which made my heart to glow;*
> *And lifting up a fearful eye*
> *To view what fire was near,*
> *A pretty babe all burning bright*
> *Did in the air appear;*
> *Who, scorchèd with excessive heat,*
> *Such floods of tears did shed,*
> *As though His floods should quench His flames,*
> *Which with His tears were bred:*
> *'Alas!' quoth He, 'but newly born*

Oxford: the Church of St Mary Magdalen

Thomas Cranmer stares out from his niche in the Martyr's Aisle on to the scene of his execution. He was sixty-seven, close-cropped but with a thick white beard, according to Foxe. Five months earlier he had watched the burning of Bishop Ridley and Bishop Latimer from the top of his prison tower. He died on the first day of spring, 1556. It was raining. Having made his amazing recantation in St Mary's, he ran to the stake through the wet street with Spanish priests trotting beside him, begging him to change his mind. It was less than five years since he had laid the foundations of a liturgy whose phraseology would influence the English language for ever. He was thrust high and dragged low in the cruel upheavals surrounding the succession, but died sublimely, his right hand blazing first. In his collect for the third Sunday in Lent he beseeches God to 'stretch forth the right hand of thy majesty, to be a defence against all our enemies'. He was a Nottinghamshire man, who never in his wildest dreams could have imagined the accidents and coincidences which would hurry him to Canterbury, and so to his dreadful death.

In fiery heats I fry,
Yet none approach to warm their hearts
Or feel my fire but I!'

'My faultless breast the furnace is;
The fuel, wounding thorns;
Love is the fire, and sighs the smoke;
The ashes, shames and scorns;
The fuel Justice layeth on,
And Mercy blows the coals,
The metal in this furnace wrought
Are men's defilèd souls:
For which, as now on fire I am
To work them to their good,
So will I melt into a bath;
To wash them in my blood.'
With this He vanish'd out of sight
And swiftly shrunk away,
And straight I callèd unto mind
That it was Christmas Day.

For today's re-workings of this metaphysical imagery we have William Golding's *Darkness Visible*, a novel in which a boy, deprived of all identity by the fires of the London blitz, family, friends, memory and his original appearance, activates love in a heartless, depraved post-war town plunged into materialism and punk sub-culture. Also Russell Hoban's after-the-bomb masterly tract, *Riddley Walker*, the tale of a charred England feebly guttering with the little that it can remember.

4

*T*he Field
Under the Hill

As children we rejoiced in frustrating the strong surge of some ditchlet by thrusting a board across its little course and seeing the pent-up waters rise and be forced to take off tangentially. At first there would be no more than a jolting, seeking, liquid worm reminiscent of our own deeply regarded pee on the arid farm-track, then the new stream would broaden, accommodate itself to a more tortuous valley – and then run fast. Bastardy was often like this. By proscribing the official channel it made life a lateral business.

Round about the year 1332 Stacy de Rokayle, one of the powerful Despensers' men, fathered a son while on a visit to the Malvern area from his home at Shipton-under-Wychwood in Oxfordshire. The Despensers were the lords of Malvern Chase and resided at nearby Hanley Castle, where there is a castle no longer, only a troubling of the earth's surface where it stood. This son was the poet William Langland. His father's father, Peter de Rokayle, had, with others, including Hugh le Despenser himself, who was executed for it, risked all in an attempt to rescue Edward II from Berkeley Castle. Thus the sad king was honoured by the grandfather of England's greatest Christian poet and by the unbelieving poet, Christopher Marlowe, alike.

Langland was most likely born at Ledbury and brought up in Colwall on a little farm by the side of the road which runs from Malvern to Ross-on-Wye. When Stacy de Rokayle refused to allow him the use of his surname, and 'de Colwall' too was denied him because the Bishop of Hereford had a house in the village and might sign himself thus if he had a mind to, the poet called himself after his mother's farm, a narrow flat holding which is still known as Longlands on the map. Except for having the old Worcester–Malvern–Hereford railway line running across it and the crumbling away of a nearby fortress-mansion, the scene remains plainly faithful to that described in *Piers Plowman*. Visiting it leaves one wordless. A grandstand view is provided from the yard of the Duke of Wellington pub: the long field which Langland disliked working in, because of his own length, he maintained, and the difficulty of bending, lies just below one a little to the left. Elizabeth Barrett Browning's and John Masefield's childhood fields almost adjoin it, and, to the right, bosky beneath the Herefordshire Beacon, is none other than the 'Field of Folk' itself, virtually unaltered after six hundred years. A thousand feet above it, topping the Beacon, is one of the best multivallate Iron Age forts in Britain, the concentric rings of it following the contours of the hill itself. Philologically a 'vallar' descends from both a rampart and from the wreath of flowers placed on the brow of the first soldier to mount it. The childhoods of William Langland, Elizabeth Barrett Browning, John Masefield and, via his mother, Edward Elgar, were all dominated by the Herefordshire Beacon and its warrior-summit, and to set 'that long, angry rumble of a poem, that never-ending summer thunderstorm', as Peter Levi calls *Piers Plowman*, at its base was a daring decision.

For, its childhood associations aside, a humpy water-meadow below the Malvern Hills was hardly the most obvious site on which to crowd all one's contemporaries. The gangling Langland on his restless tramps between London and the West Midlands must have seen scores of more suitable locations. What about the plain view from the Hills itself, a sprawling level which really does suggest a kingdom? This must have been equally familiar to someone who lived the first twenty years of his life within easy reach of those tempting ridgeway footpaths. But the great dream-writers know better than to exchange a visionary field for an open prospect. *The Pilgrim's Progress in the Similitude of a Dream* begins:

As I walked through the wilderness of this world, I lighted on a certain place, where was a den; and I laid me down in that place to sleep: and as I slept I dreamed a dream. I dreamed, and behold I saw a man clothed with rags, standing in a certain place, with his face from his own house, a book in his hand, and a great burden upon his back.

The British Camp on Herefordshire Beacon

This Iron Age hill fort, 1,114 feet above sea-level and covering thirty-two acres, was a major landscape influence on William Langland, Elizabeth Barrett Browning, Edward Elgar and John Masefield. At its foot lie the hillocks and brooks of *Piers Plowman*, one of Britain's most sacred scenes, the place where the archetypal tiller of its soil becomes Christ. Langland, like most writers, and perhaps because he knew all too well the hard facts of farming, occasionally questioned the force within him which insisted upon elevating reality to such heights, only to be told, 'I am Imagination, I am never idle . . .'

Great Malvern Priory: medieval glass in the north aisle of the chancel

Langland was at school here and there remains much glass and carving which he would have seen. The Priory was within walking distance of his mother's farm. Almost nothing certain is known of his life but the windows in the Priory church could be portraits of some of his 'folk'. It was from this society he set out for London, carrying, as country people do, an intense remembrance of his local scenes, both those of nature and of art.

'"When I was young," said I, "many years ago, my father and my friends paid for my schooling until I assuredly knew what Holy Writ meant, and what is best for the body, as the Book tells, and what surest for the soul."'

I looked, and saw him open the book, and read therein; and as he read, he wept and trembled: and not being able to contain, he brake out with a lamentable cry; saying, 'What shall I do?'

Piers the Ploughman begins:

One summer season, when the sun was warm, I rigged myself out in shaggy woollen clothes, as if I were a shepherd; and in the garb of an easy-living hermit I set out to roam far and wide through the world, hoping to hear of marvels. But on a morning in May, among the Malvern Hills, a strange thing happened to me, as though by magic. For I was tired out by my wanderings, and as I lay down to rest under a broad bank by the side of a stream, and leaned over gazing into the water, it sounded so pleasant that I fell asleep.

And I dreamt a marvellous dream: I was in a wilderness, I could not tell where, and looking Eastwards I saw a tower high up against the sun, and splendidly built on top of a hill; and far beneath it was a great gulf, with a dungeon in it, surrounded by deep, dark pits, dreadful to see. But between the tower and the gulf I saw a smooth plain, thronged with all kinds of people, high and low together, moving busily about their worldly affairs.★

★ From *Piers the Ploughman*, translated into modern English by J. F. Goodridge, Penguin, 1966.

Both dream narratives proved to be compelling and were devoured by their readers for some two to three centuries before the language of each great allegory gradually fell from popular understanding. Each writer knew that he had struck a popular vein, so much so that Bunyan followed up with a sequel, and Langland with two more versions, in the final one of which, sublimely, his ploughman hero becomes Christ himself.

Langland's Malvern was a landscape recalled, for he must have written most of all three versions of *Piers Plowman* in London's Cornhill, a very different eminence. No farm there from which a mere acolyte might have the nerve to criticize Church and state from base to apex, only a hovel containing his wife and daughter, and in which he woke, 'dressed like a beggar'. William, Kit and Colette Langland, where do they lie? Nobody will ever know. I fancy them seeded down into the Saxon depths of Wren's St Michael's, or St Peter's, or, more suitably, under 39 Cornhill, which stands on the site of the house in which Thomas Gray was born. In such a small and immensely literary country, the dust of poets and their common scenery tends to pile up, name upon name, image upon image, place upon place. A remote chance: might Gray have heard as a boy in his unhappy home in Cornhill that the author of *Piers Plowman* had lived next door? Might not this possibility and the fact that his first years were spent in London's immemorial grain-market have sown the *Elegy*?

Langland would have seen Cornhill in unavoidable ethical terms, the harvest waggons stacked high when things were good, and a large number of them never arriving at all after the Black Death. As a young man at only the first stage of priesthood, he scraped a living by singing prayers for the dead in the City chantries. This fringe vantage point, the clearly remarkable education he had received at Great or Little Malvern Priory and the intellectual climate produced by the semi-destruction of all Britain's institutions by the plague, caused him to look hard at the Church and at Christ. He saw that the first was not at all the actual reflection of the other, insist though it might. Being (just) in the priesthood, and half a gentleman, lent the necessary zest to his vagabondage. He wandered, and when the time came for him to tell the tale, he made everybody in the kingdom join him in a little meadow which, from the way in which it contin-

St Michael's Cornhill, London

The tower is the work of one of Wren's assistants, either Nicholas Hawksmoor or William Dickenson. Thomas Gray was born near by and the sound of its building filled his childhood. Below it lie the fragments of an earlier St Michael's in which Langland could have sung, for a pittance, his prayers for the dead.

'I live in London and on London. The tools I labour with for my living are pater-noster *and* dirige; *sometimes my Psalter and my Seven Psalms; and so I sing for the souls of such as help me and supply me with food. I go to their homes perhaps once in a month, and sometimes to one and sometimes to another, and I eat what they give me and take nothing away.'*

Piers Plowman

ued to haunt him even in distant Cornhill, must have been a favourite spot for escaping to when the Priory inmates at Malvern, or ploughing his mother's land, prevented him from a poet's first duty, which is to drift, observe and dream.

I always like to come to Langland's 'Field of Folk' from the Ledbury direction, so that I am facing the Herefordshire Beacon all the way. The road passes Longlands on the left, then, on the right, the Duke of Wellington inn ('Hey! trolly, lolly!'), eventually bending round to climb a foothill called Chance's Pitch. About a mile from here the road descends to the stream by which Langland fell asleep. In his day named Promeswell or Primeswell, it is now called Pewtress Spring, and flows under the main road, pumping out a daily twenty thousand gallons of water which, since 1890, has been the basis of Schweppes's carbonated tonic-water. Langland lay by the brook which rises from the spring in the valley on the left of the road.

> *But on a May morwenyng on Malverne hilles*
> *Me befel a ferly, of fairie me thoughte;*
> *I was wery, forwandrit, and wente me to reste*
> *Undir a brood bank be a bourne side,*
> *And as I lay and lenide and lokide on the watris*
> *I slomeride into a slepyng, it swiyede so merye.*

Footpaths from Pewtress Spring take one to Langland's village, Colwall, and to Colwall Stone, the much larger development which grew up around the railway. It is an extensive parish of springs, mills, Victorian enterprises (breweries, vinegar works, racing, prep schools, and the arts, as well as Schweppes) but with odd echoes of its poet everywhere. For instance, part two of *Piers Plowman* opens with William searching about all summer for Do-well, Do-better and Do-best, and falling asleep, this time under a lime tree (an avenue of lime trees now runs through Colwall Stone) dreaming about a tall man 'very like myself' who turns out to be Thought. Thought leads him to Do-well, Do-better and Do-best, the virtues he is looking for. In St James's Church at Colwall the sixteenth-century tomb of the Walwyn family has 'Doe well' carved on it. This was the time when the poem was last generally readable before the modern translations. Today's Colwall makes an effective background to the allegory, with its faint persistent hints of Langland's presence. Frank Goodridge talks of his imagination being essentially visual and dramatic, and of parts of *Piers Plowman* containing ideal film material. 'We are struck at once by the fullness and variety of his pictures of the Plain of the world, with its crowded panoramas and ugly close-ups, its noisy comings and goings and its intimate details ... Langland does not offer us the "plane mirror reflection" of the comedy of manners, but rather a comedy of humours, where single properties assume a life more powerful than that of ordinary individuals and gather into themselves a large number of observations and experiences.'

Piers the hero 'is the perfect Christian and the representative of Christ mirrored in the soul of everyman. Having failed to discover him in the priesthood of his day, the dreamer must look for his image reflected in the powers of his own soul.' Peter the ploughman, or a human being engaged at his central task of providing food, becomes first Peter the rock and then Peter-Christ, having found Love through Truth. As the middle Peter he has to build a barn (the Church) called Unity in which to store the ripe grain of Christ's true followers. But ludicrous and falsely religious creatures find their way into the barn and destroy its purpose. Peter flees this corrupted and misused edifice but not the holy idea behind its construction. He sees with a mixture of bitter humour and despair that it houses all the big business, entertainment industry and clerical trickery and silliness of his time. That Christ's 'Unity' barn is still administered with professional efficiency in spite of a priesthood which has been decimated and demoralized by successive waves of bubonic plague is no comfort to Peter its architect. It only proves the ignorance and insensitivity of the administration. There is nothing for it but for him to clear out of this hollow structure of a Church and take to the road.

> '*Bi cryste*', *quod Consience tho*, '*I wil bicome a pilgryme,*
> *And walken as wyde as al the worlde lasteth,*
> *To seke Piers the Plowman . . .*'

People who live facing views like those seen from the Malverns often feel that they must either cross them or enter them. Or even fill them. A stretching plain is a landscape with open arms. Langland, with his home on one side and his school on the other of the Herefordshire Beacon, must frequently have found his emotions rarefied by sheer distance alone. The tremendous sweeps of vale towards Wales and Oxford would have acted as clarifying agents to a man who did so much of his thinking outdoors. Even when he was farming Longlands,

> *. . . too weak to work with sickle or with scythe*
> *And too long in the back, believe me, to stoop low,*
> *Or to last any length of time working as a workman*

and maybe himself occasionally ploughing those peculiarly level strip-fields on the way to Ledbury, the scenery was such that he

would have been endlessly forced to look beyond them. It was not only the Malverns (*moel-bryn* = bare hill) which tempted him like a page on which nothing had yet been written, or nothing now worth reading, but the level ground too, which, with its new spires and parochial markings, looked so blissful from the summit, although it was full of new graves. But when the moment came to write, instead of taking his message to a far-flung scene, he had the notion of bringing everyone to Colwall to receive it. Not the kingdoms of the earth but a Field full of Folk. It was masterly. Chaucer, said Nevill Coghill, revealed England through individuals, Langland through crowds.

Four bouts of Black Death, plus the restlessness of incipient revolution, had set the kingdom scurrying like the inhabitants of a disturbed anthill. Although a necessary wanderer himself – poet's privilege – Langland deplored all this traipsing about to seek cures and pardons and opportunities. It was better to look for Truth at home than for wonders at Walsingham or Brom-

Looking across to Ledbury from
Clifton Hill: the land of the River
Teme

Then seiz'd the sons of Urizen the
plough: they polished it
From rust of ages: all its ornament of
gold and silver and ivory
Re-shone across the field immense,
where all the nations
Darken'd like mould in the divided
fallows, where the weed
Triumphs in its own destruction.
They took down the harness
From the blue walls of Heaven,
starry, jingling, ornamented
With beautiful art, the study of
Angels, the workmanship of
Demons,
When Heaven and Hell in
emulation strove in sports of glory.
The noise of rural work resounded
through the heavens of heavens.

William Blake, 'The Tillage of Urizen'

holm. Truth tells Piers that he must stay on his own field and till it. But if he *had* to make a pilgrimage, he must carry some of his own seed-corn with him, not a begging bowl. 'Carry neither purse, nor scrip [a pilgrim-beggar's wallet], nor shoes,' advised Christ. Society had to be cleansed and redeemed, but it had to be a settled society. 'I have heard Conscience say that it was natural for a man to be buried where he was christened, in his own parish.' Langland was almost certainly christened in the parish church at Colwall which was dedicated to an apostle who had reputedly died far from home, St James. Much of the building which Langland knew still stands. Piers is told that it is Christ-like to plough and harvest, and that the heathen are called such because they dwell on untilled land. However, a man can be excused for running away if he has a nagging wife, a leaking roof or a smoke-belching hearth. All the same, strolling about seeking the good life is a will-o'-the-wisp business; the good life has to be found where a man is centred. By encouraging people to seek cures for soul and body all over the place, the Church has decimated its spiritual power. The poet is exceptionally furious with the hordes of clergy walking about England, selling indulgences to the scared, meddling in parishes not their own, and corrupting what remains of the old Christian integrity with their myths. Human joys, including sexual ones, are to be celebrated, and there is a rueful note of a personal kind in his description of sexual failure due to ageing.

> [*Fortune*] *hit me under the ear, I can hardly*
> *hear; he buffeted me about the mouth and beat out*
> *my teeth, and gyved me with gout, I could not*
> *walk about. And my wife sorrowed for the woe*
> *I suffered and most certainly wished I were in*
> *Heaven. For the limb she loved and was fond of*
> *feeling, especially at night when we were*
> *naked, I could in no way make behave in*
> *the way she wanted, old age and she, to*
> *tell the truth, had so utterly battered it.**

The Fair Field of Folk is all worldly addresses when it should be man's one true address where he and his Creator-Saviour

---

* Translated by Nevill Coghill.

naturally abide. Yet it turns out to be a mart, a fairground, a crazy parliament, a folly-field, the depressingly re-occurring Waste Land of every generation. Of the countless pictures of the seven sins these, says Nevill Coghill, 'are the most lively, the most scrofulous and the most penitent'.

Like me, Coghill found his way to the foot of the Malverns by consulting Allan Bright's *New Light on 'Piers Plowman'*, a guide which, if its claims cannot be wholly substantiated, is the only one that works. In any case I have a passion for the local bee-in-bonnet hypothesis of the indigenous scholar and, as everybody knows who has read it over the past half century, Bright's signpost to both Langland's little home farm and his Fair Field is excitingly convincing. Learned families like the Colwall Brights cannot live in the territory of a great book without pacing it out sooner or later. *New Light* modestly offers a discovery as a theory. I have come to it, as it happened, on a peerless gold day between two wild and murky ones. The sun has brought out the folk in their perhaps hundreds, although these are all up above, not in the Field. Two only are there, a couple in their thirties who criss-cross it anxiously, finding it too open and too wet for what they have in mind until the man, patting a knoll, draws the woman down and urgently begins to make love. Sunday noon. The complaining sheep bunch together in fours and tens, and squelch in the fold. The birds sing and the Langland-Schweppes spring chatters in its bed. Here, wrapped up in his woolly cloak, 'as I a shep were', he had sprawled, gazing into the water until mesmerized and sent to sleep. When he woke up he was, of course, in rackety Cornhill with Kit and Colette, and dressed in mildly clerical rags.

I semi-splash through the lush pastures to where 'A deop dale bi-neothe/a dungun ther-inne/With deop dich and derk' is now sunny Oldcastle Farm and a nearby dried-up moat, as well as, presumably, the now vanished castle's fishpond. This is Colwall's foothills province of Evendine, its tilting water-table, its fountain bubbling at grass level below the coppice belts. The village extends to the crest of the Malverns where the Shire Ditch forms one of the most sensational parish boundaries in England. Gilbert de Clare, Earl of Gloucester, had this Ditch dug a century before *Piers Plowman*. Directly opposite, on the western limits of Colwall, and only a mile or so from Langland's home farm, is Hope

End, where Elizabeth Barrett lived for twenty years. 'For God placed me like a dial/In the open ground.' For her the Malverns were the 'Keepers of Piers Plowman's visions' and 'the earliest classic ground of English poetry'. In a meadow below, when she was fifteen, trying to saddle a horse without help, she fell and injured her back, inaugurating the invalidism from which Robert Browning managed to rescue her. 'On this couch I weakly lie on,/While I count my memories.' These were of Colwall, her Eden, where her father had built an oriental mansion, lost a fortune, and had nursed Elizabeth along towards literary precosity. The oriental house has partly disappeared but its grounds, a great star of trees facing the Herefordshire Beacon, remain. 'Beautiful, beautiful hills,' she wrote to Robert from Wimpole Street, 'and yet not for the whole world's beauty would I stand among the sunshine and the shadow of them any more; it would be a mockery, like the taking back of a broken flower to its stalk.' When she was nine she got the Hope End gardeners to make her a floral man, the hero of her 'Hector in the Garden'. There he 'lay supinely/A huge giant, wrought of spade' with gentian eyes, daffodil helmet, violet mouth, lily sword, daisy armour and periwinkle belt.

> *Call him Hector, son of Priam!*
> *Such his title and degree.*
> *With my rake I smoothed his brow;*
> *Both his cheeks I weeded through . . .*

For years the Barrett carriage took her along the same lane which Langland walked to school, to read Greek to the blind Hugh Boyd at Malvern. In a poem on his blindness Elizabeth hears God ordering the 'golden stuff' of the Worcestershire landscape to 'stand off' where Boyd is concerned until to his 'light-proof' eyes 'Sensual and Unsensual seemed one thing viewed from one level'. In *Piers Plowman* the Lady Holy Church tells the dreamer, the man with his eyes closed to the merely physical, 'Now I will show you the meaning of the mountain, the dark valley, and the plain full of people.' Later on he meets Nature and Imagination. The first was reasonable and ravishing, and the latter assured him, 'I am never idle.' Nature approached Piers-Langland on Mount Middle-Earth (the Herefordshire Beacon), reminded him who he was, and drew its glories to his attention.

Harvesting at Biddenden, Kent

Beasts, birds and plants surrounded him, and all of them were 'reasonable', even when they were predators or weeds. Imagination tells him to take off, as it were, from Learning, adding 'You might be a philosopher if you could only hold your tongue.' He is quoting a popular saying of the time.

How close we are now to Langland, thanks to Dr Skeat and his successors! Skeat's Early English Text Society's *Piers Plowman* did not appear until just before and after Elizabeth Barrett Browning's death in 1861, so could her knowledge of the poem have been much more than that caught from its local glow? Through the Moorish windows of Hope End, beyond the carpet-bedded Hector, she appears to have had a full cognizance of its territory and meaning, dormant though it had lain from 1561 to her time. Langland is English literature's most inspired revisionist. He works the same ground three times until his morality-play figure grows into Christ. Bright calls *Piers Plowman* a great human biography. Long Will of Colwall and his Redeemer stand in for Everyman and his fate. The perplexed medieval intelligence cannot come any nearer to us than it does on the hillocky turf below Wynds Point.

The Malverns provide an averagely hundred-feet-high grandstand from which to survey all the open country from the Vale of Gloucester to the Midlands. I walked them from where they begin to rise near Bromsberrow towards where they level out at Alfrick. Except for their much-tramped spine, they are anything but 'bare'. Their sides are soft with short, wind-reduced grass and scattered plantations, and are veined all over with tracks. At Great Malvern heavily wooded Victorian gardens climb into them. These shrub mazes created by spa-dwellers of a century ago still rustle with what Hardy called 'rencounters', the chance collisions of friends and lovers. I walked north from Midsummer Hill, with the great deer park at Eastnor and Herefordshire spread out like a kingdom on my left, and still surprisingly empty Castlemorton Common lying low on my right. Past Hangman's Hill and then a glimpse of Little Malvern Priory, one of the smallest Benedictine houses, towards which Langland would have gravitated many a time, and then, from the Herefordshire Beacon, to look down into Piers' cosmos within the cosmos, his field, both the ploughed one and the crowded one. There were distractions here, lovely kites from the famous Kite Shop above the Malvern-water fountain, dreamy hang-gliders, glittering car-tops far below, racing children and dogs, and many cries and shouts. I noticed when I was down in it that none of this boisterousness reached the Field, which remained still.

In August 1810 Wordsworth rattled past these scenes on the top of a coach and knew instantly how he should really be seeing them – with his wife, on foot.

I looked at them with a trembling which I cannot describe when I thought that *you* had not seen them, but *might* have seen, if you had but taken the road through Bristol when you left Racedown; in which case I should certainly have accompanied you as far as' Bristol; or further, perhaps: and then I thought, that you would not have taken the coach at Bristol, but that you would have walked on Northwards with me at your side, till unable to part from each other we might have come in sight of those hills which skirt the road for so many miles, and thus continuing our journey (for we should have moved on at small expense) I fancied that we should have been so deeply into each others hearts, and been so fondly locked in each others arms, that we should have braved the worst and parted no more. Under that tree, I thought as I passed along we might have rested, of that stream we might have drank, in that thicket we might have hidden ourselves from the sun, and from the eyes of the passenger; and thus did I feed on the thought of bliss that might have been, which would have been intolerable from the force of regret had I not felt the happiness which waits me when I see you again. O Mary I love you with a passion of love which grows till I tremble to think of its strength ... I am every moment seized with a longing wish that you might see the objects which interest me as I pass along, and not having you at my side my pleasure is so imperfect that after a short look I had rather not see the objects at all.

Langland would have been delighted that his dream hills should have produced such an intense desire in a man for his wife. Did they make him similarly ache for Colette? Wordsworth's erstwhile friend William Hazlitt, perhaps as a riposte to the landscape-worship of his day, would also have taken them in from a coach window. 'One chief advantage of the great and magnificent objects of Nature is, that they stamp their image on the mind for ever; the blow need not be repeated to have the desired effect.' But then his wife was not a dutiful stay-at-home like Mary Wordsworth, she was a vagabond soul like Langland, ever hiking and returning to her famously dirty house bursting with health and traveller's tales. The Malverns! Her William should see them!

Some perfect plan, rather than the usual accident of birth, could have decreed that Elgar, Britain's Christian-mystic composer, should be also a native of Langland's country. The son of a music-shop proprietor in Worcester and organist of the city's Roman Catholic church, the youthful Elgar travelled weekly to Great Malvern to teach its intellectual residents about the new music – particularly Brahms – and to earn a pittance giving lessons. In 1970 the artist Leonard Campbell-Taylor, then nearly a hundred years old, told me that Elgar had arrived by bicycle at a house where he was staying and given a girl a music lesson for half-a-crown. Had come and left without being introduced to the guests. It was the Mozart treatment on a bourgeois scale. Another pupil, the daughter of Major-General Sir Henry Roberts of Redmarley D'Abitot, the splendiferously named parish at the Ledbury end of the Malverns, married this Edward Elgar, to the embarrassment of both their families. She was a novelist and poet, not very good, but genuine. 'Love the earth a little while' was her advice to her depressed husband. After a brief flight to London to get away from all the local difficulties their marriage had created, she brought him back to the Malverns and, following one or two house failures, to Congelow in Wells Road, with views all the way to Bredon. 'Congelow', presumably somebody's else's anagram, became Craeglea (Car-Elgar), their own. *Caractacus*, based on a story which his mother had told him about the fort on the Herefordshire Beacon, had just been performed, and in Craeglea Caroline was ruling the paper for the *Enigma Variations*, *Sea Pictures*, *The Apostles* and *Gerontius*. A lot of the composition was done on a bicycle, in the porch of Queen Hill Church near Longdon, and on the high, quiet paths of the Malvern range. Like Hardy, Elgar demanded a great silence in which to make his statements. Craeglea lasted four years and then they moved to Hereford, to London again, to Sussex, and were never to be quite so happy again. Ten years afterwards, when there could be no return to what he was at Malvern, Elgar wrote to a friend,

Great Malvern Priory from the altar rail

'Of children and of glory and praise greatly I dreamed, and how old folk sang Hosanna to the sound of an organ.'

Harvesting at Thaxted, Essex

'*The harvest truly is plenteous, but the labourers are few.*' – St Matthew

'*I had to sit three hours on Monday, at the tithe-dinner, debating part of the time whether it was Puseyism to bring a wheatsheaf into church for harvest-home worship . . . we are to have a feast. It will cost £7 and it will be tea for hundreds. The Baptist minister will be invited . . . and the Dissenters are coming to church.*' – William Cory, September 1875

Yes I remember only the sweetness of it – the spring, then the beans and the hives, only I suppose I shall never see it all again or cycle over the old place.

How lovely the [Longdon] Marsh must be – I envy you your seeing it and living in it again. During these two moments I have put in – all the people seem to disappear & only the eternal hills and all the memories of the old loveliness remains.

On to Ledbury. Past Longlands and Hope End, and to the old, wide-open town on the way to Wales. St Michael's, the parish church, which is virtually an annex at a few miles' remove of Hereford Cathedral, is wide open too. But not to direct inquiries about John Masefield. I have his walking-stick at home. It is a tall ash thumb-stick and too cumbrous for East Anglia, so it lolls in the hall, clearly associative even if one did not know its history. The learned lady in the church was short about him. No, there is no memorial to him in the church (there is one to the now thoroughly vilified Edward Moulton Barrett). No, there is no plaque on his birthplace, which is a *private house* – this said very distinctly. When the talk turned to Langland the information splashed forth like a scholarly river. Well, local celebrity feeds local prejudice. If there had been a guide in St Michael's in 1483 she would probably have answered, 'Will Langland – that scoundrel?' All that business about John Masefield and the sea, why he had only been on it for five minutes!

Masefield was in his early thirties when he wrote *The Everlasting Mercy*. Evelyn Underhill thought it superb, which it is, and that it lit the dry processes of the religious psychologist, which it does. It first appeared in the *English Review* in October 1911 and has always seemed to me to counterbalance the lamb-like image which has since developed of the young villagers slaughtered in their hundreds of thousands on the Western Front, and whose names fill up the war memorials. The hero of *The Everlasting Mercy* is, as Evelyn Underhill noted, violent in body, mind and soul. It was written at Great Hampden but the location is Masefield's primal scene. Curiously, he prefaces this long, outrageous and successful Christian poem with some lines from Langland's Suffolk contemporary John Lydgate –

> *Thy place is biggyd above the sterrys cleer,*
> *Noon erthely paleys wroughte in so statly wyse,*

Ledbury, Herefordshire

The birthplace of John Masefield, and of Saul Kane, the rural ruffian-cum-penitent of his *The Everlasting Mercy*. On his eighty-sixth birthday Masefield climbed the steep hill known as Chance's Pitch, not to revive memories of the stream by which Langland/Piers slept, which flows in it, but of recollections of a fabulous mail coach which had thrilled him when a boy. The hill, the Malverns themselves and all the border landscape never lost their power over him. In 1966 he wrote,

'For some years, like many children, I lived in Paradise, or rather, like a specially lucky child, in two Paradises linked together by a country of exceeding beauty and strangeness. In one extreme I was told that the ancient joy of Britons, the woad plant, grew; and in another extreme there was the wonder, where a hill moved for three days screaming as though it hurt.'

Grace before Ploughing

Com on my freend, my brothir moost enteer,
For the I offryd my blood in sacrifise.

Saul, the roaring-boy of the Ledbury fields and ale-houses who hears the rick-burning at 'Chancey's Pitch' – the entrance to the Field of Folk – hits out at God and man until in a redemptive language unsurpassed by any similar long poem of this century he feels in his heart 'the burning cataracts of Christ'. The poem concludes with a pre-First World War ploughing scene at Ledbury as the cruel Saul is transmuted into Piers–Christ with the help of old Callow, the archetypically ideally toiling English farm-labourer. The realism is Crabbe's updated, the

East Anglia: late-summer ploughing

'You can tell by the sound of the share in the soil where you are in the field. The gravelly stony patch is harsh and noisy, the wet patch makes a slithering noise, and in yet another belt, which stretches right across the field, the earth is soft and loamy, full of organic matter, and the plough goes silent . . . There are a score of details to watch for but when everything is going well my mind slides off into speculation. Perhaps this field has been under the plough off and on for three or four centuries; maybe longer. Ploughed by men in leather jerkins driving teams of oxen pulling crude wooden ploughs, but using the same words we use.'

Hugh Barrett, *Early to Rise*

'Piers the Ploughman is my manager, my bailiff, and my treasurer, and he will receive the payments due for his pardon. Piers, then, shall be my purveyor as well as my ploughman on earth; and I shall give him a team of oxen to plough the field of Truth.'

William Langland, translated by
J. F. Goodridge

philosophy Langland's. *The Everlasting Mercy* is also a repository of all the old farming sounds – and the old small-town sounds, if it comes to that. Langland–Piers, Newman–Elgar's Gerontius, Masefield's Saul, each sets out on his soul-journey where the Malverns remain visible.

> A ploughman's voice, a clink of chain,
> Slow hoofs, and harness under strain.
> Up the slow slope a team came bowing,
> Old Callow at his autumn ploughing,
> Old Callow, stooped above the hales,
> Ploughing the stubble into wales;
> His grave eyes looking straight ahead,
> Shearing a long straight furrow red;
> His plough-foot high to give it earth
> To bring new food for men to birth.
>
> O wet red swathe of earth laid bare,
> O truth, O strength, O gleaming share,
> O patient eyes that watch the goal,
> O ploughman of the sinner's soul.
> O Jesus, drive the coulter deep
> To plough my living man from sleep.

5

How to Make a Pilgrimage Without Leaving Home

It is ironic that the landscape which provided the features for this country's finest spiritual allegory should be that of one of its least regarded counties where scenery is concerned. More, that Britain's most popular journey of the soul should have been made among views that have mostly been passing ones for earth-bound travellers, both ancient and modern. In the old days, the great roads running north and south tended to hurry everyone through Bedfordshire with a minimum account of its existence, and in our own time it offers the kind of motorway and main-line panorama which streams past the retina like a green Nowhere. And yet this is where John Bunyan's pilgrims walked and in their footsteps, for the better part of three centuries, walked all the English-reading world. Generations, millions walking in what they sensed was 'a vain shadow', followed the sacred map which he transposed on his native fields in order to reach the City of God. Never before or since has the geography of heaven and earth received so direct a literary integration. Except in the Scriptures themselves, of course. It was the newly published Authorized Version of these which took total charge of Bunyan's existence. They told him that he and his Midland contemporaries had no option but to set out for Christ or for Apollyon the Destroyer from their own flat lands. They insisted that no man living could avoid taking some path or other. Bunyan spun these options out – 'Still as I pulled it came' – in *The Pilgrim's Progress*, plainly and vigorously, and for a vast public, even in his own day. Indeed it was the runaway success of his Christian (*The Pilgrim's Progress* is two linked novels) that seems to have decided him on his Christiana – this and his need to honour women. The preface to the sequel shows Bunyan's unconcealed delight in the wholly unexpected popularity of the first volume.

> *My pilgrim's book has travelled sea and land . . .*
> *In France and Flanders where men kill each other*
> *My pilgrim is esteemed a friend, a brother.*
> *In Holland too, 'tis said, as I am told,*
> *My pilgrim is with some, worth more than gold.*
> *Highlanders, and wild-Irish can agree,*
> *My pilgrim should familiar with them be.*
> *'Tis in New England under such advance . . .*
> *As to be trimmed, new clothed and decked with gems,*
> *That it might show its features, and its limbs,*
> *Yet more; so comely doth my pilgrim walk,*
> *That of him thousands daily sing and talk.*

Already, in his own lifetime, Bunyan's Bedfordshire turned Holy Land had become the territory of an international Puritan quest. It is a prison book and a dream book. For years denied his wanderings across country to village meetings or to repair household utensils, prevented from preaching, cooped up, Bunyan's reaction to Bedford Gaol became that of an unstoppable river which, dammed in its natural course, floods its banks. All prison writing, from St Paul's to Breytenbach's, does this. There is little that could be called a longing for his local haunts in Bunyan's prison books. All his longing is for the Celestial City and he merely routes a way to it for others through the most familiar territory he knows. Did not Christ do the same? Roger Sharrock, the modern authority on Bunyan, sees him illuminating or recasting traditional symbols to some extent. 'The figure of the lonely wayfaring man, the simple honest foot-traveller with his pack on his back, goes back to the middle ages: Langland's Piers Plowman sets out thus on pilgrimage to find Truth after he had ploughed his half-acre. The modern imagination perhaps tends to see man more as a prisoner than as a traveller, but the image of the purposeful journey through life still has great evocative power ...' Where Bunyan differed from both the medieval pilgrimage-writer and from ourselves was in what Sharrock calls 'the psychological dynamic' of his Calvinism. 'Puritanism has been misconceived as restrictive moral prohibitions, weighed down by sexual guilt; in the mid seventeenth century it was a fiery religious and social dynamic resembling contemporary Marxism more than modern Fundamentalism.' Bunyan's advantage, he says, was that as a convert to Puritanism from a reformed earlier faith (which he adored when a boy), he was able to draw on the spirit of both in his writing.

That he did so unreservedly in *The Pilgrim's Progress* is the reason why he hesitated to publish a book which simply ran away with him. As the author of a number of profoundly serious works, including *Grace Abounding to the Chief of Sinners*, a spiritual autobiography which ranks with those by St Augustine and St Teresa, and as leader of of the Bedford congregation, it has an enchanting, entertaining aspect to it which clearly bothered some of his friends. His preface to it in the form of a poem admits everything, how he was at work on another book when he 'fell' into this one – a dilemma which has overtaken many writers – how he wrote it for self-gratification, his literary genius getting the better of his moralizing, and then his delightful offering it for the approval of his fellow Christians.

> Some said, '*John, print it*'; others said, '*not so*';
> Some said, '*it might do good*'; others said '*no*'.

He concludes, no author offering his new work more truthfully, that,

> *This book will make a traveller of thee,*
> *If by its counsel thou wilt ruled be;*
> *It will direct thee to the Holy Land,*
> *If thou wilt its directions understand* ...

And it does. So does Bunyan-Christian's entire life in far from dull Bedfordshire. It is safe to say that it is best to know nothing of Bunyan if you want to tour this county under the usual topographical conditions. If not, it is the land of Last Things, of a sublime metaphor, of paths to paradise, of everything you couldn't see on the Inter-City or M1 rush through the whole length of it. Bedfordshire needs a special exploration. But give it its earthly dimensions first, although not before adding that there is something to be said for those consistently passed-over places on the tourist route, for, not always being pressed and recommended, they are able to speak up for themselves when visited. Bedfordshire says many an unexpected thing. It is at first

The Pilgrims' Way, near Wrotham, Kent

'*When the sweet showers of April have pierced the dryness of March to its root and soaked every vein with moisture whose quickening force engenders the flower; when Zephyr with his sweet breath has given life to tender shoots in each wood and field ... then people long to go on pilgrimages ... In England especially they come from every shire's end to Canterbury to seek out the holy blessed martyr St Thomas à Becket, who helped them when they were sick.*'

The opening of the 'Prologue' to *The Canterbury Tales* by Geoffrey Chaucer, translated by David Wright

glance a wide open swoop of land which descends from the chalky barrier of the Chilterns (880 ft/268 m) to below sea-level as it runs into Huntingdonshire and its black peats. Bunyan's quags and plats and bottoms have been called to order by modern agriculture and engineering, but are clearly only just below its tidy surface. Although a broad country, it is well hemmed in. The London Brick Company's works, once the largest in the world, fume away to the south of Bedford, whilst the Ouse, a big, handsome river, winds right across the central plain on its way to King's Lynn. Bunyan once accompanied his father on the long boat trip to Lynn to fetch metal for their trade. They were skilled pewterers and ironmongers, and of more superior stock than either of them ever realized, descending from yeomen who had lived in the district for centuries. Tinkers, they were called, and Bunyan made no attempt to improve this description. Similarly, the real facts of his native countryside, natural or historical, rarely got into his writing. For him, Bedfordshire's ecology was a series of hallowed or unhallowed places, its every feature telling a heavenly or a hellish tale. Born on the North Beds clayey mud, for him the chalk hills became infinitely preferable, not because they offered an easier working environment for a villager, but simply because they were white. He thought that the chalk which constituted the Chiltern ranges which stretched from Totternhoe to Barton and from Warden Hill to Dunstable Downs was like 'the Child of God ... White in his life, easily wrought upon'. Exquisitely carved clunch from the Chiltern quarries was everywhere. It was a material which gave itself up completely to a creative hand. He wrote,

> *This stone is white, yea, warm, and also soft,*
> *Easy to work upon, unless 'tis naught.*
> *It leaves a white impression upon those*
> *Whom it doth touch, be they Friends or Foes.*

Gradually, this milky escarpment beyond the huge and, in his time, ill-drained vale of clay, blue with distance and with an unseeable world behind it, became the mountains carrying the soul of man upward to the level at which it could dwell with God. The peaks of the world have always been the seats of the Holy Ones, whether they be Kilimanjaro, Olympus or Cader Idris, but the blessed heights of Bunyan's landscape are different.

It is their modest ascendance at the limits of all that was familiar to him which gives his sublime story its human scale. Men are pilgrims and, as such, must encounter experiences ranging from happiness to terror in their journey to the divine presence. But they do not make this journey outside their own country. The universal success of *The Pilgrim's Progress* was due to its routeing countless readers past all the strongest image-bearing geographical delights and hazards of their personal localities, reliable stretches of straight old road, meandering footpaths, the marketplace, the rectory, the welcoming inn, the low-lying spots full of the horrors, the warm, flowery meadows, those places which enlighten you and those which half-kill you. Everyone, from the unlettered peasant listening to it being read by the hearth, to the sophisticated person, knew exactly what it meant and how it applied privately to him. In order to live, he had to lift up his eyes unto the hills. Allegory, having made an extremely popular twentieth-century bow in terms of Tolkien and C. S. Lewis, is not the academic thing it was until recently. All the same, veiled moralizings are not the literary adventures they were, and those who read Bunyan now, do so differently to their grandparents. What was the most urgent and profound traveller's tale in the world to them, is just an astounding piece of prose to us. How was it done (we could ask)? By knowing that it had to be done, in the same way as a great rescue operation has to be done. John Bunyan, pot-mender, itinerant preacher and prisoner of conscience, who first tried his hand at popularizing his own spiritual autobiography, eventually succeeded in producing a superb novelized Rule for Puritans. Roger Sharrock puts it most faithfully: 'A seventeenth-century Calvinist sat down to write a tract and produced a folk-epic of the universal religious imagination.'

Before entering some of the scenes which lent their contours to this folk-epic, and most surprisingly extant and little altered they are, we should perhaps glance at Elstow, where Bunyan was born and brought up, and at Bedford, a mile or two away, where he wrote. Although the road which links the two places is now built along – that same road in which, during his twenties, the tormented young man asked God to perform miracles through him by altering the position of its puddles – both town and village have managed to keep their distance. Bunyan saw

Elstow as the scene of his early degeneracy and Bedford, although it was the scene of his salvation, as the 'City of Destruction'. For him it was a town of very mixed blessings. Although it locked him up for many years, it could truly, with hindsight, say that it did so for his own good. For had it let him preach there would have been no need for him to write. He was a brilliant speaker and at first in the gaol all he tried to do was to put his silenced sermons on to paper. His pen then ran away with him into realms of natural literary expression. The quality of his writing was instantly recognizable to his contemporaries, and whatever else may have happened to him under the Clarendon Acts by way of humiliation and privation, he was never a prophet without honour in Bedfordshire. He was 'Bishop Bunyan', the spiritual father of his people, and the author of some sixty books, two of them masterpieces, and, from the moment of his arrest, a revered local man.

Briefly lumped by the conventional clergy with the ranters, Bunyan rapidly moved to a position in which he wrote for Englishmen of all classes. He was a phenomenon, a map-maker of Everyman's spiritual terrain. After so much confusing theological direction, here was a tough but sensible way of getting

Stevington, Bedfordshire: The Church of St Mary the Virgin

Waters flowing from the limestone outcrop on which this partly Saxon church is built made Stevington a centre for blindness cures and eye-disease remedies. The holy well is set in the churchyard wall, just below the buttresses. The path leads to the Ouse. Bunyan trod it many times. When the notorious Five Mile Act made it illegal for nonconformists to worship in Bedford, crowds of them joined the Stevington congregation in secret midnight meetings in the riverside wood and meadows here. The lane leads up to the market-cross and with its wall, 'sepulchre' (holy well), climb, etc. provides the exact details of the place which Christian ascended, lost the burden of his sin and from which he journeyed to God.

'... that Wall is called Salvation. Up this way therefore did burdened Christian run, but not without great difficulty because of the load on his back.

He ran thus till he came at a place somewhat ascending; and upon that place stood a Cross, and a little below in the bottom, a sepulchre. So I saw in my dream, that just as Christian came up with the Cross, his burden loosed from off his shoulders, and fell from his back; and began to tumble, and so continued to do till it came to the mouth of the sepulchre, where it fell in, and I saw it no more.'

to Heaven set out in a language which everybody could understand. In order to live for ever more a man had to lift his sights from what normally elevated him, including church steeples, and take in his real prospect, which was nothing less than Christ's Kingdom itself. It beckoned on the edge of the home scenery. The journey to it was to be via the local track, not the stars. 'Have you never a hill Mizar to remember? Have you forgot the close, the milk house, the stable, the barn, and the like, where God did visit your soul?' *Grace Abounding*, a book which Bunyan intended to be no more than his own private traveller's tale of finding the way into the Kingdom, is full of precise Bedfordshire locations. We can see them feeding his imagination and his terror, but eventually nourishing his conviction that he was on the right road. We can see too that the fields and architecture of his boyhood were more than sufficient for all that a great writer needed during his childhood as founding facts and images for later creativity. As a Calvinist Bunyan would have abandoned all that belonged to his unredeemed self, but since it was traditional for such a convert to make a complete inventory of what he had turned from, *Grace Abounding* contains as intimate an account of a young man's view of the early-seventeenth-century countryside as can be found anywhere. We know that although one's early life can be turned from, it does not go away. Bunyan's old and new lives rest one upon the other in *Grace Abounding* as the young man of merry England searches for the turning which will take him to immortality. When he discovered it, his eagerness to travel along it led to a coarsely rich simile which his contemporaries would have appreciated. 'My mind was now so turned, that it lay like a horse leech at the vein, still crying out, Give, give ...' But had he a permit to enter the divine realm? This was his dilemma.

The mile or two of lanes and fields between Bedford and Elstow are both John Bunyan's playground and his *via dolorosa*. Here he ran wild with his friend Harry ('I now shook him off'), danced, rang all the bells, exploited his strength and good looks, and got a roaring-boy's reputation. And here, in exactly the same place, he got the sudden urge to find the redemption which produced his breakdown. At first, amidst building and paths that exist to this day, it was, 'Oh these temptations were suitable for my flesh, I being a young man, and my nature in its prime', then it was deep spiritual crisis and envying laughing old women of Bedford because they 'were set on the sunny side of some high mountain ... while I was shivering and shrinking in the cold'. Here, somewhere between the roads running out of Bedford to Ampthill and Hitchin he 'moped in the fields', desperately repeating over and over again, 'Thou art my love, thou art my love, thou art my love', his eyes full of tears and his conscience telling him, 'God hath been weary of you these several years ... your bawlings in his ears hath been no pleasant voice to him.' Terrifyingly he came to believe that he had committed a special sin which was *outside* those for which Christ died, and he wished that he had been born a fish or a bird. And then, wandering once more in the Elstow fields – the reprieve! 'Christ! Christ! there was nothing but Christ that was before mine eyes ...' Later, sitting by the fire with his newly married wife, and realizing that, if there *was* a way to God, one would naturally have to travel along it, he asked her if she knew a text which said, 'I must go to Jesus'. She said she would see, but, two or three minutes later, a verse from Hebrews 12 'came bolting in upon me'. It was verse 22,

But ye are come unto mount Sion, and unto the city of the living God, the heavenly Jerusalem, and to an innumerable company of angels.

Bunyan had hit upon his Way, as well as, though some years hence, the journeying theme of *The Pilgrim's Progress*. 'That night was a good night to me, I never had but few better!' It was both natural and supernatural for a man to struggle out of his home clay towards those distant white heights and cerulean pinnacles. One can see how the Chilterns had attracted his upward stares as a child.

His actual birthplace is now no more than a corner of an empty field. The house site itself is a rough little copse by the side of a rivulet which supplied water for his family for centuries. The house, like the family, was originally more substantial than Bunyan ever understood. 'For my descent then, it was, as is well known by many, of a low and inconsiderable generation, my father's house being of that rank that is meanest and most despised of all the families in the land.' The Bunyans were in fact yeomen reduced to itinerant whitesmiths and John himself was a tall, well-built and impressive man whose education, if at

Bedford Grammar School, would have been similar to that of Shakespeare. The total disappearance of his house excepted, Bunyan's home fields must be among the least changed surrounding the home of any major British writer, for they still can only be reached by the footpaths which he used, one of which follows the stream from Harrowden road and the other of which leads to Elstow. This little bit of country is soaked in association, Tinker's Hill, Bunyan's Field, Bunyan's Farm, and with references such as that written by the vicar of the neighbouring parish of Houghton Conquest: 'Memorandum – That in Anno 1625 one Bonion of Elsto clyminge of Rookes nests in the Bery wood found 3 Rookes in a nest, all as white as milke and not a black feather in them.' It lies on the Bedford side of a curiously large almost roadless rectangle which stretches from the town's suburbs to Wilshamstead, and with still more than a hint of the unenclosed ploughlands which the writer would have seen. But delectable (an adjective which Milton liked to use for trees) additions to what must always have been an unadorned native situation fill the horizon; Ampthill Heights and the mixture of a little palace and a parish church which post-Reformation builders created at Elstow. Artistry and Hebron shone across these flats. Coming to the isolated spot, marked now just by sloes, scraps of tile and a recent memorial, one is pressed between wheat and blackberries with unusually large flowers which edge the brook. This ditch runs into Cardington Brook, which is a tributary of the Ouse. Thus Bunyan can be said to have drunk for the whole of his youth the water in which he was baptized and through which he passed, metaphorically, in death. Also, to be less symbolic, twice nearly to natural death by drowning, once at Lynn.

The church of St Mary and St Helen at Elstow whose Laudian services Bunyan once so much enjoyed, and in which he was christened, stands at the top of a fine green. Its history is a witty and worldly one, and his account of his early life reflects a tradition of colourful goings-on in the neighbourhood. For the church, the ruined mansion beside it and the curious separate tower nearby are all part of what was until the Reformation a magnificent Benedictine abbey founded by William I's niece Judith and ruled over for centuries by a succession of litigious and elegant ladies. An extravagant secularization of the abbey had taken place just before Bunyan's birth, when the nuns' cathedral-like church had been mutilated to suit ordinary parish requirements and all the rest of their fine architecture demolished to provide stone for a glorious Inigo-Jones-like house for a local magnate, Sir Thomas Hillersdon. Throughout Bunyan's writing there is the alluring concept of the place of domestic ease, hospitality, earthly refinements and love being *en route* to the dwelling of God. Inside Elstow Church, amidst drastic 1880 changes, there is still much that Bunyan saw and touched. In the south aisle are the altar and rails at which he received the Sacraments, and in the north aisle the huge Perpendicular font to which his parents carried him from their poor old house across the meadows on 13 November 1628 to be named after his father. Here too his daughters, one of them the blind Mary who daily brought him hot soup during his long imprisonment, were baptized. Although Bunyan underwent adult baptism by immersion, he never forced it on his family or on others as a condition of faith. 'It is Love,' he said, 'not Baptism that discovereth us to the world to be Christ's Disciples.' All around the church are the medieval carvings which haunted him as a boy and which filled his dreams. Here among the corbels and trefoils reprieved by the Victorian rebuilder are the art forms which first pressed themselves on the imagination of one of the world's most influential dream-writers. William James, in his *The Varieties of Religious Experience* (1902), said that Bunyan's 'was a typical case of the psychopathic temperament, sensitive of conscience to a diseased degree, beset by doubts, fears, insistent ideas, and a victim of verbal automatisms, both motor and sensory. These were usually texts of Scripture which, sometimes damnatory and sometimes favourable, would come in half-hallucinatory form as if they were voices, and fasten on his mind and buffet it between them like a shuttlecock. Added to this were a fearful melancholy, self-contempt and despair.'

This game analogy is an apt one. Bunyan, like many village men, was mad about sport and recreation generally. When we wonder over his guilt concerning dancing and bellringing, we have to realize that it is the anxiety felt by a mature person at the hold which play continued to have on them. Bunyan possessed an outsized gift for enjoying himself, a zest for amusement. The time given up to watching, discussing and following games in the twentieth century is enormous but on the whole self-guiltless. Not so for the Puritan, for whom it was a trivialization of his mortal existence. What Bunyan was unable to comprehend was that for him recreation, playing, spilled over into art, into music, and into nourishing his fantasies. To appreciate how a sermon against playing games on Sunday, which was about the most hackneyed rebuke which could come from a seventeenth-century village pulpit, could have put Bunyan into such a state of spiritual turbulence as to allow him to see 'the Lord Jesus looking down upon me, as being very hotly displeased with me', we have to understand that it was an overwhelming criticism and affront to his natural light-heartedness and artistry combined. What was he, if he was not of what he excelled at?

The landscape of this divine criticism remains little altered. At one end stands the parish church whose north door (now blocked up!) is the Wicket through which Christian passed to the House of the Interpreter, and nearby the tempting belfry, the castle from which Beelzebub shoots arrows at all who dare to approach the Straight Gate.

Now, you must know, that before this I had taken much delight in ringing, but my conscience beginning to be tender, I thought such practice was but vain, and therefore forced myself to leave it, yet my mind hankered ... I began to think, how, if one of the bells should fall. Then I chose to stand under a main beam, that I might stand sure, but then I should think again, should the bell fall with a swing, it might first hit the wall, and then rebounding upon me, might kill me for all this beam, This made me stand in the steeple door; and now, thought I, I am safe enough; for if a bell should fall, I can slip out behind these thick walls, and so be preserved notwithstanding ... Another thing was my dancing; I was a full year before I could quite leave that ...

Below stretches the green where Bunyan danced and played games and attended the May fairs, the medieval Green House, now called the Moot Hall, with its arcaded shops, and West End Lane leading to Ampthill and the 'stately palace named Beautiful'. It was on Elstow Green, surrounded by all kinds of buildings and paths which he was to weave into his allegory, and which survive to this day, that, about to strike the 'cat' in the game of tip-cat, he heard God ask him the direct and dreadful question, 'Wilt thou leave thy sins and go to heaven, or have thy sins and go to hell?' His first reaction was that of a man who decides that he may as well be hanged for a sheep as for a lamb. He had, he says, 'a great desire to take my fill of sin, still studying what sin was yet to be committed, that I might taste the sweetness of it; and I made as much haste as I could to fill my belly with its delicates, lest I should die before I had my desires.' This sensuous craving Bunyan confesses in the opening pages of *Grace Abounding* because, he declares, it is 'more usual amongst poor creatures than many are aware of'. And so he fed on his pleasures 'with great greediness' and 'playing the madman', so much so that a woman shopkeeper let fly at him, telling him to his face that he was a source of corruption in the village. This coming from a person known locally for her own looseness shook him and he began to pull himself together, only to hate and despise what he was now seen as, a primly respectable young man.

Salvation may have uttered itself in the wilderness of the Bedford–Elstow fields and during lonely walks along their pot-holed lanes, but its language was that of books. Immense books like the newly translated Bible, a ragged, falling-to-pieces book called *A Commentary on Galatians* by Martin Luther which astounded Bunyan because, he said, it seemed to 'have been written out of my heart', and a couple of pious homilies which, although 'they did not reach my heart' can now be seen as part of his literary awakening; one was called *The Plain Man's Pathway to Heaven*. Even as he stumbled about, alternating between wild and sedate behaviour, we can see that details of his own immortal contribution to the literature of human life as an essentially solitary passage through a physical universe to a perfect spiritual destination were creeping into his subconscious. Although much later on, as a celebrated local preacher and popular author, Bunyan rode to engagements all over the East Midlands, and occasionally to London, the landscape experience which fills his poetry and prose is that of the walker. As a walking craftsman summoned by householders living within a twelve-mile radius of Bedford to repair their precious copper, brass and pewter, he would naturally have taken all the short-cuts possible to the farms, halls and cottages, unconsciously absorbing their privacy and intimacy, and, as Kim Taplin says in her study, *The English Path* (the best explanation of a neglected subject), equally unconsciously sorting out his ideas.

The image of life as a journey is so old and so persuasive that it is easy to forget it is one; but there is yet great emotional power in the contrast between a grim journeying and a state of house-keeping, settled content towards which, or out from which the traveller goes. English rural writers have often visualized the road of life as a country footpath ... *Solvitur ambulando* – the old Latin tag means something like, 'You can sort it out by walking.' Working out, finding out, unknotting and freeing are all possible connotations of the word *solvitur* ... A companionable path was more apt for a curative release than a road, since solitude, peace, and close contact with nature, as well as the action of walking, are all important ingredients. Problems unravel as the feet cover the miles, but through the body's surroundings, as well as the body's action.

She quotes the country priest-poet Andrew Young in his *A Traveller in Time*:

> *Where was I? What was I about to see?*
> Solvitur ambulando.
> *A path offered its company.*

In his *Silver Ley*, the novelized autobiography of a young man farming in Suffolk, Adrian Bell supports the concept of the footpath, or 'narrow way', as the true thoroughfare, as it were, to where one must, at all cost, get. It is the snowy Christmas of 1928 and the main transport of the village, the bicycle, has been made obsolete overnight. Staring out of his window at the quiet white scene, he notes 'the reason for the dying away of footpaths in this our land. For now people are seen plodding straight for their object across the fields, whether it is the church spire, snow-encrusted, or the smoke of a cottage chimney. Who are they? Not travellers from far, for they would not venture out today – in fact the travelling area is suddenly restricted in time as it was a century ago. These are those parish workers who, when times are normal, take the serpentine routes of by-roads on bicycles.' 'Take the gentle path,' advises George Herbert in his poem *Discipline*. Although Bedford and Elstow between them are able to muster an extraordinary number of sites and associations connected with Bunyan and have few equals where a writer of his genius is concerned, still the closest one can come to him is via the little tracks criss-crossing the entire area. These are what stimulated both his rich introspection and his vision of the blue and high horizon as a sacred view. A simple way to become a 'heavenly footman' is to walk this earth.

So tread in his steps along the footpath running from Old Harrowden Lane to his birthplace, taking in all that is close at hand and all that is most distant. Find a good map and pick out its ancient cross-country ways to Haynes, Flitton, Pulloxhill, Marston Moretaine, Astwood, Oakley, Clapham, Mogerhanger, Old Warden, Wootton, Steppingley, Ridgmont, Ravensden and old isolated farms and mills, secret reaches of the Ouse, ancient protective woods and especially any path leading up to an eminence which would allow the eyes to feast on the Chilterns, for these are where, walking between customers and congregations, Bunyan recognized himself and his God. 'Where was I? What was I about to see?' Any of us following him around should go on asking these questions. For it is a country whose answers do not lie on the Ordnance Survey, help though it is.

But we cannot drive off without touring the Bedfordshire basis of Christian's progress. Even in an age which knows little of the book, it is still a profoundly affecting experience, this visiting the actual geography out of which was created a religious metaphor which served a worldwide Protestant philosophy for three centuries. 'These are the words of the Lord,' wrote the prophet Jeremiah. 'Stop at the crossroads, look for the ancient paths; ask, "Where is the way that leads to what is good?" Then take that way, and you will find rest for yourselves. But they said, "We will not." Then I will appoint watchmen to direct you, listen to their trumpet-call.' Bunyan doesn't mention this text but it seems to contain the very plot and inspiration of *The Pilgrim's Progress*. It fits across his Bedfordshire like a template, and one can still stop at a particular crossroads, trace certain ancient paths, see the house from which the writer's own trusted watchman set him right, as country people say when they have given a traveller information, and stand by a wide river across which nightly he heard a trumpet-call. The tracing of that most famous of all English journeys from despair to bliss via both the busy main roads and silent lanes which lead from the centre of Bedford to the Chiltern Hills is one of Britain's major literary landscape adventures.

One of the most compelling aspects of the Gospels for the Puritan reader was their restlessness. The age itself, radical and seeking, roaming and energetic, thrust its way past all kinds of things which previous centuries had regarded as ends in themselves. Obedience to old institutions became of no consequence in comparison with obedience to Scripture. Reading the stupendous new translation of the life of Jesus, the Puritan encountered a perfectly rational human intelligence as well as the Christ. The Gospels were so full of action and movement that they became a dynamic which began to drive the whole social fabric. The most appalling question for many, and for Bunyan and the saints of his Bedfordshire plain, was, were they a predestined part of this sacred vitality, or were they just being dragged along in its wake with no guarantee that they would ever reach its blessed destination? Individually, and with intense relief, he and countless others decided that although they were indeed predestined for God's presence at the last, they had no right to believe that they could arrive in it without following his Son's instructions to the letter. It was then that they recognized the human as well as the divine scale of Christ's law – 'For the Son of Man is as a man taking a far journey, who left his house, and gave authority to his servants, and to every man his work, and commanded the porter to watch.' What could be clearer? He had left them with his commission and their task, but as he had also said, 'Follow me', they had to carry them out while making a lifelong progress to where he waited for them in the Celestial City.

Bunyan's feat was to correlate the long walk which Jesus made through Palestine with the typical walk through life made by a seventeenth-century Englishman. *The Pilgrim's Progress* inaugurated a whole new love and understanding of Christ, because men found that there were long stretches of the way where they could keep step with him. But the conditions for going Christ's way were severe; Bunyan-Christian, the vulnerable hero of the story, gets lost, gets terrified, gets into every kind of predicament before he and his friend Hopeful cross the River, enter the Gate and are able to 'look their Redeemer in the face with joy'. Jesus's walk through this world was both touchingly natural and wondrously supernatural. Its natural progression took in sights and experiences which were often very little removed from those of Bunyan's rural contemporaries. Although born into an ancient civilization of settled temples and courts, Christ remained from birth to death a being of passage. His birth was crowded with journeys and his death followed a long walk to the scaffold. In between, the references to his unsettled state are ceaseless, and unsettlement is what he commanded of his followers. The Saviour walks on and on through villages, towns, fields, meadows, past wells and pools and the great lake, and in his human exhaustion envies the foxes and birds their cosy homes. He travels to the wilderness for self-examination and climbs the mountains to be near his Father in prayer. He sees wheat, thistles, figs, trees, mustard, brambles, colts, pigs, fish, grapes, barns, friends' houses, inns, shepherds, beggars, soldiers, prostitutes, children, disease, beauty, everything of the best, everything unmentionable. It is a life of endless encounters and withdrawals. He loves Palestine and when he prays he always gives thanks to the Father of heaven *and* earth. He talks of cleansed men walking through dry places, seeking rest. 'Nevertheless,' he tells his companions, 'I must walk today, and tomorrow, and the day following ...' He urges them to 'Walk while ye have the light, that ye may be the children of light ... Whither I go ye know, and the way ye know ... *I am the way.*' His direction is the ultimate one. 'He that doesn't take his cross and follow me, isn't worthy of me.' On this journey a man must leave behind his stave, scrip, food, money and spare coat, must leave his wife and children if necessary.

Christian did. Bunyan too was accused of making his family suffer for the sake of refusing to promise not to preach and thus having to stay in prison instead of looking after them. Bedford became his Nazareth, the Ouse his Jordan-Lethe, the Chilterns the high road to the New Jerusalem, the Elstow fields his wilderness, Stevington his Calvary and the homes of his friends his Bethany. Soon, in his own lifetime, huge numbers of the Gospel-absorbed world would be reading his allegory and translating it into their native scenery. Sion would lie beyond Snowdon or Brown Willy, or just the blue of any distant rise; ploughmen squelching and struggling through the undrained bottom of a field were powerfully reminded of the sin of despair. Fine new Tudor houses, many of them constructed from old abbeys and priories, rather than churches, foretold the 'many mansions' which awaited the people of God. Rivers became sacred again for the first time since the days of the ancient nature gods, due to their secret use for baptism by immersion. Twice in a lifetime their waters had to be braved, once when the Christian symbolically died to the 'world', once when he departed from the earthly scene. All over the country, whether they were modest streams like Suffolk's river Box and Shropshire's river Tern, or

St John's Rectory, Bedford (Charles Hall)

In 1653 the Bedford civic authorities invited the homeless Independents to take over St John's Church and Rectory. Their pastor was an ex-royalist major (and ex-criminal), John Gifford, now a reformed and charismatic figure. Bunyan came to consult Gifford in this house after he had seen the happiness of some women who had found the true Christian path. Gifford taught Bunyan the way, and his Rectory became the 'House of the Interpreter' in *Pilgrim's Progress*, Gifford himself becoming 'Evangelist'. Gifford baptized Bunyan at night in the little backwater of the Ouse which now lies between the weir bridge and Duck Mill Lane car-park. The St John's congregation was in fellowship with the Stevington Christians. Gifford, Interpreter-Evangelist, died only two years after coming to St John's and was succeeded by a pastor nominated by Cromwell himself, so important now was the Bedford Meeting. But soon it was Bunyan who dominated the youthful Independents throughout the county.

The Rectory was originally a medieval hospital and Bunyan and Gifford talked in the refectory and in the ancient garden. It was here that Bunyan discovered his amazing gift for preaching which, when it was silenced by the town gaoler, immediately re-routed itself into literature.

the broad Thames and Severn, they now spoke of inescapable tests and of eternity. No single work of English literature has so 're-symbolized' a local landscape as *The Pilgrim's Progress*.

The Puritan cosmos claimed each man's home ground, and caused him to be confined to the limits of a moral and spiritual map. 'For the Kingdom of Heaven is as a man travelling into a far country.' *A* man – not generations, not populations, not generalized humanity – this was the accent on Bunyan's traveller, an individuality through which each separate reader could see his own progress, or lack of it. As in a great novel, the reader becomes one with the central character. Where Bunyan shows his genius is in seeing that his heaven-bound man, woman or child, although guaranteed a safe eternal lodging at the last, never wanders away from their earthliness into realms of fantasy. If Bedfordshire and its inhabitants are one's earthly lot, then it will be they, not some tempting Elfland and its creatures, which will provide life's ups and downs until the struggle is over. Roger Sharrock points out that it is not the landscape and characters of *The Pilgrim's Progress* which have reached a position where we can no longer easily identify with them, but its theology. For generations of his readers the life-cycle rolled on, in or out of obedience, with a doctrine of Redemption which even the ignorant intuitively recognized and accepted but which today few know anything about. The grandeur of the book, in popular terms, is thus lost.

But a tour of its setting is still an incomparable spiritual experience. The country of those folk we still know so well, Pliable, Obstinate, Worldly-Wiseman, Talkative, Faithful, Hopeful, Madam Bubble, Mr Honest, Mr Stand-fast, Mr Great-heart, Giant Despair and all the rest of them (and us), lies open to anyone with a copy of the allegory and a copy of Sheet 147 of the Ordnance Survey. Some of its sites, Stevington, for example, are as moving to discover as those of martyrdom. Others, like Houghton House, charge the sightseeing imagination. But there are too Bunyan's witty generalizations throughout the book, such as when Christian runs into a fellow-traveller called Mr By-ends of Fair-speech, a gentleman of rank *en route* to Paradise, who loves to walk with religion in the street if the sun shines. Which one of us, who, after reading Mr By-ends's airy description of his pedigree will ever be able to take the average claims of local magnates without a pinch of Leveller's salt? – 'to tell you the truth, I am become a gentleman of good quality; yet my great-grandfather was but a waterman, looking one way and rowing another: and I got most of my estate by the same occupation ... my wife is a very virtuous woman, the daughter of a virtuous woman. She was my Lady Faining's daughter, therefore she came of a very honourable family, and is arrived to such a pitch of breeding that she knows how to carry it to all ...' These are lines which wouldn't come amiss on the Restoration stage. Although some people in his book called Christian 'Fool and Noddy', Bunyan's remains an often painfully sharp English intelligence.

Begin then in Bedford itself, where the book began 'in the similitude of a dream', and in the town gaol which stood at the corner of High Street and Silver Street, and where the dreamer beheld 'a man clothed with rags, standing in a certain place, with his face from his own house [Bunyan's was only five minutes away in St Cuthbert's Street], a book in his hand, and a great burden on his back'. There in a little town of then no more than two thousand inhabitants, which in his allegory he has unified with his birthplace Elstow, we can follow the anxious

Bunyan-Christian about, and see why he was terrified that he would be pressed down into Tophet (Hell) by the weight of evil that he was carrying. Here are scores of houses which he would have known, but most importantly that of his friend John Gifford, St John's Rectory, south of the river. Here Gifford explained and taught an entirely Bible-bound faith to the worried young tradesman who immortalized it as 'the House of the Interpreter'. The two of them talked in the main room which was once a medieval refectory and, according to legend, under the cedar and mulberry trees which still thrive in the garden. When at the Restoration Gifford was ejected from the living as an 'intruder', he and his friends were unceremoniously described as 'one Bunnion, a tincker, Burton a coachsmith, and one Gifford, all schismatics'. A few steps from St John's flows the Ouse and the Duck Mill backwater where, late at night, Bunyan received baptism from his 'Interpreter'. From the small religious community which was formed under John Gifford in 1650 there has sprung one of the most celebrated independent Christian churches in the world, the Bunyan Meeting. Its home in Mill Street contains relics of the writer so intimate and so clearly invested with his presence still, that all the rationality of Calvinism fails to rid them entirely of their relic-like power. His meeting-house chair, his iron violin, his anvil, probably the very one he lugged with him all the way to Ampthill and his 'House Beautiful'; the door of his prison cell, his walking-stick, the table he wrote on in the gaol, and the table at which he presided during Communion, the warrant for his arrest and scraps of wood from his various pulpits, the latter in particular proving the persistence of relicry even to the emancipated, all are here. Bedford produced a great saint and has always known it. The doors of the Meeting reveal a further example of Puritanism's ability to accept what it is popularly believed to detest, ecclesiastical imagery of the highest order in the form of a pair of bronze doors by the Victorian artist Frederick Thrupp on which, inspired by Ghiberti, ten high-relief panels picture *The Pilgrim's Progress*. Given by the 9th Duke of Bedford in 1876 and hung to the singing of Handel's Hallelujah Chorus, their magnificence is only now being comprehended. If anything, these lovely doors witness more than anything else to the generally unsuspected ecumenicity of the Bedford faithful, who from the start have always allowed both infant and adult baptism, with all that these two concepts imply. Bunyan, who received the interpretation of Christ which he could accept at St John the Baptist's Rectory, would have enjoyed the coincidence that an English work of art based on *The Pilgrim's Progress* should have evolved from the youthful Thrupp's contemplation of Ghiberti's 'Paradise Doors' which opened on to the Baptistry of St John in Florence.

Tracing *The Pilgrim's Progress* makes a memorable beginning to the discovery of Bedfordshire. Easily the most startling halt by the way is Stevington, a cruciform village five miles from

Stevington Cross (Charles Hall)

The scene, some believe, of one of Bunyan's own great moments of enlightenment, after which, he 'led me into something of the mystery of the union with the Son of God' (*Grace Abounding*). Here Christian in the allegory felt the heaviness of evil falling away from him. (Bunyan did much of his travelling humping heavy tools, including the huge anvil which can be seen in the Bedford museum.)

Bedford along the Sharnbrook road. A medieval market cross rises from its hub and below, down a dipping lane which peters out into water-meadows, stands the parish church with its Saxon tower. Both church and houses are built on rocky lime outcrops. From the one which supports the church a limestone spring with an immemorial reputation for curing blindness gushes. A holy well. When I was there, little girls were splashing its water against their bright eyes 'to see better'. The valley-descending lane becomes a muddy track at this point and half lost under the butterbur (*Petasites hybridus*). Neither the ubiquitous flower festival taking place in the church, nor its architectural guide, had the faintest reference to the fact that Stevington was the scene of a salvation experience which, next to those in the Bible itself, had more influence on post-Reformation England than any other. For it is believed that this village, to which the young Bunyan frequently walked to preach to the Independents at their secret meetings in the Holmes Wood, crossing over as he did so, and ironically for him, Dancing Meadow ('and then there was my dancing . . .'), was the place where Christian lost his burden. It is the incident in the allegory, next to that in which Mr Valiant-for-Truth passes over the river of death and has 'the trumpets sounded for him on the other side' (Bunyan heard a trumpeter sound the curfew each night by Bedford bridge), which most thrilled countless readers, and at Stevington one can walk through its imagery from beginning to end.

Christian, having been told by the Interpreter the road he has to go, and accompanied as all Celestial City-bound travellers are by the Comforter, ran with difficulty, because of his heavy load of sin, up the highway. 'He ran thus until he came at a place somewhat ascending [the lane leading from Stevington church]; and upon that place stood a Cross [the present market cross, and the one which Bunyan probably had in mind when, in his tract *The Heavenly Footman*, he writes that 'the cross is the standing way-mark by which all they that go to glory must pass by'], and a little below in the bottom, a sepulchre [the holy well]. So I saw in my dream, that just as Christian came up with the Cross, his burden loosed from off his shoulders, and fell from off his back; and began to tumble, and so continued to do till it came to the mouth of the sepulchre, where it fell in, and I saw it no more. Then was Christian glad and lightsome, and said with a merry heart, "He hath given me rest, by his sorrow, and life, by his death." Then he stood still a while, to look and wonder; for it was very surprising to him that the sight of the Cross should thus ease him of his burden. He looked therefore, and looked again, even till the springs that were in his head sent the waters down his cheeks.' Later, it is by the wall of Stevington church that Christian encounters Simple, Sloth, Presumption, Formalist and Hypocrisy.

For John Bunyan, the village of Stevington was associated with intense personal meaning and emotion. The notorious Five Mile Act which forbad nonconforming Christians to assemble in Bedford had swelled its open-air meeting and the record kept of the services gives a vivid picture of what it was like to worship late at night in the soaking meadows below the church 'when the females screened their minister's head from the damps of the night with their aprons'. In many parts of England nonconformists, especially Quakers, were being hunted; breaking up their assemblies and routing them from their hiding place had

Stevington: the Ouse fields (Charles Hall)

Where Bunyan prayed and listened to the preaching in the cold and darkness.

Tell them that they have left their house and home,
Are turned pilgrims, seek a world to come,
That they have met with hardships in the way,
That they do meet with troubles night and day . . .
    The Pilgrim's Progress, part II

become a loutish sport. The Holmes Wood at Stevington is a potent mark on the Bedfordshire map for it is where Bunyan began to understand himself, and discovered that he possessed a power with words, spoken ones first and then, when these were silenced, words on a page. His discreet and threatened walks, there and to other secluded spots, contained a drama and excitement which fed his literary imagination – 'hedges have eyes' – and helped to lay the foundations of his masterpiece. Vera Brittain in her biography says that 'Bunyan made Bedfordshire's homely villages and peaceful streams shine with the light of Heaven itself and turned the life of an ordinary man struggling to overcome his daily temptations into a journey as heroic as Jason's quest for the Golden Fleece.' She adds that it was a supreme example of unconscious achievement, 'for he neither knew nor cared that at a single step he had created the English novel'. She saw him as a naturally tolerant man existing amidst national intolerance and that 'he wrought an unrecognized miracle in his cell above the gateway of the county gaol'. Kipling called Bunyan 'The Father of the Novel/Salvation's first Defoe', and Disraeli, 'the Spenser of the people'.

The essence of this divine peregrination is to realize always that wherever his hero went, whether they were the heights and depths of the spirit or of Bedfordshire, its author had gone before. *The Pilgrim's Progress* has sanctified an English county in a manner which no other book has done before or since. Christian was never made to travel beyond the bounds of a Bedford Meeting saint, literally or figuratively, and ever since his life has remained an astonishing lesson on how an ordinary person can intensify the home scene. Don't get bogged down in it, as Bunyan's contemporaries frequently were in both senses as they grasped for money and social standing on their ill-drained, swampy plain. Get up and go to the visible heights of love. He took stock of this prospect from the window of a palace whilst mending a bath, his 'House Beautiful', Lord Ailesbury's seat on Ampthill Heights (Hill Difficulty), for two centuries now a soaring, empty shell called Houghton House. It was a view which loomed large when, many years of imprisonment and twenty-two books later, he gave in to an urge 'to use those metaphysical descriptions which Hosea called "similitudes"' (Vera Brittain) in a tale which would make millions look up from the daily round

Houghton House, Ampthill, Bedfordshire (left and right)

The House Beautiful in *The Pilgrim's Progress*, whose treasure-filled rooms and view to the Delectable Mountains made a profound impression on John Bunyan when he journeyed here from Bedford to mend some utensils in one of its upper rooms. In winter the scramble up to it, carrying his heavy tools, made him dub its approach Hill Difficulty. From the portico twelve miles of the Vale of Bedford stretch away to the chalk heights. This magnificently situated building which, for the writer, was the house of art and hospitality, civilization and taste, and which existed to refresh humanity on its way back to the Creator, has a non-allegorical history of blight, tragedy and abandonment. But its outlook makes as stunning an impact on today's visitor as it did on the man who wrote,

'When the morning was up they had him [Christian] to the top of the House, and bid him look south; so he did, and behold, at a great distance he saw a most pleasant mountainous country, beautiful with woods, vineyards, fruits of all sorts; flowers also, with springs and fountains, very delectable to behold. Then he asked the name of the country; they said it was Immanuel's Land ...'

to a transcendance which, with 'a little grace, a little love, a little true fear of God', could be theirs.

Other *Pilgrim's Progress* places are Millbrook on its hill, below which lies 'The Valley of the Shadow of Death'; Cardington Brook, 'the Slough of Despond'; the Vale of Flit, 'the Valley of Humiliation', and Watling Street and the Baldock-Biggleswade stretches of Roman road, the 'strait' path. John Bunyan's allegory supplanted in popularity in the Protestant esteem John Foxe's *Book of Martyrs*, a work which he knew backwards. In

the latter the Italian martyr Algerius is quoted as saying, 'In this world there is no mansion firm to me, and therefore I will travel up to the New Jerusalem, which is in Heaven, and which offereth itself to me without paying any fine or income. Behold, I have entered already on my journey, where my house standeth for me prepared, and where I shall have riches, kinsfolk, delights, honours, never failing.'

Bunyan defended his superb allegory from accusations of its

being a frivolous version of the faith by citing Christ himself who 'in olden times held forth by types, shadows and metaphors'. In August 1688, a wild, wet month, he set out yet again towards the Delectable Mountains, this time on horseback, riding below them across the Aylesbury Plain to Marlow, Henley and Reading to London, where he had promised to preach for a friend. He was sixty and the burly strength which both he and his followers had for so long taken for granted was failing him. He arrived in the capital soaked and exhausted, and died a few days later from pneumonia. Thus it was that instead of a resurrection-awaiting grave by the wide Ouse, he was taken to what Southey called 'the Campo Santo of the Dissenters', Bunhill Fields, where he lies beneath a blitzed memorial near William Blake, Susannah Wesley, Daniel Defoe, Isaac Watts and thousands more who, it is no exaggeration to say, would have

The Chilterns (Bunyan's Delectable Mountains) seen from West Wycombe churchyard (opposite)

Great things are done when men and mountains meet;
This is not done by jostling in the street.

William Blake, *Gnomic Verses*

Chiltern country near West Wycombe – 'Immanuel's Land'

known his book by heart. There was to be a further suitability, for just west of Bunhill Fields is Bunhill Row, where John Milton completed *Paradise Lost*, England's major Christian epic. These two extraordinary instances of Puritan genius were published within a year of each other.

Among the closing lines of *Paradise Lost*, which Milton wrote only a short walk from Bunyan's grave, are these. Michael is reconciling Adam to the next best thing to Eden. Having been brought 'To dwell on even ground' because of his sin, he is not to despair, for

> *. . . doubt not but in Vallie and in Plaine*
> *God is as here, and will be found alike*
> *Present, and of his presence many a signe*
> *Still following thee, still compassing thee round*
> *With goodness and paternal Love, his Face*
> *Express, and of his steps the track Divine.*

And did that face see and those feet walk England's green and pleasant land, Blake was to ask. Humanity usually searches for its deity on the home ground.

Elstow, the epicentre of Bunyan's spiritual disturbance and the heart of *Pilgrim's Progress*, has now been designated a suitable place to deposit nuclear waste.

6

George Herbert and
the River Valley Route

George Herbert retains his role as sacred enchanter. That spell which he cast over a handful of friends and simple country people while 'keeping God's watch', as he called it, is as potent now as ever it was. When Christ became for him such a serious pleasure, and Christian practice the most delightful of all the world's activities, he was able to say as much in a perennial language. As a wit addicted to central truths which could be encapsulated in maxims, proverbs and brief tales, his written faith is a similarly precise revelation. It rings and shines like a flawless glass and contains all. He is intense and at the same time playful. Though Christ is wholly and tremendously 'my King', he is also an intimate friend. Herbert's poetry veers happily from the veneration of its subject to the talk of close friends. Just a few lines of it have a way of making a clearing in the dense theological woods where the Christ-seeker, often with awe and embarrassment (for in spite of Herbert's literary tricks God is usually quite inescapably present there), discovers what he is looking for. Whether the finder is in anything like the state required for the keeping of the prize is another matter. Herbert hurries us to Christ, and although the introduction is witty, courteous and affectionate, the meeting is most profound. One hardly knows what to say. First-rate religious poetry, and leave it at that? Or love poetry, even, and leave it at that? But Herbert escapes this kind of docketing. If his work was only all about heaven, it would be easier, but as he is the supreme English poet of the Incarnation, and thus all about earth as well, he continues to affect us spiritually as few other writers can. Which is why his tiny church in a Salisbury suburb continues to be a beckoning shrine. Aubrey described Bemerton as a 'pittiful little chappell', and Charles I as 'a very neate Curious Chappell' and these early reactions, though seemingly contrasting, remain relevant.

For one who enjoyed the sacred conceit of all good things being contained in a box, rather like the cube and double-cube rooms his family were to build at Wilton after his death, Herbert would have approved of our choosing, out of all the mostly splendid buildings in which he spent his life, that humble, closed-in little church of which he was rector for less than three years, and which encapsulated the total length of his priesthood. Although a church-builder of the utmost perfection – the one he built at Leighton Bromswold in Huntingdonshire is nothing less than his own exquisite Christianity carried out in wood and stone, besides being a masterly expression of the purest form of Anglicanism – Herbert's ultimate divine edifice is humanity itself.

> *My God, I heard this day,*
> *That none doth build a stately habitation,*
> *But he that means to dwell therein.*
> *What house more stately hath there been,*
> *Or can be, than is Man? to whose creation*
> *All things are in decay.*

For us, then, the living dwelling place of the Creator, the natural world is 'either our cupboard of food/Or cabinet of pleasure' – and both in Herbert's eyes are for the legitimate taking. Unlike Peter Abelard and many another singer of the eternal who used the imagery of the temporal, George Herbert extolled the bliss of mortal existence. 'The earth is not too low' to 'sing, My God and King!' Before sin fooled him, man ('I mean myself') encountered God naturally in all things – 'At some fair oak, or bush, or cave, or well' – and was himself a garden within a garden. But this tended, perfect order was wrecked and now man needs to search hard to discover with a disciplined insight where God is. It is no longer within our nature to meet him as naturally as we meet plants and weather, or even time itself. Although Herbert wrote many 'seeking' poems, including one which anticipates Bunyan, *The Pilgrimage*, in which the country-side is very like the Lincolnshire through which Herbert rode on the way to see his married sister Frances, to us he is a 'finding' poet. And so, contrary to much of what he confesses about the shy, elusive nature of God in his own experience, we come to Bemerton, Wiltshire, his brief parish, in order to be in a place where one of the most wonderfully written authentications of the discovery of the naturalness of the friendship of Christ was made.

Since many such discoveries are made in cells, the likelihood that most of George Herbert's were made in broad landscapes lends them a quality which is both airy and homely, lyrical and conversational. Christ is the supper-guest, the delighted listener to the Salisbury choir, the daily companion on the path from Bemerton to Fugglestone, Herbert's other minute parish, and especially in the rectory garden itself, which was more a growing larder and medicine-chest for the village than the elaborate cultivations which had surrounded his various homes before he became a priest. One of the curious things about George Herbert, or perhaps about us, is this concentrating of him at the tail-end of his life in two small unremarkable buildings which face each other across a busy road, when nearly all the sites and scenes of his entire experience are still here for the savouring. His geography is one of rivers and riverside gardens, the Severn and its tributaries at Montgomery, his birthplace; the Thames always close by his mother's various houses at Oxford, Charing Cross and particularly at Chelsea where her second husband Sir John Danvers designed his famous Italian garden; the Roding at Woodford, the home of his favourite brother Henry; the Avon at Dauntsey, the Wiltshire village where he retreated to think about his future; the Kym at Leighton where he built his inimitably Herbertian church; the Cam at Cambridge, where he was officially domiciled for close on twenty years and the Nadder at Bemerton, which ran below his lawn and witnessed the climax of his genius and saintliness. For all that, if we are to judge them by the few references to them in his work, rivers were not a potent analogical force.

> *Rivers run, and springs each one*
> *Know their home, and get them gone.*

He notes the perverse aridity of river valleys in summer – 'Most herbs that grow in brooks, are hot and dry' – and it is only in his lovely Christmas hymn, 'The shepherds sing; and shall I silent be?' that river scenery becomes at all beneficent.

> *The pasture is thy word: the streams, thy grace*
> *Enriching all the place.*

This hymn was written at Bemerton when he was walking twice a week through the water-meadows to Salisbury Cathedral, and probably with the Advent music in which he had been taking part still ringing in his ears. Otherwise, rivers, because of their transitory drift, or maybe because they do not provide the best climate for a consumptive, or possibly because in spite of the regular strolls along the banks of the Nadder to the cathedral Herbert was always far more equestrian than pedestrian and came to enjoy the kind of landscape where one could gallop, such as the open sheep country around Old Sarum or the West Suffolk heathland, seem dispiriting elements. He calls on them chiefly when 'My grief hath need of all the watery things'.

However, it is because of rivers that first-person confession must take over from third-person comment. Which is how it always has to be with Herbert anyway. In order to hear him, one speaks and listens to him, not talks about him. In the days when public poetry readings were still thought of as a test of what people would endure by way of cultural entertainment, a clergyman friend of mine, Harold Sparling, suggested that I should arrange such an event in his church. I thought of Vaughan, Milton, Traherne – or Hopkins – just as a suitable subject for such a setting. Trying Herbert out for sound and length in the church was a curious experience. Herbert's words became song, became confidence, became grand simplicity, became a perfect formulation of a religious pleasure which I had frequently but incoherently felt, became, in fact, as they have with most people who have read him, an articulation of the faith that was native to me but which had previously sheered away from such lucid expression.

I set about this reading with the aid of that very Herbertian and unjustly neglected poet, James Turner, and the Irish poet, W. R. Rodgers. We read first at Langham and then at Little Easton, and it was quite accidental that there happened to be a Herbert link in each of these Essex villages. For Langham was one of the livings of Dr Fisher, the future Bishop of Salisbury, who was an amateur artist, and who thus became interested in a youth living in the next parish whose painting was on quite another scale – John Constable – and so began the patronage which was to bring the great landscapist to Salisbury and to paint those riverside scenes which Herbert knew so well. And Little Easton was once the living of Thomas Ken, whose daughter married Izaak Walton, Herbert's biographer.

Constable's naturalistic approach to landscape (he called it 'scientific') was underlyingly religious, as well as being proprietorial, he belonging to so many farms, mills, barges and family acres. Penetrating these agricultural family vistas were spires and towers which could be claimed as 'his' by virtue of his wife and friends. Throughout his life he found it hard to work where, as he said, he had not been able to make a place his own. Langham, where we read Herbert in the church, was to be the subject of his painting to commemorate the Bishop of Salisbury's kindness to him. It was also Constable's favourite height for viewing the Stour valley. In May 1819 he wrote to his wife back in London,

> I have been this morning for a walk up the Langham Hills, and through a number of beautiful fields & by the side of the river – and in my life I never saw Nature more lovely ... Every tree seems full of blossoms of some kind and the surface of the ground seems quite lovely – every step I take and on whatever object I turn my eye that sublime expression in the Scripture 'I am the resurrection and the life' &c., seems verified about me.

Here he was repeating something which Wordsworth had said to him on another walk in an earlier spring.

What Constable called his 'Great Salisbury', 'Salisbury Cathedral from the Meadow', is an extraordinary uniting of a native and of an adopted scene, for here the thrilling spire and storm-swept facade of the latter soar up virtually from the elements of 'The Hay Wain'. The shallows of the Avon and the Stour are a similar palette shape in both pictures. In each the middle ground is taken up with a farm waggon and three horses, a skiff and, to the left, with dense foliage. Both paintings have middle-distance water-meadows with a screen of trees cutting off any further view of the plain, and each has its brisk little dog and the rotting river-logged posts which Constable loved. He said,

> There has never been an age, however rude or uncultivated, in which the love of landscape has not in some way been manifested.

And how could it be otherwise? for man is the sole intellectual inhabitant of one vast natural landscape. His nature is congenial with the elements of the planet itself, and he cannot but be sympathizer with its features, its various aspects, and its phenomena in all situations.

Constable's studies of Stonehenge and Old Sarum have an archaeological innocence. For him, as for Herbert galloping below them on the Roman road, they represented ancient moods that remained impenetrable. For both brief Salisbury-dwellers the spiritual and material actualities of their lives had always been associated with river-bank civilizations, Constable's with the magnificent towns and villages which affluent medieval clothiers had strung along the Stour Valley in Suffolk, Herbert's consisting of a series of exceedingly beautiful river-side homes at Cambridge, Chelsea, Dauntsey and Bemerton. It is Constable's authoritative treatment of the contemplative yet workaday geography around Salisbury, and the way in which he contrasts the placid (his favourite word) countryside of the stream with that of the wilderness, which makes him such a perfect guide to the final scenery which George Herbert saw. Constable's views may be far from contemporary but they are nearer to those which the poet experienced within the immediate orbit of the cathedral, which is where he spent those Christ-exultant last years, than anything we can see now. Cows in the Close, raggedy cottages, rotting river-staging, rough paths and old tumbling trees, swallows skimming the river for flies, shepherd and flocks below Old Sarum, the detail and atmosphere of the 1820s are hardly in any way removed from those of the early seventeenth century. So, staring into Constable's Salisbury pictures we can take a close look at Herbert's last landscape. These are the water-meadows in which Herbert walked while writing *A Priest to the Temple*, that rule for the English clergy which in its common sense and goodness is in the great tradition of guides to the pastoral vocation, and which, although its style might daunt today's ordinand, is as relevant now as ever it was. Imagine the shadow of Constable's spire pencilled across that same mile or two a few generations earlier and that tall, elegant, ill rector following it to knock on doors:

The Country Parson upon the afternoons in the weekdays, takes occasion sometimes to visit in person, now one quarter of his Parish, now another, For there he shall find his flock most naturally as they

Salisbury Cathedral, Wiltshire

The meadows through which George Herbert walked every week to join the 'singing-men' in the choir. The Cathedral and Bemerton church provided the architectural extremes of splendour and simplicity in the mile or two of countryside in which he constructed the last poems for *The Temple*.

Let th' upper springs into the low Descend and fall . . .

are, wallowing in the midst of their affairs: whereas on Sundays it is easy for them to compose themselves to order, which they put on as their holy-day clothes, and come to Church in frame, but commonly the next day put off both. When he comes to any house, he first blesseth it, and then as he finds the persons of the house employed, he both commends them much, and furthers them when he is gone, in their employment; as if he finds them reading, he furnishes them with good books; if curing poor people, he supplies them with Receipts,★ and instructs them further in that skill, showing them how acceptable such works are to God, and wishing them ever to do the cures with their own hands, and not put them over to servants. Those that he finds busy in the works of their calling, he commendeth them also: for it is a good and just thing for every one to do their own business . . . he hears the children read himself, and blesseth them, encouraging also the servants to learn to read, and offering to have them taught on holidays . . . If the Parson were ashamed of particularizing in these things, he were not fit to be a Parson: but he holds the Rule, that nothing is little in God's service: if it once have the honour of that Name, it grows instantly. Wherefore neither disdaineth he to enter into the poorest cottage, though he even creep into it, and though it smell never so loathsomely. For both God is there also, and those for whom God died . . .

The popular notion of George Herbert, a writer who is increasingly accepted as England's principal devotional poet, is of a brilliant young seventeenth-century aristocrat who, after seeing his 'court hopes' dashed by the deaths of patrons, had some kind of spiritual crisis, turned his back on the world and became a simple clergyman. Albeit, a clergyman of literary genius. This has never been my view of him. I have always thought of him as someone for whom the delights of Christ had been obvious from childhood on, but that the especial glamour of his social position at Cambridge and the tempting possibilities of careers of all kinds quite naturally, given his youth, wit and protracted self-discovery, deflected him temporarily from a path which had been quite recognizable to him almost from the very beginning. This is why I am as much drawn to the scenes of his early years as to that famous scene of climax at Bemerton. For a long time now, during occasional journeys to the Welsh border counties, I have sensed him in the air, and not just because I know he was

★ Prescriptions, recipes for making up herbal medicines.

probably born in a now vanished house called Black Hall which stood just below the family castle at Montgomery, but because sharing such a landscape with such a fascinating mother during the first six or so years of his existence adds something infinitely more compelling to his legend than a date.

Most importantly for the making of both saint and poet, it was Magdalen Newport's country as much as that of Richard Herbert. She was carrying their tenth child when her husband died in 1596 and from then on until the turn of the century, when she moved to Oxford to look after the older boys' education, life alternated between Montgomery and Eyton, her own Shropshire village. The River Severn flowed past both, the first of a long sequence of Herbert's riverside addresses. For all that, his imagery is much of plants and rarely of rivers. Perhaps as a sufferer from the 'quotidian ague', that malarial fever which was one of the horrors of Cambridge before the Fens were drained, he had a reason for not liking them very much. His mentions of them are sparse and dismissive. 'The river past, a God forgotten', was among the proverbs he collected.

The road to Bemerton itself began to be mapped out as long ago as the Wars of the Roses, when Herbert's ancestor was made Earl of Pembroke for supporting Edward IV. The earl's grandson married Ann Parr and so became brother-in-law to Henry VIII, who gave him one of the most magnificent properties which the crown had confiscated during the Dissolution of the Monasteries, Wilton Abbey. Thus it was that when the third earl's pious kinsman eccentrically decided to become a priest in his mid-thirties, an ignominious profession at that time for anyone of his rank, he was instituted into the living of Fugglestone-cum-Bemerton, two broken-down parishes on the edge of Wilton Park, presumably in the belief that curates would be paid to run these whilst Herbert himself acted as chaplain to the great house. As we know – it is the most widely admired aspect of his legend – Herbert did nothing of the kind. Instead, he imitated, so far as he could, which was to a profound extent, his God-King to the letter, and so set in motion, via a single book of poems, and a book of clerical instruction, a religious intelligence which permeates English Christianity to this day. The Welshman's words proved to be exact ones for three centuries of Englishmen in search of Christ.

Plaish, Shropshire

A glance across part of Herbert's childhood world and into Housman's land of lost content. These fields slope away from Wenlock Edge towards the Wrekin.

Except for one short stay in Kent when he was thirty-two, the actual place probably unknown for ever, it is possible to accompany George Herbert, geographically speaking, from beginning to end of his life. Although I deliberately set out with him in Wiltshire and was intrigued to discover how near one can still get to him during the whole period of his life there, and how, like some minute Compostella, Bemerton itself did bring me to a wondering standstill at the end of the road, the haphazard encounters with him which I had made in Shropshire and Wales have always retained their own significance. Perhaps because they disturb the calmer picture I have of him – this seeing him in his native element of quarrelling border territory running between the massifs of the Cambrian Mountains and Wenlock. Also, it has always struck me that his genius did not stem from the fierce, thrusting, grabbing, politicking Herbert line at all, but from his intellectual mother, Magdalen Newport, whose influence over him was so like that of Monica over her son Augustine. This is why Shropshire, Housman's land of regret, and not Wales, is for me one with Herbert's land of first associations. For a Tudor boy of his rank, those first half dozen years spent at Eyton-on-Severn would have been crammed with learning and, for a son of Magdalen Herbert, controlled by a not at all usual pleasure-through-piety discipline. George Herbert not only acknowledged his love of literature to his mother but, more unusually, his 'second birth' or kinship with Christ. He wrote of her:

> *To thee I owe my birth on earth –*
> *To thee I owe my heavenly birth –*
> *As thou didst lead I followed thee;*
> *Thou wast a mother twice to me.*

Magdalen's virtues have been so eloquently listed by her sons and her poet friends, including John Donne, whom she met when George Herbert was still a child, that she often sounds like an alabaster Jacobean tomb woman, stiff with rank and excellence. But her charm, intelligence, practical Christianity and artistry were genuine enough to attract to her house – 'a court in the conversation of the best' – an enthralling crowd of scholars, gardeners and poets, as well as the thoughtful new Christians who were emerging from the political arguments and violence of the Reformation and Counter-Reformation decades. When, in his *A Priest to the Temple*, Herbert set out his recommendations for domestic life in an English country rectory, he was doing no more than adapting his mother's household rules. Cleanliness, decent food and manners, prayer and pleasure, everybody to be taught to read and write who wished to, whatever their position, and especially children; a knowledge of medicine, and a professional accomplishment in music and welfare. What Magdalen Herbert inculcated was a subtly confused daily programme of religion, high culture and the workaday. At the age of forty, and with her ten children variously settled at school, at Court, at the university, and in marriage, she herself remarried, her new husband a boy of twenty and so handsome that people stopped to study his complexion in the street. This was in 1609, the year in which John Donne had addressed to her his impertinent 'The Autumnall':

> *– No* Spring, *nor* Summer *Beauty hath such grace,*
> *As I have seen in one* Autumnall *face.*

Such was the person who, more than any other, founded George Herbert's character and who began to form his thought during his Shropshire boyhood. Thus one can say that the true beginning of all that he was to become took place at Eyton, near Wroxeter, and within sound of those same medieval bells which Housman heard. And then, at the very start of the new century, with Magdalen's typical practicality, came the move to Oxford and the inauguration of all those very different events which were to draw this large Herbert clan away from its border homelands for ever. The scattered graves, George's at Bemerton, his brothers', Edward at St Giles-in-the-Fields, Thomas at St Martin-in-the-Fields, Henry at St Paul's, Covent Garden, William in Flanders, Richard in Holland, and Magdalen's herself (in spite of the painted effigy lying beside her first husband's in Montgomery parish church) lost somewhere in St Luke's, Chelsea, tell of freshly branching out energies rather than the break-up of some old settled power. The infancy of saints and poets bears so directly on their achievements that, now and then, it is as well to go back to the beginning. Because of Magdalen, Herbert was set on the road to Bemerton during those critical years of her Shropshire widowhood where she began to direct his life in such a way that it was bound to end up at some such destination. That lovely spread of the Severn valley below the Wrekin where Watling Street runs straight to Uriconium, and where Shrewsbury is caught in a great loop of river, and all of it so curiously a version of the Avon below Old Sarum, this was George Herbert's first view of the world. Once, after giving a lecture at Shrewsbury School, I was taken to the library and shown one of its treasures, a herbarium, or a huge album of pressed flowers, all of which had been picked in the Severn meadows during the seventeenth century, many bright-petalled still. It rushed me to that huge family a few miles downstream, to Edward, who was to allow Cromwell's troops to take over Montgomery Castle in order to have his books, which had been seized in London, returned to him; to Henry, who was to become Master of the Revels to James I and to their brother George, who was to write:

> *A wreathed garland of deserved praise,*
> *Of praise deserved, unto thee I give,*

I give to thee, who knowest all my ways,
My crooked, winding ways, wherein I live,
Wherein I die, not live: for life is straight,
Straight as a line, and ever tends to thee,
To thee, who art more far above deceit,
Than deceit seems above simplicity.
Give me simplicity, that I may live,
So live and like, that I may know, thy ways,
Know them and practise them: then shall I give
For this poor wreath, give thee a crown of praise.

It was certainly a 'straight as a line' spiritual progress which sent Herbert to Westminster School as a day scholar in 1605 where, due to the appointment of Lancelot Andrewes a few years before, he was instantly absorbed into the very nerve of those religious practices and language which were to create Anglicanism. Magdalen had by this time brought her children to London and become hostess to the musicians, priests and poets involved in creating fresh devotional patterns. Lancelot Andrewes, John Donne, who met her about this time, John Bull, William Byrd, some of the scholars engaged in translating the Bible for the King, Francis Bacon, the eight sons who still lived at home and their friends and tutors, created a dazzling company, and the extraordinarily intelligent and beautiful Christian atmosphere which predominated both at home and at school must have made George Herbert wonder what kind of temptations there could be to lure him away from it. This is where he learnt to play the lute and thus, indirectly, to form the rhythms of his poetry. Magdalen Herbert's domestic arrangements, so far as she could make them, were intentionally paradisal. Her *Kitchen Booke* is as crammed with accounts of prayer, brilliant religious society and intellectual disciplines as it is with the domestic detail which one would expect in the records of such a large household. Where her house stood in relation to what now sprawls at Charing Cross, none can say. Hardly a step from the summer-stinking, winter-fog river, to be certain.

From it Herbert walked daily to Westminster School and there, and in the Abbey itself, those in pursuit of his topography can tread very exactly in his footsteps. Lancelot Andrewes had arrived four years earlier and, as dean, had totally transformed

Westminster School, Little Dean's Yard

The school, founded by Queen Elizabeth I, succeeded a pre-Reformation school belonging to the Abbey, and uses many of the monastic buildings which originally surrounded gardens. When George Herbert attended it the atmosphere was one of renewal and renaissance. Its pupils make an embryonic poets' roll-call – Ben Jonson, Abraham Cowley, John Dryden, Matthew Prior, William Cowper, Charles Wesley, Robert Southey ... The Thames damps, along with the future Cam and Nadder damps, were the very worst climate for him. Did the multitudinous Abbey tombs, although far fewer than now, and the crowded dormitories fill him with thoughts which would be expressed later?

When boys go first to bed,
They step into their voluntary
  graves,
Sleep binds them fast; only their
  breath
Makes them not dead:
Successive nights, like rolling waves,
Convey them quickly, who are
  bound for death.

the spiritual and cultural atmosphere of both the school and the Abbey. A combination of linguist, patristic sage on the grand scale, preacher of genius, high ritualist and lowly man of prayer, and soon to head the 'Westminster Ten' appointed by the king to assist in making his own authorized version of the Bible, Andrewes was irresistible. The court, the ordinary Londoners, the schoolboys he taught, not in classrooms but informally on long walks or as special guests in his house, the Elizabethan writers, all succumbed to his magic. The Word was expressed in unsurpassable words, as well as in a rite that suited the English to perfection. Those who required a rite, that is, for alongside it there was already building up, like an unstoppable ocean swell, something more direct and determined to rid itself of these ancient nuances. George Herbert was always too absorbed in his royal, simple, friendly Christ to argue the point. Such a sacred delight! – what path could lead to a better God? No ceremony whatever was required when one spoke to him in the garden, when riding or, most intimately and entrancedly, in one's room. However, to be his guest at the divine banquet necessarily involved one in a stately etiquette, music and language.

Dean Andrewes, whose manner of teaching was casualness itself when he strolled with his trailing class along the river bank from Westminster to Chelsea, entered his private chapel for his daily communion with his Redeemer as the most strictly caring table-servant. In the translation of Mark's Gospel by King James's scholars Jesus tells his friends Peter and John to go to a 'furnished and prepared' room and 'there make ready for us'. This was what Lancelot Andrewes did to the letter. Best behaviour, and the best of all that one possessed in order to serve the holy feast. Decorum, glory, ultimate nearness to the ultimate host. There is a description of what George Herbert saw in Lancelot Andrewes's private chapel. The poet never, as has been pointed out by biographers of his own day and ours, insisted that ritual had any greater importance than as an ordering of the symbols of his faith. For him, rite was hallowed usage, an intuitively and imaginatively understood framework to be filled out with new prayer, new recognitions. The beauty of it alone made it a positive factor, for it invaded the senses. When the Dean communed with his Saviour, the furnished and prepared room was as follows.

Very quiet, with an altar three feet and a quarter high lit by two tapers on each side of a velvet cushion which held the service-book. Arranged before these was a silver-gilt basket for the wafers which was lined with cambric lace, a tonne or flagon set in a wicker cradle, a chalice covered with a pure white linen napkin called an 'aire', an incense boat, and a tricanale containing water. At the side was a credence table and before it a faldstool on which he knelt to read the litany. The atmosphere in the chapel was still and unfussed, and had an instant effect upon anyone who entered it. When Andrewes spoke, his extraordinary ability to embue tradition with originality, causing old familiar things to scintillate in the minds and emotions of his congregation, threw the conventional worshipper off balance. What was this religion which every Englishman claimed? Not what they had been previously told, it seemed. Both Queen Elizabeth and King James remained fascinated by Andrewes as, year after year, at Christmas and Easter, and in a voice and language which stunned their courts, he repeatedly set out before them the huge tale of redemptive love. He was their Isaiah, learned, simple and eloquent beyond belief. To catch the tone of his learning and style one has only to open Genesis, or the Books of Kings, or Ruth in the Authorized translations. Herbert, reading the first thirteen books of the Old Testament in a version of the Bible which was to shape, first Britain's character and then that of a large part of the world, must have experienced the curious sensation of having a voice he had listened to at his mother's table, during tramps along the Thames footpaths and at school, strangely in duo with the voice of the Creator himself. Born at a unique moment in Christian affairs, in his elevated position he was bound to have a unique education. But then so did his brothers and his youthful stepfather, and countless others, and few of them acquired his clear view of Christ. Herbert was nineteen when the Authorized Version was published and he and all the Westminster schoolboys of his year would have recognized among its multiple scholarship the special cadence of their '*Stella Predicantum*', as they called Andrewes, that unmistakable voice. Herbert's actual experience of Dean Andrewes at Westminster itself was brief, as he left to become Bishop of Chichester soon after the poet arrived, but they were always to keep in touch, and the Abbey itself remained permeated for many years afterwards by his intelligence and goodness. So, to find George Herbert, go to Westminster, where the Dean prayed for him thus:

> *The Youth among us,*
> *Students in Schools,*
> *Those under instruction,*
> *Children, Boys and Youths,*
> *Charge formerly or now.*

Herbert was later to acknowledge that

> *I know the ways of Learning: both the head*
> *And pipes that feed the press, and make it run*

and it was here that his 'sudden soul caught fire'.

Not until 1876 was Westminster to put up a monument to its poet-saint, and then only because an American paid for it. It is in the form of a window in the baptistry which overlooks the school and Herbert shares it with another Westminster boy, William Cowper. Herbert, dressed in his cassock, stands at his church porch at Bemerton, Cowper in his dressing-gown in his Olney garden with hares at his feet. Cowper is gazing at his dead mother's portrait and saying, sadly,

> *O that those lips had language! Life has passed*
> *With me roughly since I heard thee last*

and Herbert is blessing his parishioners and advising them,

> *If thou do ill, the joy fades, not the pains;*
> *If well, the pain doth fade, the joy remains.*

During one of the terrible depressions which once drove Cowper to attempt suicide he discovered Herbert's poems and 'Gothic and uncouth as they were, yet I found in them a strand of piety which I could not but admire. This was the only author I had any delight in reading. I pored over him all the day long; and although I found not here (what I might have found) a cure for my malady – yet it never seemed so much alleviated as while I was reading him.' Herbert the spiritual healer would have been delighted by this testimony. Ill all his life, he had himself used poetry as a defence against pain. Cowper, praising their school, says, 'in the firmament of fame still shines a glory by poets raised by you', and knew that Herbert was the chief part of this glory. There was a special emphasis on Greek and music at the school in Herbert's day. During the Abbey services he found himself both in church and in music's 'house of pleasure' and with a guide who knows 'the way to heaven's door'. If one can look beyond the vast accumulation of tombs of the last three centuries, to him mainly preposterous memorials which severed 'the good fellowship of dust', to the purest of Early English arches, to the roof and the window traceries, the cloister walks and the shrine-graves of the Middle Ages, as well as to a liturgical language which in countless phrases is identical to that which he sang daily, one could hardly come closer to a poet and saint in the making than to the teenage Herbert in Westminster Abbey.

From Westminster we can follow him to Cambridge but, considering that he was to spend by far the lengthiest part of his career there, less palpably than in London. In 1609, accompanied by his friend John Hacket – their headmaster Richard Ireland said that he 'expected to have credit by *them two*, or he would never hope for it afterwards' – he went up to Trinity. Neville was still rebuilding the college and there is a tradition that his mother arranged for him to have rooms in the just-completed New Court, but nobody now knows exactly where he lived. He was fifteen, handsome, clever, conscious of his rank, dandyish but never very well. He played no games but spent all his spare time walking, riding and practising music. His prayer-life was centred at Trinity Chapel but this is so altered that there is little there now that he might have seen, and yet it is a fact that for almost twenty years during term time George Herbert worshipped in this building. The altar at which he made his Communion survived the Puritan cleansings which occurred after his death – only to catch fire in 1660, the year of the Restoration.

> *Immortal Heat, O let they greater flame*
> *Attract the lesser to it: let those fires,*
> *Which shall consume the world, first make it tame;*
> *And kindle in our hearts such true desires,*
> *As may consume our lusts, and make thee way.*

In 1616, the year of Shakespeare's death, he took his Master's degree and became a Fellow, and shortly afterwards was made Public Orator of the University, an office which was a conventional stepping-stone to a position at Court. As Orator, part of Herbert's task was to make ornate proclamations on behalf of the University when royalty visited Cambridge, or when some national event required a formal response from a great seat of learning. Herbert's orations, made in Latin, of course, were extravagant to a degree and one senses that both King James and this elegant academic, a number of whose relations were courtiers, were well aware that at times they were taking part in a comedy. The king was often at nearby Newmarket and Royston, and frequently rode into Cambridge, whose mixture of learning, spectacular hospitality and attractive young men he found irresistible. If he ever had to live there, he said, 'I would pray at King's, eat at Trinity, and study and sleep at Jesus.' One of Herbert's first duties as Orator was to congratulate the king's lover George Villiers on his rise from earl to marquis. In it, Herbert hoped that Villiers would run through all the degrees of earthly dignity to an everlasting reward, which was more or less what happened to him. When the full Senate met to thank the king for presenting his treatise on the art of government, *Basilikon Doron*, to the University, it was the task of the seventeen-year-old Herbert to voice its thanks. These contained the exact note of preposterous youthful wit and charm to please the author and is worth quoting from.

Amidst such convulsions on earth, hast thou leisure to compose a book? Scotland was too narrow for thee: even the empire of the British Isles is not wide enough for the expansion of thy wishes. By this book thou dost compass the world ... We have borne thee in our hearts; thou wishes to be held in our hands ... We are besprinkled with Royal ink ... We embrace this thy offspring, thy second Charles, this embodiment of wisdom, the King of books. Mansions are destroyed. Statues are thrown down. Thou dost overcome time and decay ... When scholars come to Cambridge, and boast of the treasures in the Vatican and Bodleian Libraries, we say, 'All *our* Library is contained in one book.'

It was this fanfare of a review which brought Herbert to the notice of his sovereign, which no doubt was what it was intended to do.

An even funnier oration awaited James's son Prince Charles after he and George Villiers, now Duke of Buckingham, had returned from the débâcle of the Spanish marriage negotiations in Madrid in 1623. After congratulating the prince for arriving home safe and sound with the wedding-ring, Herbert defends Charles's extremely unpopular attempt to wed a princess of a land which for decades had been England's chief enemy. No harm has been done (the Spaniards never took the matter seriously and kept the little suitor and his glamorous suite hanging about in the most undignified manner) and 'Charles has come back laden with honours, like a bee with thighs full of thyme.' But alongside the hyperbole and the official dutifulness runs a deeper statement about the true nature of kingship, about sexuality and about war. All three subjects reveal Herbert's hardening personal attitudes to the conventions. Kings must remember that their title derives from a word which means 'I can, I know, I dare.' Marriage is a solemn, sensual business as much for princes as ordinary men. He reminds his listeners that Charles 'is a man, not a marble statue', just as when, years later announcing his own betrothal to Jane Danvers, he reminds those who are already beginning to think of him as a model of Christian virtues that, 'I am made of flesh, not brass'. But this oration also contains something altogether more challenging to people like Charles and Buckingham, and the common thinking, a strong attack on war which is as powerful in its way as Wilfred Owen's was in 1917, and the kind of pacifist criticism which is always most unwelcome to the state. Why should Herbert have sandwiched this daring tirade between pictures of his romantic prince losing nothing by travelling all the way to Madrid and back to woo a princess whose father turned him down? Because two of Herbert's brothers had died recently in battle, and death in other ways was playing havoc in his close-knit circle. Thus, while the Cambridge bells and bonfires, and its Orator, did their best to welcome back the luckless Prince Charles from Spain, as well as to disguise in celebration the country's relief at not having to welcome a Spanish princess, a darker note was being sounded. Herbert himself had been so ill a few months before that his own death was thought inevitable. Now, in recovery, he turned on those who dealt in death as a branch of politics. Charles's journey may not have produced a bride but it had undoubtedly produced a halt to the long hostilities between England and Spain, most of them senseless.

War is thought glorious, but peace is devoutly to be preferred. In peace sons bury their parents; in war fathers bury their sons. In peace the birds warble; in war the trumpets bray. In peace there is safety in the fields; in war not even in the towns. Peace has opened the New World; war destroys the Old World. How great a blessing to our republic, to our University, is peace! How would our colleges, our libraries, our manuscripts, our literature fare under the murderous discharge of the sulphureous cylinder? Learning like a delicate flower must be handled gently. While Archimedes was tracing problems on the ground, the sword of the Roman soldier reached his heart, and his dead body effaced the lines he had just described. Read the pages of human history: fields are drenched in human blood; noble cities are burnt to ashes; hunger, misery, sickness and wounds rage among the people ... In the grave there is no difference between the monarch and the subject, and the stench from the rotting carcasses of slaves makes as loud a thunder as from the putrifying corpses of kings.

Such opinion in an official oration is not likely to recommend its author for any kind of preferment at a seventeenth-century court. Walton, Herbert's first biographer, said that the poet's 'court hopes' were dashed by the sudden deaths of the handful of men who would have helped him rise from Cambridge to Whitehall, and including King James himself, but the more one discovers about Herbert during all those years at Trinity College, the less one is convinced by this explanation. A different king was already in command, causing him to be reckless with 'ambition', enchanting him, offering him delights – a favourite word – above anything to be found at the Stuart court.

And then there was the friendship with a young man of his own age, Nicholas Ferrar, who put Herbert's position as someone who makes his own decision on essential matters very plain. 'Quitting both his deserts, and all the opportunities that he had for worldly preferment, he betook himself to the Sanctuary and Temple of God, choosing rather to serve at God's altar than to seek the honour of State-employments.' No dropping into the Church due to failure in other directions here. Cambridge is the scene of their companionship, which resulted in as influential a series of conversations and actions as any which the Church of England records. A fellow of Clare College, Ferrar was a year older than Herbert, and it was he who, immediately after his friend's death, was given the responsibility of seeing his works, the finest Protestant poetry in the language, through the press. Calling the collection 'The Temple', from the verse in Psalm 29 which says, 'In his Temple doth every man speak of his honour', Ferrar took the book to Thomas Buck and Roger Daniel, the University Printers, who produced an edition worthy of its contents. Thus, Cambridge establishes itself with even greater centrality to Herbert's past and unimaginable future. Was it here that he and Nicholas Ferrar decided upon the motto that each of them were to take for both Little Gidding and Bemerton? It was 'Less than the least of God's mercies' and it was taken from the words which Jacob spoke after his mysterious struggle with the angel.

Although Cambridge saw the birth of a book in which Richard Crashaw said, 'divinest love lies' and which announced a writer T. S. Eliot thought might justly be called a major poet, it would almost certainly have seen an even earlier death for Herbert had he remained there. Ironically, it was during the time when its damps were playing havoc with his lungs that he found himself the University's spokesman against the only measure which would improve the health of the place generally, the proposed draining of the Fens. The University believed that if Parliament granted a patent to the Corporation of Bedford Level to drain the close on half a million acres of swamp which surrounded the town, and which stretched into Lincolnshire, Northamptonshire, Cambridgeshire, Suffolk and Norfolk, that the Cam itself would disappear. This classic little stream which runs into the Ouse was as much a college amenity and pleasure in Herbert's day as in our own, and was already lined with gardens, glorious trees, beloved meadows, boat-houses and cultural and emotional associations of every kind. No matter that the Dutch engineers could bring prosperity to what was a vast mosquito-y dereliction, some four miles of academic limpidity must remain. Herbert's orations to those influential enough to 'save the Cam' (it was never in any danger of being lost, of course) must be one of the first examples of conservationist special pleading on record. It is the familiar argument between feeling and expertise. Here is how J. J. Daniell, the first of Herbert's twentieth-century biographers, summarizes these conservationist pleas. They are actually flowery thanks in advance for assistance which did not materialize, for of course the Dutch did drain the Fens to every East Anglian's and don's benefit.

First Herbert thanks King James for securing to Cambridge the waters over which the Muses delight to reign. Then he tells Sir Robert Naunton, the Secretary of State, that the University rejoices that her son should preserve for his mother the fountains at which he himself had once drunk. Sad would it be for so noble a mother to suffer from dry teats. For if the Cam be drained, and from want of water the colleges be abandoned, and the Muses, like withered widows be bereft of children, can any doubt that England would shed tears enough to cause another river to flow? Then he thanks Lord Brooke for 'preserving our river Cam by the river of thy eloquence, and has washed away the drainers from the marshes, who have been at work as if the sun had ceased to draw up exhalations from bogs: we offer thee the river of our thanks.' He also writes to his friend Francis Bacon, but here Herbert touches on deeper threats to Cambridge. As his reticence on the very long period he spent there is so marked, this letter is of some significance:

That river, on the banks of which so much learning and poetry flourish, which flows through our College gardens, and strews flowers all around, is of far higher value than all the swamps and morasses in the land. Fortunately the season has been so dry that it has mocked the grand concern, and done more for us than a thousand speculators could have done. Some of our foes are envious not only of our river, but of our sovereign immunities, and these, not only the ignoble masses, who think there can be no religion with learning, but persons of gentle birth, who cry out aloud against deep scholarship, as waste and useless.

As J.J. Daniell adds, 'But not withstanding all the opposition aroused and presented by the University, Parliament granted a patent to the Corporation of Bedford Level; vast drainage works went on for many years; deep canals were cut, miles of embankment raised, mosses and meres drained; rivers turned into new channels, roads laid and bridges built, and thousands of acres of valuable land reclaimed, and brought into cultivation. And the Cam flowed on in the same volume as before.' The Fens as we now know them were being created. George Herbert's is a strange utterance to hear in this context but one of the most fascinating things about him is the continuing relevance to ourselves of so many of the arguments of his day. Although his distinctive voice was heard lecturing, orating, praying and singing in numerous existing Cambridge buildings, it is not in these that I overhear it across the centuries, but, interlaced with that of Ferrar, on the bridges and banks, and along the Newmarket road as he rode into Suffolk and a better climate.

It was while he was at Cambridge that he began to be absorbed in proverbs. He and his younger brother Henry made a special study of them and eventually Herbert was to publish over a thousand in his *Outlandish Proverbs*. For him, as for the anthologist of the Book of Proverbs, their pleasure was in dealing with a subject which showed how many kinds of tested knowledge could be reduced to a few words. For Herbert, wisdom, whether Christ's wisdom, a scholar's wisdom or a ploughman's wisdom, was all an essentially homely matter. The incisiveness of the Book of Proverbs taught him compression and simplicity as a poet, and again at Cambridge one hears his divided voice, correctly florid when Orator (although frequently saying things that were challenging and unwelcome), and 'terrifyingly lucid', as one critic has described it, in its sacred homeliness. Here the master of English literature's plainness can be felt withdrawing himself from the baroque dais and pulpit. At Bemerton he preached once only in what might be called his Cambridge manner; ever after it was in Christ's style, so far as it was imitable. The villagers were enchanted by it, tying up their ploughs or leaving their household tasks the moment the Bemerton bell spoke the approach of a service in the little clockless community. Like his bell, a proverb had its resonance. It was a statement of plain truth which hung around in one's hearing, setting up an intricate kind of thoughtfulness.

As well as dozens which are still in daily use, George Herbert's *Outlandish Proverbs* contains hundreds of pithy little sayings, each one of which is like having his early seventeenth-century England briefly lined up in a camera shutter. Many are the maxims by which the first settlers lived in the New World.

A cake and ill customs must be broken.

When a friend asks, there is no tomorrow.

Love and a cough cannot be hid.

A fair wife and a frontier castle breed quarrels.

Everyone stretches his legs according to his coverlet.

Of all smells, bread: of all tastes, salt.

Milk says to wine, welcome friend.

I wept when I was born, and every day shows why.

It is a great victory that comes without blood.

Advise none to marry or to go to war.

There are more men threatened than stricken.

The best mirror is an old friend.

God comes to see without a bell.

The charges of building and making of gardens are unknown.

Good finds good.

Building is sweet impoverishing.

Virtue now is in herbs and stones and words only.

Prettiness dies first.

Gluttony kills more than the sword.

Living well is the best revenge.

Thursday come, and the week's gone.

In every country the sun rises in the morning.

Nothing lasts but the Church.

Love and business teach eloquence.

When a man is on horseback he knows all things.

Gentility is nothing but ancient riches.

It's a dangerous fire which begins in the bed-straw.

No love is foul, nor prison fair.

It is good to have some friends both in heaven and hell.

Woe be to him that reads but one book.

Critics are like brushers of noblemen's clothes.

Soldiers in peace are like chimneys in summer.

A man's destiny is always dark.

Whatever is made by the hand of a man, by the hand of a man is overturned.

There also flooded into Herbert during these long Cambridge years all his lifelong passions, which ranged from the need to possess a Christ-centred artistry in words and music, to dieting and gardening, the latter interests having for him certain essential connections. As well as of Faith, Herbert is the singer of alternative medicine and botany. It was not only his young stepfather who taught him the excitements of the aesthetic and practical uses of English plants, but also his philosopher-poet brother Edward, who confessed to him that he 'delighted ever in the knowledge of herbs, plants, and grass, and in a few words, the history of nature; I consider it a fine study and worthy a gentleman to be a good botanic'. George Herbert agreed, recalling that

Our Saviour made plants and seeds to teach the people: for he was the true householder, who bringeth out of his treasure things new and old ... that labouring people (whom he chiefly considered) might have everywhere monuments of his Doctrine, remembering in gardens, his mustard-seed, and lillyes; in the field, his seed-corn, and tares; and so not to be drowned altogether in the works of their vocation.

There can be little doubt that if the liturgical discipline of Westminster Abbey and Trinity College was to so astonishingly transfigure a rough, workaday little village like Bemerton, the ordinary health of the parish must have improved out of all recognition due to Herbert's advanced understanding of the plant world, nutrition, healing properties, etc. Herbert described herbs as 'Nature serving grace both in comfort and diversion' and it is impossible for anyone who has read him and who then traces his paths through the English cities, villages and open countryside which he loved, not to run into all that marvellous floral geography, some on East Anglian clay, most of it on Wiltshire chalk, which he gathered to himself to feed both body and senses. Not a petal or stalk is to be ignored.

> *Nothing we see, but means our good,*
> *As our delight, or as our treasure;*
> *The whole is, either our cupboard of food,*
> *Or cabinet of pleasure.*

Balsam, garlic, rhubarb, roses, crown imperials, plantain, St John's wort, adder's tongue, hyssop, valerian, shepherd's purse, knotgrass, elder, comfrey, smallage, melilot, yarrow, trees, all the scents and colours and tastes of both the cultivated and wild places fill Herbert's language. Also the everchanging English weather, the latter so much so that Aldous Huxley saw it as a force within the poet himself – 'The climate of the mind is positively English in its variableness and instability. Frost, sunshine, hopeless drought and refreshing rains succeed one another with bewildering rapidity. Herbert is the poet of this inner weather.'

One of the reasons for Herbert's passion for flowers was that, influenced by one of those recipes for a long life which advocate vegetarianism, in this instance a book by an eighty-three-year-old Italian named Luigi Cornaro, the poet was able to cure himself of a particularly severe attack of 'quotidian ague' by giving up meat and following a spare diet. Other people, including the Ferrar family at Little Gidding, were reading Herbert's translation of Cornaro and eating balanced vegetable diets too, and when one connects this recovered awareness of healthy

Little Gidding, Huntingdonshire (Kurt Hutten)

Here in 1626 Nicholas Ferrar brought his family, a community of some thirty people, to live a life of prayer, craftsmanship and healing. His tomb – T. S. Eliot's 'illegible stone' before the 'dull facade' – guards the door. Inside is the brass font which is part of the worthy fittings Ferrar introduced after finding the place ruinous and used as a barn. Nicholas's brother John and Arthur Woodnoth oversaw the rebuilding of George Herbert's church at Leighton Bromswold, five miles away, riding there once a week. It was here that Herbert's poems were prepared for the press. 'Little Gidding', the last poem of *Four Quartets* and Eliot's finest achievement, is, among other things, a great meditation on landscape. In it the violence of the fires caused by the London bombing in 1941 echoes the violence of the destruction of the religious experiment at Little Gidding by the Parliamentary troops. But nature's seasonal changes and man's spirituality remain indestructible and

> *You are here to kneel*
> *Where prayer has been valid.*

eating with the intense new interest in gardening which captured early seventeenth-century England, the many examples of plants as divine composites of the utilitarian and the beautiful in Herbert's work can be more fully appreciated. A walk through George Herbert's England is a contemplation of gardens as well as of God.

From late 1624, when he gave up his office at Cambridge and became a deacon, to that famous moment four years later when he set about repairing the simple rectory at Bemerton, Herbert was homeless, although not in any sense as was his Lord when a Palestine village refused to receive him. Throughout this drifting period we can catch both glimpses and full sights of him. One of the glimpses is when John Donne writes, 'Mr George Herbert is here', meaning that glorious house in Chelsea. Present-day Danvers Street marks a spot which John Aubrey describes as follows.

As you sitt at Dinner in the Hall, you are entertaind with two delightful Vista's: one southward over the Thames & to Surrey: the other northward into that curious Garden . . .

You did not enter directly out of the Hall into the Garden: there was a low semicircular wall to hinder the immediate pleasures and *totall* view primo introitus. But you first turned on the right or left hand, down a paire of staires of ten steppes which landed you in a kind of Boscage (Wilderness) of Lilacs, Syringa's &c. (Sweet Briar &c. Holly – Juniper): and about 4 or 4 Apple trees and peare trees. In the west end of this Boscage was the figure of the Gardiners wife in freestone coloured: at the east end of the Gardiner's the like: both accoutred according to their *Callings*. The east and west ends of this little darke, shadie Boscage delivered you into the stately great gravelled Walkes of the garden, East & West.

And one should be able to capture more than glimpses of Herbert at Woodford and in Epping Forest, and also in Kent, where he retreated to think his future out, but the facts are scanty, and my own tracing of his steps after Cambridge took me straight to Wiltshire and then finally to Huntingdonshire, and to those remote fields where his poetry was given to the world by his friend Nicholas Ferrar, and where stands that incomparable parish temple at Leighton Bromswold, a building so Herbertian that it leaves one gasping.

The Thames near Chelsea Bridge

Immediately after their marriage, an event which shocked society because he was twenty and she over forty, Sir John Danvers took George Herbert's mother to live in a mansion on the river bank near here, whose rare and curious furnishings and atmosphere were very like those of Bunyan's 'House Beautiful' at Ampthill. Danvers Street marks the site. Around the house, and making much of the views of the Thames, Sir John made an Italian garden which became one of the wonders of the river. Both Herbert and his brother Lord Herbert of Cherbury, the philosopher-poet, were keen gardeners and were inspired by their stepfather's genius at Chelsea. He liked 'sudden arbours', or garden surprises, and what were then called 'sweets', or heavily scented flowers. All three men saw gardens as dispensaries, particularly George, who was so continually ill. It was Sir John Danvers's brother Henry who founded and endowed Oxford's famous Physic Gardens. Plant imagery fills George Herbert's poetry and much of it was learnt here during his teens. The neighbouring lawns of the Royal Hospital now annually attract the gardening world to the Chelsea Flower Show.

So first to Wiltshire, and Dauntsey, a serene little place on the banks of the Avon halfway between Swindon and Chippenham. Here in 1628 came the thirty-five-year-old poet and deacon, no longer to think things out but to take those deliberate steps which led to Bemerton. It is significant that what brought him to the county which his few years spent in it makes sacred to the modern traveller in search of hallowed earth, was not Herbert's magnificent family at Wilton but the distinctly unusual and curious family into which his mother had married. At no

Dauntsey, Wiltshire (Charles Hall)

Dauntsey House, where George Herbert came to live with his kinsman the Earl of Danby. The great house was his home from 1629 to 1630, and it was from its hospitable base that he stepped off, as it were, into matrimony and then his life as a priest at Bemerton. The Avon, his step-uncle's celebrated garden and plenty of good riding country (and most of all the peace of heart which came from his decision to be ordained), made him regard Dauntsey as a very special milestone on his Christian path. Faint echoes remain of his happiness here, of his singing and lute-playing.

My God, I heard this day,
That none doth build a stately
  habitation,
But he that means to dwell therein.
What house more stately hath there
  been,
Or can be, than is Man? to whose
  creation
All things are in decay.

From 'Man'

time in his life can there be discerned Wiltshire tugging at him, yet his arrival there was a spiritual homecoming. Which is why, when we reach the bridge at Dauntsey and see the Georgian mansion which boxes in, in a way which would have amused him, the mansion he knew, and then pass what Pevsner calls its 'absolutely unenriched' gateway, and then see St James's church among its sycamores, we can give way to some holding of the breath. For this village marks the first big step. Dauntsey is cool and unemphatic about it, making it all the more tangible. For the reader of the poetry, the whole place rains emblems, symbols, intense little views of Lord Danby's guest of three and a half centuries ago, the sophisticated and still-young man from Cambridge and the fringes of the Court, having in the most complete sense imaginable his sabbatical. His total leisure and, at the same time, his total preparation, hang in the air. If there can be a geographical version of the anteroom, then Dauntsey is George Herbert's, the place from which he stepped to his fulfilment as priest and poet. It is certainly the place to read and contemplate him on a June day.

We arrived from Malmesbury, looking like a walled Burgundian wine town on its escarpment, and our immediate introduction to Dauntsey was blue and flashing – a kingfisher vanishing

Dauntsey, Wiltshire (Charles Hall)

St James's Church, (*opposite*) the porch leading to the Norman doorway through which Herbert passed to say his daily offices. Villagers would have heard him composing lute-hymns. It was almost certainly his influence which persuaded Lord Danby to restore the church in 1632. Among the poems which Herbert is thought to have written in the church are 'To All Angels and Saints', 'Church Monuments' and 'Laus Deo'.

across the piers of the old bridge, amber in the shallow river. A warm southern wind set up a soft roaring in the sycamores and tilted their leaves. Nothing announces itself, in pilgrimage terms, as do Bemerton and Little Gidding. But holiness at Dauntsey, as at Leighton Bromswold, civilly requests a mite of erudition. So first Lord Danby who gave Herbert any part of Dauntsey House 'as might best sute with his accommodation and liking'. He was the poet's stepfather's elder brother. Very soon the widowed stepfather himself, remarried and steadily moving into a politics which would allow him to sign King Charles's death warrant, would be living at nearby West Lavington. This was the village in which Sir John Danvers created the second of his glorious gardens, although none of it remains now. The most eloquent relic of the unlikely man to have given George Herbert so much moral and practical assistance in life is the tomb in the church of his twenty-one-year-old son, who is literally dying in marble, his book slipping from his fingers. This youth was six when his father became a regicide. They belong to a post-Herbert world, one which, if he felt it was coming, he gave no hint of the fact. But it remains a dramatic addendum to his Wiltshire, and those seeking him here might care to wander on to West Lavington where a later poet, Edward Thomas, saw a street of 'about two miles of cottages, a timber-yard, a great house, a church and gardens, with interruptions from fields', and heard a little, half-seen river running parallel with the lane, 'very clear and thin and bright', all of it a sight which Herbert, cantering through these deeply recessed roads, would have noted from his saddle.

At Dauntsey it is no more than a lawn from house to church. This is where, twice daily, he would have walked to say his office, for he was now a deacon and the pattern of his worship was to be synchronized with that of his friends at Little Gidding, 'I and dear prayer would together dwell'. Entering by the garden-side door for Matins, the daybreak office, he would have passed through the present porch to kneel in the chancel –

> *I cannot ope my eyes,*
> *But thou art ready there to catch*
> *My morning-soul and sacrifice:*
> *Then we must needs for that day make a match.*

and again for Evensong,

> *Yet still thou goest on,*
> *And now with darkness closest wearie eyes,*
> *Saying to man,* It doth suffice:
> Henceforth repose; your work is done.
> *Thus in thy Ebony box*
> *Thou dost inclose us . . .*

Would he have seen the lurid, dismantled Doom which now stands discreetly against the north wall? Judgement as a gruesome raree-show was not for him. To be terrified into loving, this would have been a persuasion which was outside his comprehension. His 'Doomsday' is a very different occasion, a divine springtime.

> *Come away*
> *Make no delay.*
> *Summon all the dust to rise,*
> *Till it stir, and rub the eyes;*
> *While this member jogs the other,*
> *Each one whispering,* Live you brother?

But the little dead people tied top and toe in their shrouds, just as about this time John Donne was to tie himself in his to model for his tomb-maker, would have caught his attention. During the Middle Ages it was a popular belief that everybody would be aged about thirty-three, the same age as the risen Christ, in both heaven and hell, and so children and old folk are rarely seen tumbling into the devil's vermilion maw. Herbert seems to recollect this in his cheerful poem 'Death'.

> *For we do now behold thee gay and glad,*
>   *As at dooms-day;*
> *When souls shall wear their new array,*
> *And all thy bones with beauty shall be clad.*

Sitting in St James's church at Dauntsey, surrounded by fine Laudian furnishings whose design is so perfectly echoed in Herbert's parish masterpiece at Leighton Bromswold, surrounded by objects and patterns which burnt themselves into the heart of his creative force as he luxuriated in a freedom which he had never known before and directed himself to the priesthood and to poetry, there comes a sudden recognition of where one actually is – it is in his 'Temple'. Here, at Dauntsey, to this very day, is

> *My Light, my Feast, my Strength.*
> *Such a Light, as shows a feast:*
> *Such a Feast, as mends in length;*
> *Such a Strength, as makes his guest.*

The little churchyard then would have been almost clear of memorials, a humpy sheep-nibbled swell of turf. Now the baroque table-tombs of Georgian farmers and gentry tilt and plunge in its grasses, ornate boxes very much after Herbert's own heart in which what is confined is paradoxically both caught and free. They are engagingly tender, like that of John Baker on which sad, tubby children dry their eyes on the hem of their dead mother's dress. Their contemporaries, the Rogers, Vines, Whales, topple all around under the drifting sycamore leaves. In Herbert's time, to place poison in an ebony box was thought to rob it of its power, and in spite of the carved tears, there is a decided optimism about these handsome stone enclosures. A very fine box indeed crowds the Danby family chapel. In it lies the poet's kindly host and on it is carved the epitaph written by Herbert years before either of them had to 'take acquaintance of this heap of dust'. The rector during his stay at Dauntsey was Mr Elias Woodroofe. Did he daily accompany his visitor in

> *This glorious and transcendant place,*
> *To be a window, through thy grace?*

Between Aubrey and Izaak Walton we catch a vivid personal glimpse of him at this moment. That his complexion was fine and consumptive, that he was tall and very straight and 'lean to an extremity', that he was very cheerful, and he 'was a very good hand on the lute, and that he set his own lyrics or sacred poems'. And so one sees him gaunt and happy among the Dauntsey saints, Magdalena, Katharina, Margarita, Dorothea, Anne and Fridismunde, at prayer and at his art. Penetrating the church then as now, a backing to his lute, was the sound of weir water, wind and birds.

A monstrous asbestos flue now runs the full length of Lord Danby's lovely 1630 tower and (as at Leighton, of all places!) the altar itself conceals a pile of verger's junk, yet nothing matters except that George Herbert paused here for a few months between one set of duties and another, was well here, was at leisure here. Leisure, rather than rest, was what he hoped to find in paradise. Between the canonical hours of ten and four he wrote or revised his poems, explored the Avon valley – and courted a girl named Jane Danvers who lived some twenty miles away at Baynton, and who was, according to that old gossip John Aubrey, 'a handsome *bona roba* and ingeniose'. Surprisingly, they were married in mid-Lent and the next year of the long and gradual progress to Bemerton Rectory was spent at his wife's home. The marriage, Jane was taught, did not make her a great lady but a priest's partner, for Herbert was then setting out his sternly joyful rule for country parsons in which their wives are to be rankless intelligent women who are village educators and nurses, 'curing and healings of all wounds and sores with her own hands'. Jane was his stepfather's cousin and, with Lord Pembroke now searching around for somewhere to place this extraordinary kinsman who was so bent on following Christ to the letter, the Wiltshire commitment was complete. From Dauntsey through to Edington, the handsome church in which the wedding took place. Five miles from Westbury and built all at one go in the fourteenth century, set below the downs and architecturally magnificent, it is the antithesis of what Herbert was to find at Bemerton, one of those palace-temples which nest in the border foliage of a medieval Book of Hours, not homely at all but designed to stimulate wonder. It was built by a native of this village who became Bishop of Winchester in 1345 as the prayer centre of some priests known as the Bonshommes, who followed the Augustinian rule. Its architecture is extraordinary, for it is nothing less than a compound of the two great medieval styles, Decorated and Perpendicular, at their moment of transition. George Herbert strolled or rode down to it by the steep lane from Baynton House many times, and what Aubrey says of him at Dauntsey – ''Tis an honour to the place, to have had the heavenly and ingeniose contemplation of this good man' – applies equally to Edington. These are the temples which he entered daily when he was writing his *Temple*, and all around them lie the natural origins of his imagery, the seasoned timber, bees, plants, paths, groves, skies, animals; a local ecology which he wove into the imagery of the poets of the Psalms, his most

profound literary influence. His friend John Donne reckoned
that David was a greater poet than Virgil, but what drew Herbert to the Psalms, their sacredness apart, was that here lay a
language for singing.

> *Heark, how the birds do sing,*
> *And woods do ring.*
> *All creatures have their joy: and man hath his.*

What more arresting thought could the interiors of Dauntsey
and Edington parish churches provide than that once George
Herbert sang his Christ-songs in them to his lute?

Being Herbert, he left behind there an artefact to prove it. It
is the ring which John Donne gave him and which is now the
property for ever of the successive priests of Warminster. It
consists of a 'heliotropian' (bloodstone) set in gold whose device
is the body of Christ crucified on an anchor. This is not 'the
famous stone, that turneth all to gold' of Herbert's most celebrated hymn, which is a reference to the philosopher's stone
which was so long and vainly searched for by medieval alche-
mists, but a stone which, in Herbert's day, was believed to turn
or bend itself towards sunlight. Many things were thought heliotropian, or sun-turning, including sundials, marigolds and
sunflowers. In Wiltshire the poet himself became included in the
heliotropian band whose nature was to stare straight back at the
source of its being. But not with the old dread – this was the
best of it. 'Of what an easie quick access, My blessed Lord, art
thou!' Unlike previous generations of mystics, Herbert is never
ashamed or embarrassed by the flesh, or longs for the day when
it is not there and he is all spirit. Face to face with a Light which
he must reflect, and being the image of God, how can his body
be other than 'all symmetrie, Full of proportions'? Riding,
whether to Newmarket or on Salisbury Plain, the landscape
exhilarates him. It is good to be alive.

> *For us the windes do blow,*
> *The earth doth rest, heav'n move, and fountains flow.*

As a consumptive, and with his extreme distrust of doctors
and his strict regime of dieting and exercise, Herbert, during the
last years of his life, seems to have clasped the chalky, sweeping,
secretly intended, airy, ancient spread of Wiltshire to him with
the rapture of a Richard Jefferies, who also was thirty-nine when

he died. To Herbert's mind, God had, in his inexplicable generosity, provided man with two paradises, one for his brief earthly life and the other for his everlasting spirit, and the only complication was that the countryside of southern England was so enticing (a favourite word of his) as to make the superior claims of heaven often quite impossible to believe. But it was all part of the blessed playfulness of his King, the ruler of both.

On 16 April 1630 Herbert was presented by the Crown. ('Most willingly to Mr Herbert, if it be worth his acceptance,' agreed Charles I, voicing the general surprise that such a man should apply for such a living. Being much at home at Wilton House, the king could have been familiar with these two forlorn little chapels and their ruined rectory.) On 26 April, St Mark's tide, Herbert was taken first to Fugglestone and then to Bemerton by the Bishop of Salisbury and, although he was still only a deacon, inducted. The astonishment which his friends felt when they looked through the windows of St Andrew's, Bemerton, to find out what was keeping him, and then to discover him prostrate before the altar, only proves to illustrate into what a mere convention the ceremony had fallen. He was thirty-seven and amazingly happy. In the two years left to him he was to give these churches and their rectory, which at that moment was uninhabitable, a significance that makes them a watershed in Britain's Christian history.

Bemerton in particular conveys to perfection the Anglican definition of a shrine, which is a spotless structure for listening to words in. Nobody from Herbert's day to our own first sees it without receiving something of a shock. The church now clings stubbornly to what is not much more than a traffic peninsula, and Herbert's tiny village is now Salisbury's largest suburb. His initials twist and flash above the weathercock but the single bell in the turret which tolls against the roar of cars and lorries is that which tolled for his services. The south door is the one which he opened and the chalice that from which he and his country communicants drank. Yet excessive care over the years has had the effect of obliterating the object which had to be cared for. The poet himself lies somewhere beneath the parquet and with the minimum of a memorial, as he required it, just a ceramic tile with a cross and 'G.H. 1632'. In a way it would have amused him, this carrying out his injunctions on

cleanliness and neatness, and polishing him out of sight. A middle-aged man repairing the churchyard fence who couldn't help observing that I had arrived at an important destination, had to ask why I was there, at Bemerton. He excused his ignorance by telling me that he came from the New Forest.

'A poet named George Herbert used to be rector here.'

'George Herbert,' he said slowly, having never said it before. Then 'Lately?'

'Oh, no. A long time ago.'

'I don't read a lot,' he said.

I praised his fence, which was worth praising.

Vans and cars manipulated the chevron of roads created by the churchyard, and any procession from the house to chancel at ten and four today would need to be cautious. The propinquity of Herbert's home to his altar still makes its point in spite of the traffic, and the site of those regular steps across the lane seems to be more protected than obliterated by tarmac. Bemerton means 'the town of the trumpeters'. Could it have been a music school for Old Sarum? What a sound by the river!

Bemerton, George Herbert's Rectory

The Rectory Garden, which Herbert planted as a dispensary. He died in a room facing the garden. The River Nadder flows under his windows.

Christ hath took in this piece of ground,
And made a garden there for those
Who want herbs for their wound.
From 'Sunday'

Bemerton, Wiltshire (Charles Hall)

St Andrew's Church, where George Herbert was priest from 1630 to 1633. No one knows how drastic were his restorations, for the building was in a scandalous mess when he came to it but, knowing as they did his association with it, later restorers should have mended it once more with nothing less than sacred respect for what he saw and touched. But such a consideration never entered their mind. However, his fine door still lets us in.

A broken Altar, Lord, they servant
*   rears,*
Made of a heart, and cemented with
*   tears;*
Whose parts are as thy hand
*   did frame;*
No workman's tool hath
*   touch'd the same.*
              From 'The Altar'

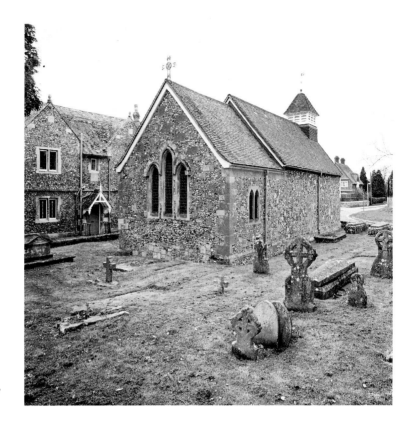

I know the wayes of pleasure, the sweet strains,
The lullings and the relishes of it;
The propositions of hot bloud and brains;
What mirth and musick mean; what love and wit
Have done these twentie hundred yeares, and more . . .

So this is the spot where he set up and briefly delighted in his own holy household after a lifetime of belonging to institutions and being a peregrinating family guest. This is where he laid down his sacred version of the domestic law so 'courteously', as he would have described it, that what happened here between 1630 and 1633 vibrates in the imagination to this day. Herbert's household consisted of himself and his young wife, his three teenage nieces who had recently been orphaned, two men-servants and four maids. Together they made an impressive group for him to lead across the lane twice a day for prayer and song. On the other side of the rectory lay his long medicine-chest of a garden, the River Nadder and a view of Salisbury Cathedral. Both the rectory fig tree and medlar are traditionally said to be his, and the prospect which he would have seen from his bedroom window is little changed. He taught, he preached – though not one of his highly popular sermons remains. Most of his parishioners were ordinary field-workers, 'thick and heavy, and hard to raise to a point of zeal, and fervency, and need a mountain of fire to kindle them ...', so rather than attempt to whip them up by means of dramatic oratory, Herbert's method was to 'give them stories and sayings they will remember'. Had not Christ done exactly this? The poet never preached for more than an hour and he always tried to preach 'something worth learning'. He insisted on kneeling and silence during prayers, and he deliberately created a profound atmosphere in his church by the manner in which he moved and spoke. It was his unaffected mixing of high solemnity and the practical and workaday which beguiled his congregation, who came to love his Matins and Evensongs so much that they would tie up their ploughs to the hedges when his bell rang and hurry to hear him, just as they were. Making it his 'business', a word he liked, to know all he could about agriculture and the ordinary working-life of the countryside, he seems to have established a genuine authority towards his people.

During his last months Herbert completed his 'Rule' for Britain's country clergy. In it, quite plain to see, although *en passant*, his own living of Fugglestone-with-Bemerton, exactly as it must have been when he took it in hand in 1630, reveals itself, warts and all. Only a country rector of his unselfconscious sanctity (Herbert insisted that holiness was much more a normal, rational requirement than a rare achievement) would have had the nerve to compose such a 'Rule' when he himself was so new to the job. This and the fact that he was now a priest in a hurry. Although never more perfectly alive, death was at his heel. There could be no settling down to leave his special godly mark, as some good rectors did. His had to be a fleeting incumbency whose imprint would be of another sort. A century of reformation, plus many centuries of folk attitudes, had obscured the nature of the priest of Christ and before Herbert encountered death, no longer ghastly but

gay and glad,
As at dooms-day;
When souls shall wear their new array,
And all thy bones with beauty shall be clad

he intended to reinstate this familiar and oft-derided village figure as a sacred force. Fugglestone-with-Bemerton would not be able to look back (although it did) on his brief pastorate as they would have on some dutiful shepherd who, as they say in Suffolk, 'had wintered us and summered us' for generations, but the English Church itself might *live* because he had lived. In order to illustrate a priest's common rural experience, Herbert drew on what he saw on his rounds near Salisbury, what he heard, what he himself actually did. *A Priest to the Temple* is thus an autobiography as well as a tough analysis of his flock. A highly unsuitable flock, it would seem, for a sickly, patrician man of letters. But in his 'Rule' the poet is indifferent to the suitability of parishes for certain types of clergymen. Wherever they are, in whatever kind of society, they have to be nothing less than 'the deputies of Christ for the reducing of man to the obedience of God'. And since being a priest of Christ is the ultimate honour attainable by man, an ordinary, sincere village clergyman, although the simplest of people, is equal to the so-phisticated divines of the university and palace. At the end all that he needs to say, as Christ did, is, 'I sat daily with you teaching in the Temple.'

It is a dramatic way of foreshortening time to read *A Priest to the Temple* at Bemerton and Fugglestone. Motorways recede and river-valley tracks and lanes take up the old ground. Three temples, Salisbury Cathedral, Bemerton chapel and Fugglestone church, and a palace, Wilton, give the local scale as Herbert would have known it. The voices along this route are his most eloquent ones and those of the rich and poor – chiefly the latter – which fill his book. T. S. Eliot wrote about 'the spiritual stamina of his work' and when Herbert says that a country parson has to care for his people 'as if he had begot the whole parish', this strength is demonstrated. Here is no detached moralist and kindly welfare worker but a father in God upon whom every child in God in his parish depends for its spiritual nourishment. They are an earthy, materialistic lot, these toilers of the fields which still break up the house plots of modern Salisbury, and 'because country people live hardly, and therefore as feeling their own sweat, and consequently knowing the price of money', their priest has to be 'exceeding exact in his life' and 'an absolute master and commander of himself'. It is crucial that he does nothing to 'the dishonour of his person and office'. He has to be 'not witty, or learned, or eloquent, but Holy'. He, of course, was all four in one and could not be otherwise. We catch a glimpse of the rectory interior, fresh as a Vermeer. It has to be the house beautiful on which all Fugglestone's and Bemerton's houses should be modelled, its furniture 'very plain, but clean, whole and sweet as his garden can make it' (herbs and cut flowers), and with Christ's words painted on their walls. In them, time must be found from all the field and housework to read and write, sing and, most particularly, for prayer.

Herbert, it could be said, brought this place to its knees with disciplines and pleasures which few of his people would have previously associated with praying, and his elevation of prayer to the peaks of human activity makes uncomfortable reading for the average worshipper now. It needs much more time than we can spare for it. 'Hurry is the death of prayer,' says Francis de Sales, but it isn't hurry that is our weakness but our ignorance of how to direct time towards timelessness. This is what Herbert taught his little community to do, even if its time was not much more than seasonally varied dawns and dusks. 'I value prayer so,' he said,

> That were I to leave all but one,
> Wealth, fame, endowments, vertues, all should go;
> I and dear prayer would together dwell,
> And quickly gain, for each inch lost, an ell.★

Kneel in St Andrew's, Bemerton, and imagine what kind of Christian worship was conducted in this temple by a rector who had declared himself on prayer thus:

> Prayer the Churches banquet, Angels age,
> Gods breath in man returning to his birth,
> The soul in paraphrase, heart in pilgrimage,
> 　The Christian plummet sounding heav'n and earth;

★ An ell is 45 in (114 cm).

> *Engine against th' Almightie, sinners towre,*
> *Reversed thunder, Christ-side-piercing spear,*
> *The six-daies world transposing in an houre,*
>   *A kind of tune, which all things heare and fear;*
>
>   *Softnesse, and peace, and joy, and love, and blisse,*
> *Exalted Manna, gladnesse of the best,*
> *Heaven in ordinarie, man well drest,*
>   *The milkie way, the bird of Paradise,*
>
> *Church-bels beyond the starres heard, the souls bloud,*
> *The land of spices; something understood.*

The country parson, he insisted, 'has a special care of his church, that all things there be decent ... walls plastered, windows glazed, floor paved, seats whole, firm and uniform, especially that the pulpit, and desk, and Communion Table, and Font be as they ought ...' Unfortunately – if one can use such a word of criticism – this part of Herbert's Rule has been obeyed over and over again at Bemerton, so much so that one is stunned by the sheer mercilessness of this 'special care' which has carpented and plastered most of what he cared for out of existence. However, here it is, the holy room in which the ploughmen and better sorts crowded, and where he stood with arms extended, uniting them in 'a kind of tune', in 'the land of spices', offering them 'a banquet', leading them to 'where God's breath would return to them', the thoroughly hallowed little building in which for a year or two he sang and coughed, a reassembled essence of the faith as he understood it. Here, at the east end, his coffin was placed under the floor on Quinquagesima Sunday, the Epistle for which has St Paul looking through a glass darkly and speaking of tongues ceasing. Herbert understood.

> *A man that looks on glasse,*
> *On it may stay his eye;*
> *Or, if he pleaseth, through it passe,*
> *And then the heav'n espie.*

Could the glass which held his attention have been a medieval window through whose art he could stare into the blue sky beyond? Both images of the eternal would have delighted him. It was correct behaviour in church to dream yourself into and through both man and God's creations. He is the poet of gratitude. There was so much on which to 'stay his eye' that both his poetry and his rule for English country clergymen contains an underlying commentary and description of the places and objects which a loving and witty providence had, for a little under forty years, strewn around him for his 'pleasure'. Commons, enclosures, apples, pears and grapes, 'great estates' and 'stately habitations', churches everywhere, of course, and architectural detail, especially windows, flowers, trees, grasses and 'greennesse', horses, sheep, birds, gardens, parks and courts, and 'bushy groves', hills and valleys and 'sweet walks', clouds, dew, rain and always the sun, 'these are thy wonders, Lord of Love'. Herbert celebrates an England which he believed God had made 'a land of Light, a storehouse of treasures and mercies', and his work ceaselessly tracks down every link it can between earthly experience and paradise. It is the poetry of a blessed continuum, with Wiltshire sprawling, quite naturally, across the frontiers of heaven. At Dauntsey, Edington, Baynton, Fugglestone, Bemerton and, twice a week at Salisbury, Christ the King was present with the poet in a close companionship whose subtleties amused them both. Who was guest, who host? Herbert's genius, three hundred and fifty years later, is to let us see the imprints of their parochial travels, and to listen to their intimate conversations. He asks, his God answers; the country sounds and sights penetrate their holy talk. Bells, lutes and trumpets play to delight them both. Divine love animates this world and the next. Riding up the old Roman Way to the north of Bemerton, and out on to Salisbury Plain, was often a giddy business, as creation and Creator sped through his intelligence. On his way he would have seen 'his flock most naturally as they are, wallowing in the midst of their affairs', and made them, if only for a few minutes, look up, which is not something which land-engrossed sheep, whether human or quadruped, are much given to doing. But he would have approved 'the great aptness of country people for thinking that all things come by a natural cause ...' Their Saviour too, as it happened. On the lower levels of Old Sarum he would have smiled at the 'cock-sure farmers' and on the summit amidst the ruins have felt his broken lungs working a bit more easily in the fine air.

The contrast of Herbertian simplicity at Bemerton and Herbertian splendour at Wilton provides perennial lessons. Those who have come a long way to see the shrine will go on to see the Pembrokes' palace and, what with Stonehenge and Salisbury Cathedral adding their uniquely influential contributions to the local scene, one soon sees that the great Christian poet reached the end of his own way of perfection in the context of some extraordinary neighbouring power centres. I, too, joined the conducted tour round Wilton House. It is a successful essay in magnificence, very grand, very beautiful. Sir William Chambers's triumphal arch topped by an equestrian Marcus Aurelius – 'The universe is transformation; our life is what our thoughts make it' – is the opposite of that 'unenriched' arch at Dauntsey and prepares one for what follows, which is as much richness as walls can take. The effect is one of richly dulling gold. We crocodiled, as thousands do all summer long, past the Van Dycks and Rembrandts, the Inigo Jones swags and Kent and Chippendale furniture. Past objects which could have been witnessed in Italy by Marcus Aurelius and by George Herbert. At the end, ungratefully, it must have sounded, having been shown so much, I asked our guide if there was anything of Herbert's to be seen? 'No.' Her answer was final and unapologetic. Had she not shown us art out of mind and glory beyond compare, domestically speaking? Not to mention more than enough to keep us going in the intimate sense, a lock of Elizabeth I's gingery hair, wan at the roots, an actual chair from the Roman senate, letters, telling little odds and ends which smelt of their owner's brief hour, rather than of posterity? However, if it is true, it does seem a serious omission. Impossible to imagine a continental princely house with a saint in the family not placing him above the décor and this world's achievements.

In August 1865 the poet William Cory ('Heraclitus') was a guest at Wilton House and although he approved the social concern of the Pembrokes – 'the wealth here is flowing freely over the estates' – and found the luxuries of 'this famous palace' more defensible than those of King's College, Cambridge, he left a sharply critical account of George Herbert's little world, then just beginning to attract the modern pilgrim. It has always intrigued me, because it has a claim to be amongst the first comments of the modern tourist to this holy place.

'Aug. 6. At 5 p.m. I walked in the grounds alone; stepped out the circumference of the ilex at the south-west corner of the

house – eighty paces of shadow ... I think I should get tired of
this flat valley, where the magnificent timber hides the hill, and
there is no sky, very little air, no sense of infinity ... Aug. 8. At
noon, A. called at our schoolroom and marched me off, by
appointment to Bemerton.' On the way he saw the new church,
St John's, designed by T. H. Wyatt in 1860 and, not yet containing its pretty mosaic of Herbertian medlar trees, the work
of Nellie Warre the rector's daughter. 'This isn't George Herbert's church,' said the elderly village woman who was cleaning
it to me. 'It is a *Victorian* church. But it is a good example.' She
was an example of that legion of countrywomen who, more
than any other group, and certainly more than the restorers,
have been housekeepers to Christ in the best way possible, caring
for his temples much as they care for their own homes, dusting
and polishing, setting out flowers and maintaining works of art
unawares. All the same, this *is* George Herbert's church so far as
the nineteenth-century Pembrokes were concerned. They built
it as 'a monument of so excellent a man, a renowned poet, a
chaste priest, a good citizen', and I think he would have been
surprised and delighted by it. William Cory was not delighted
by it, as he saw it glaring in its newness five years after its
consecration. It is 'all very well, though the tower is too dumpy'.
But this criticism was as nothing when he saw Bemerton. Here
he seethed with indignation. His is an all too rare glimpse of
what a cultivated and spiritual mid-Victorian felt when coarse
restoring hands got to work on an ancient edifice. 'But the old
church, George Herbert's church, is almost destroyed. There are
a few ribs of the roof, stumps of windows, a floor heaped with
rubbish. They may call it "restoration" if they like. At the
parsonage the wife showed us the trees which Dyce drew for
the picture of Herbert meditating: one is a medlar which the
good man planted close to the pleasant little river – its trunk
was coated with lead.' Later, he saw 'a go-cart stopping for a
flock of sheep' which 'kicked up no dust, owing to the rain, and
their valuable feet made pretty rakings and harrowings over the
dark soft roads'. Herbert would have liked that 'valuable feet'.

> *The shepherds sing; and shall I silent be?*
> *My God, no hymn for thee?*
> *My soul's a shepherd too; a flock it feeds*
> *Of thoughts, and words, and deeds.*

Thy pasture is thy word: the streams, thy grace
Enriching all the place.
Shepherd and flock shall sing, and all my powers
Out-sing the day-light hours.

No pretty rakings and harrowings over the dark soft Bemerton roads now, but the Salisbury meat lorries hurtling past 118 Lower Road, or Herbert's rectory. And yet and yet, the pastures, the stream, there they are still, limpid and maintaining their damp paths to the right, and stretching onwards as they did in his time to the edge of the city. As he walked to the Cathedral to join the choir twice a week, these and the Lower Road would have been his composing tracks, those regular strolling places where poetry works itself out. Edward Thomas, describing the Herbert landscape beyond Wilton, the 'waved green wall of down, the castle among the marsh-marigolds of the flat green meadows, the moorhen hurrying down the swift water, the bulging wagons of straw going up a deep lane to the sheepfolds ... A trap weighted with two ordinary men and a polished, crimson-faced god of enormous size drove off. Lord Pembroke's cart followed, full of dead hares ...' would have understood.

Not entirely surprisingly, since his wife had a cottage in Winterslow, William Hazlitt, a Christ-respecting agnostic, adds his description of Herbert's countryside just at the same time as Constable painted it.

I remember once strolling along the margin of a stream, skirted with willows and plashy sedges, in one of those low sheltered valleys in Salisbury Plain, where the monks of former ages had planted chapels and built hermits' cells. There was a little parish church near; but tall elms and quivering alders hid it from my sight, when, all of a sudden, I was startled by the sound of a full organ pealing on the ear, accompanied by rustic voices, and the willing quire of village-maids, and children. It rose, indeed, 'like an exhalation of rich distilled perfumes.' The dew from a thousand pastures was gathered in its softness; the silence of a thousand years spoke in it ... It filled the valley like a mist ...

But the climax of George Herbert's geography must be that hill in eastern England where, centuries before, synods and law-courts met, thus eventually bringing to its summit a prebendial church of sufficient importance for it to be dismantled by Henry VIII's commissioners at the Reformation. The great stone where these ancient judgements were handed out still lies there. Leighton Bromswold's history was most likely a closed book to Herbert. All he understood was that he, a newly ordained deacon, had a desecrated shrine on his hands. There were countless such all over the country. Only five miles from Leighton, at Little Gidding, the Ferrars had found their church turned into a barn and full of pigs and hay. Shakespeare's 'bare, ruin'd quires' criticism need not be confined to the unroofed abbeys. Everywhere, even at humble chapels such as Bemerton, could be seen the same collapse and mess. Often it was not so much lack of funds to keep the sacred fabric in order as a forgetting of the sacredness itself. Herbert shocked his friends, and his mother particularly, – 'George, it is not for your weak body and empty purse to undertake to rebuild churches' – by the swiftness with which he disassociated himself from what had become a tolerance of ruin. To give Mr Hughes, the vicar of Leighton, his due, he had made an effort to restore his church but the cost was beyond him. Set now on his thrilling new path (ordination closed most other careers, anyway), Herbert recognized that the cost of *anything* where Christ was concerned must never prevent its acquisition. And so over the seven years remaining to him he collected the money together, some £2,000, and, under the guise of repairing and making decent a neglected parish church, set out in stone and carpentry an architectural version of his soul.

It was not quite finished in his lifetime. Did he visit it? There are divided opinions. We know that John Ferrar, Nicholas's brother, riding three times a week from Little Gidding along the twisting lane which still links the parishes, oversaw the work. We know too that this building took on for Herbert a significance which was not unlike that of the reconstruction and rededication of the Temple at Jerusalem for Nehemiah, and that when he was dying he asked Nicholas Ferrar to make it the 'chiefest' care of all the responsibilities which he would leave him. As these included the publication of his poems, we can gather what Leighton must have meant to him. Izaak Walton wrote, 'Being for the workmanship a costly mosaic, for the form an exact cross, and for the decency and beauty I am assured it is the most remarkable parish church that this nation affords.' And so it is in its way.

St Mary's Church, Leighton Bromswold, Huntingdonshire

The Laudian ideal, created by George Herbert on a hilltop, and as perfect now as when it was completed in the 1630s. It was ruined and neglected when the Bishop of Lincoln made him its prebend, and he was under no obligation to touch it, but Izaak Walton says he 'became restless till it was finished'. Instead of an architect's plan we have a long sequence of poems giving full symbolic instruction on how to build a Christian shrine according to the most devoutly understood English precepts. To comprehend Leighton Bromswold we have to read 'Church-monuments', 'Church-lock and Key', 'Church-musick', 'The Church-floor', 'The Church-porch', etc.

To reach it with full effect one should climb up Staunch Hill which, with its stagged oaks and suspicion of stateliness and huge views, is like an overture for something unforgettable to come. There is a cold little stream, the Kym, and almost within sight to the rear, Kimbolton, Queen Catherine of Aragon's prison. Curious to find in this Huntingdonshire borderland the seedlings and cuttings which made so much English religious growth of all kinds, Cromwell, the divorced wife, a king on the run. This is the landscape which T. S. Eliot describes in *Little Gidding*.

If you came this way
Taking the route you would be likely to take
From the place you would be likely to come from,
If you came this way in may time, you would find the hedges
White again, in May, with voluptuary sweetness.
It would be the same at the end of the journey,
If you came at night like a broken king . . .

Charles was a long way from being broken when Herbert was building his church. It is likely that he would have heard of it from the Ferrars and might even have been taken to see it. The interior could hardly have looked more pristine than it does today, the pale oak seats and twin pulpits – 'they should neither have a precedence, or priority, of the other; but that prayer and preaching, being equally useful, might agree like brethren, and have an equal honour and estimation' – the altar and its rails, the children's benches. Scarcely a missing hinge or latch, hardly a scuff-mark, the Jacobean-romanesque cabinet-work still as fresh as a daisy. No staining, few armorials. Everywhere an intellectual happiness and completion. What a gift to a country parish. Trees move faintly through Herbert's greenish glass. Dauntsey ideas are all over the place, in the finials, in the width of the aisle, which is far more like Isaiah's holy highway than anything else. You feel that Herbert wanted Christ's people to pour along it. Although built thirty years earlier, it is really the 1662 Book of Common Prayer turned into an edifice. One Angevin face, a statue bracket maybe, stares down from the Middle Ages. The list of incumbents with names straight out of Mervyn Peake, Roger Skirville, William Roughthorn, Robert Gurnwardeby, Nicholas atte Anvel, and the alabaster Tyrwhitts, the governess to Elizabeth I and maid of honour to Catherine Parr, are enclosed in the finest of all Herbert's divine boxes. All round the churchyard stretches a low broad wall, comfortable for sitting on in the sun. The tower, Dauntsey again, is first-class masonry with its edges still sharp as a knife. There are Alice in Wonderland standard roses and, still functioning on the nave walls, Herbert's elegant lead rain-water heads. It is a stunning creation and without parallel.

St Mary's, Leighton Bromswold: the interior

Equal pulpits for prayer and preaching. To the left the alabaster tomb of Lady Tyrwhitt, Queen Elizabeth's governess and maid-of-honour to Queen Catherine Parr. Flawless seating made in the reign of Charles I. A frequent notion of Herbert's was to see a church as an inn, with Christ as host. They were to be welcoming, beautiful, refreshing. Love bade each guest 'sit and eat' the sacred 'banquet' and be escorted by music to heaven's door.

What Church is this? Christ's Church. Who builded it?
Master George Herbert. Who assisted it?
Many assisted: who I may not say,
So much contention might arise that way.
If I say Grace gave all; Wit straight doth thwart,
And says, All that is there is mine: but Art
Denies, and says, There's nothing there but's mine:
Nor can I easily the right define.
Divide: say, Grace the matter gave, and Wit
Did polish it . . .;
In building of this Temple, Master Herbert
Is equally all Grace, all Wit all Art.
Roman and Grecian muses all give way:
One English poem darkens all your day.

Herbert's poetry is about what Christ himself called 'the temple of the living God', the human body; its earthly lodgings and its house of prayer. It can thus be seen as a poetry of total landscape involving all divine and human creativity, all nature and all art. It is still the best spiritual guide to an English place.

7

The Lands of Do Different

George Fox was twenty-eight years old on that famous May morning of 1652 when, in spite of feeling faint because of lack of food and having with him a companion, Richard Farnsworth, who was too injured to accompany him, he obeyed a sudden urge to climb Pendle. He tackled it from the 'Big End', and with difficulty, and was rewarded with a sight, not only of the sea bordering upon Lancashire, which meant that it must have been an especially clear day, but of the potential of the inhabitants of the limestone land which sprawled below him. Convinced (his operative word) that he had been shown the country from which he could draw his evangels, he was 'moved to sound the day of the Lord'. This 'sound' lay in a profound silence, yet I like to imagine that the elation which comes from gaining the heights and glimpsing the possibilities was of a youthful shout which echoed all across Bowland, and that he bounded down to the crippled Richard, noisy with discovery. Fox's dictated account of the climb and its consequences was given twenty years later, and with impressive economy, very similar to an incident in St Mark's Gospel. 'As I went down I found a spring of water in the hill, with which I refreshed myself ... At night we came to an inn, and declared the truth to the man of the house.' In a dream he saw 'a great people in white raiment by a river that parted two counties, coming to the Lord'. The river was the Lune, the dwellers by it the founder-members of the Society of Friends and its missionaries. This 'Galilee of Quakerism', as it is called, has been best topographically described in David Pownall's *Between Ribble and Lune*.

Fifty minutes' fast driving and you will be through it. Sitting with 70 m.p.h. on the speedometer as you cross the M6 bridge over the

Ribble at Preston, there is barely time for a glance at the broad grey swing of water which flows from the east after the long Samlesbury loop before the eye is obtained by the Henry Mooresque cooling towers of Ribbleton. From here to the end of the land between Ribble and Lune at Tebay in the old Westmorland fells is fifty odd miles of ups and downs, flashes of sea and mountain, moors shouldering the sky in the east, the coastal plain sliding away into the west... This is the far north-west of England.

He ends his book in a way which would have appealed to Fox:

I think I will finish with the final landscape, the one which could once be seen in the eyes of the people, in their stance, talk and charac-ter. There were hill-folk and plain people, shore-souls and river-writers. The final aid I get in my struggle to know the land I live on is through friends. In their faces are all the corners and spires, trees, horizons and houses. In twenty years' time if I am living on the other side of the world, it will not be a photograph of bricks or fields which will bring back this living time, but that nose, that bald head, the bags under those eyes, that moustache and the memory of never-still mouths. In their expression exists this landscape, combined in such fashion that only I can see it.

That always was the true landscape – the head ... Whether of stone or bone, they are all spheres, revolving inner mysteries. The way one echoes the other and then unrolls its thoughts on to a hill or field, making its eye into a sea or a plain, giving the animal face back to the inanimate cradle, is one of the most satisfying connections to be con-templated.

William Penn, describing Fox on Pendle Hill, said that he behaved 'as if he had been in a great auditory', adding that he was 'a strong man, a new and heavenly minded man, a divine and naturalist' who was able to see from its summit 'people as thick as motes in the sun'. Critics have added the equivalent of 'he would, wouldn't he?' as the distant, glittering Lune led on to the territory of the Westmorland Seekers, an idealistic group whose fame had spread far and wide. In other words, that George Fox was knowingly tramping to where he would be best understood, but doesn't say so. But he would hardly have wandered through the Midlands for nine years, clearly with no shape to his journeyings beyond that created by his impulse to challenge various town and village 'steeple-houses' and their priests and 'professors', as well as to find his own spiritual direc-

Easedale near Grasmere, Westmorland

The country of the 'statesman-farmers' of the dales, many of whom were Seekers, and from amongst whom George Fox chose his missionaries. Rewards of five shillings to five pounds were offered by the local magistrates to anyone catching a Quaker. The people, though very poor, ignored the rewards. 'That is George Fox,' they said, and did nothing.

Wordsworth and his sister Dorothy came to live in Grasmere in 1799, and the landscape of the Seekers and the first Quakers became that of the Romantic Movement.

Their cottage on a plot of rising ground
Stood single, with large prospect, north and south,
High into Easedale, up to Dunmal-Raise,
And westward to the village near the lake;
And from this constant light, so regular
And so far seen, the house itself, by all
Who dwelt within the limits of the vale,
Both old and young, was named the Evening Star.

W. Wordsworth, 'Michael'

tion, had he believed that the Westmorland Seekers were his people. On the contrary, it is Fox's sturdy solitude between the ages of nineteen and twenty-eight, and his meticulous setting down of his groping progress to the 'very great hill' where he received his mandate, which give authenticity to his account of how he arrived in Lancashire.

Early seventeenth-century Britain was teeming with alternative-society-ists and the Establishment everywhere was dragged into debate by them. Fox writes all the time of question sessions in the churches, with some poor clergyman being bated by itinerant Seekers, Ranters, Baptists, etc., and finding it impossible to defend either his own or the state's religion, which were not usually identical, from the attacks of those who had thrown overboard the entire historic structure of conventional belief, rank, manners, the law and morality. To Fox, in his total rejection of the Anglican clergy, a priest 'looked like a great hump of earth' – like Pendle in fact, a huge gloomy protuberance whose remaining function it was to provide something for him to stand on to reveal the true light. The clergy retaliated by having him beaten up when he interrupted their services, throwing him down the snowy steps of York Minster and describing the proto-Quaker meetings as 'mumbing and dumbing'. Fox and his Friends gave as good as – and often much more than – they got, except where the common viciousness of the average English citizen and villager was concerned. To this they simply gave themselves up, out of saintliness, it could be said, but as one reads the *Journal* and sees what savages the ordinary people of this country could be, also out of knowing how useless it was to try and protect themselves. Fox's cool picture of his England is a scathing indictment of the impotence of nominal Christianity where, to use one of his favourite words, 'tenderness' is concerned. When he courteously declined a commission in Cromwell's army, he was taking a stand against the social toleration of violence in men, having witnessed it and felt it everywhere he went. When he railed against the current preoccupation with what was and was not 'lawful' in the Church, it was because he longed for all its members to return to the only thing that mattered, its Holy Spirit. When he advocated simple, rational dress (his being such an incessant traveller must surely be taken into account here) it was to cut across the whole policy of how we grade ourselves by what we wear. In this last instance he would have been astounded to know that Carlyle, in his mock-Germanic philosophical essay on clothes, *Sartor Resartus*, could have taken over the notions of his faith, his anti-clericalism and his sensible leather breeches, and produced the following:

Perhaps the most remarkable incident in Modern History is not the Diet of Worms, still less the Battle of Austerlitz, Waterloo, Peterloo, or any other Battle, but an incident passed carelessly over by most Historians, and treated with some degree of ridicule by others: namely, George Fox making to himself a suit of Leather. This man, the first of the Quakers, and by trade a Shoemaker, was one of those, to whom, under ruder or purer form, the Divine Idea of the Universe is pleased to manifest itself ... Sitting in his stall; working on tanned hides, amid pincers, paste-horns, rosin, swine-bristles, and a nameless flood of rubbish, this youth had, nevertheless, a Living Spirit belonging to him; also an antique Inspired Volume, through which, as through a window, it could look upwards ... The Clergy of the neighbourhood, the ordained Watchers and Interpreters of that same holy mystery, listened with unaffected tedium to his consultations and advised him ... to 'drink beer and dance with the girls'. Blind leaders of the blind! For what end were their tithes levied and eaten, for what were their shovel-hats scooped out, and their surplices and cassock-aprons girt-on; and such church-repairing, and chaffering, and organing, and other racketing, held over that spot of God's Earth ...? Fox turned from them, with tears and a sacred scorn, back to his Leather-parings and his Bible. Mountains of encumberance, higher than Aetna, had been heaped over that Spirit ... how its prison-mountains heaved and swayed tumultuously ... 'Will all the shoe-wages under the Moon ferry me across into that far Land of Light? Only Meditation can, and devout Prayer to God. I will to the woods: the hollow of a tree will lodge me, wild berries feed me, and for Clothes, cannot I stitch myself one perennial suit of Leather!' ... Thus from the lowest depth there is a path to the loftiest height ...

Pendle Hill needs an extra 179 feet to qualify as a mountain, yet there is something about it which makes it more than any hill need be. It is as though an entire moor had been laxly heaved up on tentpoles. Treeless but evenly covered with cotton-grass, ling, mare's tail, butterwort, and with here and there a low bush of the aptly named cloudberry, it has a long sloping flat top and chasmic sides. It must have confronted George Fox, as it does most people seeing it for the first time, and as it did me, as an enigma more than a view. Hills do not customarily make one ask, 'Why?' but Pendle does. Even when one has noted their geology. It has something to do with the way it crouches in its immensity on Bowland, so at odds with the scale of the surrounding fells. Raindrops the size of old pennies began to fall as I started to climb the main old path up from Barley, which was the one which Fox would have taken. It was October, not May. In a few minutes I was back in the womb of the car whilst Pendle was diagonally lashed by torrents of silver-black water which thudded on its turf with very much the same dull roar as hail on tarpaulin. During a brief let-up I ventured out once more and heard Pendle's rivulets clinking and gobbling their way down to the moorland villages, and saw the Big End where Fox had stood – for how long? – as in his auditory. It made a sullen dais from which to take such heady stock.

The car nosed cautiously round it, splashing in and out of its base-line villages, Pendleton itself, Sabden, Higham, New-church, Barley, Downham, Worston, each preoccupied with the great hill, now streaming. As always, I thought of men's necessary and unavoidable tramping about before trains and cars and bikes. I would be on Lindisfarne in the morning, bone-dry, needing to walk, mildly wearied only by floods making a few miles' detour necessary. Other than his view from Pendle, Fox spares his literary energy for giving a tough account of the difficulties of getting about, and says little of sightseeing. Most travellers did the same, so presumably their readers were not very interested in what the country looked like, only in the state of its roads and the neatness, or otherwise, of its towns. Fox rambled on and on until the end of his life, usually by the abysmal tracks which were the King's (or Lord Protector's) Highways, but sometimes as the crow flies: 'I went by my eye over hedge and ditch.' On and on, from Pendle to Cornwall, and eventually through Holland, Germany and eastern America, where the going was never very good, and more often dreadful, with 'the ways being very deep, and the waters out'. Only in New England does Fox become geographically expansive and gives us, in his *Journal*, one of the earliest glimpses of New Jersey, Virginia, Maryland and the Carolinas. His patrician convert William Penn had actually given him a thousand acres of what was to be Pennsylvania but for Fox, the own-nothing, the gift remained an abstraction. He knew he possessed a reputation and on his restless travels the only sound he cared to hear was 'The great Quaker of England is come to town!' And that not from pride but because he knew that his was one of the acknowledged voices of his time, hear it or temporarily smother it. Eight times the judges attempted the latter, the worst when they threw him into Launceston gaol and left him ankle-deep in human excrement for a fortnight and poured urine over him from cracks in the floorboards overhead. Fox is the cool recorder of legal squalor. A clean man, always washing himself in brooks, refusing to have his fair, lank, shoulder-length hair cut, with a good head on him, as country people still describe an intelligence which cuts through cant, he maddened his enemies.

The Friends' Burial Ground near Charsfield, Suffolk, in the country of George Fox the Younger (Ursula Hamilton-Paterson)

The Akenham burial scandal occurred near here in the late nineteenth century. It highlighted the difficulties which could be encountered when non-Anglicans were refused burial in the local churchyard. The Quakers minimized all funeral practices and found that a piece of waste by the lane-side was as decent a place as any to lay one's bones. Their dust here supports an apple orchard and chickens.

Cromwell received him and for an hour or two these divergent radicals from the Midland fens listened to each other. 'O.P.', as Fox called Oliver Protector, had tears in his eyes and said, 'If thou and I were but an hour of a day together, we should be nearer one to the other.' Later, Fox was to watch with amazement the mock-royal farce of Cromwell's funeral. England astounded him, and to the end. On Pendle he saw the size of his task, as well as the only people who would be capable of helping him to complete it. They were to be known as 'the valiant sixty' and nothing quite like their mission had been seen since Iona, Lindisfarne and other Celtic prayer-houses had sent their emissaries forth a thousand years earlier. Yeomen and farm-workers – and their wives – from Swarthmoor, Askrigg, Brigflatts, Kendal, Sedbergh, Grayrigg, Preston Patrick, Dragley Beck, Underbarrow and all those seeking centres between the Yorkshire dales and the Cumbrian fells went forth in eloquent silence. These folks found themselves, as one of them, Francis Howgill, said, gathered, caught by the Kingdom of Heaven 'as in a net'.

Having pinpointed this land of promise from Pendle, Fox's arrival in it was swift. On 9 June he was at Sedbergh hiring fair shouting to the huge crowds that the barriers were down between man and God. That same night he met the first Seeker and stayed with him at a farm called Draw-well. It was by the silver river, the Lune, hard to find and still standing. The next Sunday he preached what was to be his splendid inaugural Quaker sermon from a rock on Firbank Fell. He spoke for three hours to a thousand Seekers and established the Society of Friends. After it, an excited young man pressed his pipe on him, crying, 'Come, all is ours!' Although a non-smoker, Fox accepted, explaining, 'But it came into my head that the lad might think I had not unity with the creation, for I saw he had a flashy, empty notion of religion; so I took his pipe and put it in my mouth and gave it to him again, to stop him lest his rude tongue should say I had not unity with the creation.' Three weeks later he was with Judge Fell and his wife Margaret, eventually to be Fox's wife, at remote Swarthmoor Hall, and the astounding spiritual journey was both completed and begun. George Fox, the uncomfortable young man from Leicestershire, had walked in circles, as had Moses, to a God-filled territory which was waiting for such a stranger. 'The 1652 country', it came to be called.

I saw it briefly but lastingly, its ragged outcrops, and the Trough of Bowland full of curlews crying in the rain. Just passing through it was a sufficient corrective to a muddled notion of George Fox which had confused me since childhood. For we also, in Suffolk, laid claim to a 1650s country and over the

Easedale

years scraps of it, a name here, a burial-ground there, were pointed out to me to prove it. George Fox, I was told, was born in Charsfield, the village next to which I lived and which became the centre of the personal rural experience which I called 'Aken-field'. As churchwarden of its modest steeple-house, I occasionally mused on the fact of his furious rejection of it – that same modest Tudor brick tower and flinty nave, he had shaken his fist at them. But this was George Fox 'the Younger in Truth' who had, metaphorically, stood on Pendle in 1651, the year before the other George Fox had, by some divine coincidence, come to exactly the same ideas. They were very much the ideas of the German Jacob Boehme, carried, as many seeds are carried, on mild winds. Like George Fox the Older in Truth, Boehme was a shoemaker and mystic, and a heretic, naturally. He was in personal communion with God and believed that everybody should be. His first book (*c.* 1612) was called *Aurora or Red Morning* and was followed by *The Threefold Life of Man, The Signature of all Things* and *The Way of Christ*. For England's 'Behmenists', as Boehme's readers were called, these works were the quite miraculously simple way out of a labyrinthine muddle of claims, orthodoxy, laws and pretensions known as the Church, and they took it. Among other things, Boehme believed that the universe, the Earth, the land and its climate and plants and creatures, was God displayed. Some of his answers may not have settled the questions but they finished off many an old certainty. ' "Where does the soul go when the body dies?" – "There is no need for it to go anywhere." '

I like to think that George Fox the Younger in Truth walked past my little farmhouse at Debach, which is a mile from his birthplace, with his nose in a translation of *The Signature of All Things*, perhaps on some Matins-despising Sunday with the bell-sounds following him. One bell is inscribed 'Box of sweet honey, I am Michael's bell', although this would not have charmed him. George Fox the Older in Truth was equally adamant where it came to the mellifluousness of the established Church, and was not to give it a good word. The rector of Fenny Drayton who had known him from childhood, and who seems to have done his best, complained, 'George Fox is come to the light of the sun, and now he thinks to put out my starlight.' Did the vicar of Charsfield feel similarly outshone by his George Fox? What plain speaking there must have been. The parsons were told that they should be priests of Christ without tithes. This would have made the farmers think. The oldest tombstone in Charsfield is for a farmer who was contemporary with our George Fox. I stopped them shifting it for the sake of

Woodbridge, Suffolk.

The Friends Meeting House, built in 1678 and recently metamorphosed into a house. Here, in February 1849, Edward Fitzgerald stood at the graveside of his old friend Bernard Barton, the 'Quaker Poet'.

a motor-mower. Along a hilly lane near Earl Soham stands the meeting-house-cum-farm where the two Foxes' converts met in secret and behind it lies a little orchard where their funerals took place at night. At Colchester, in the Norman Castle made of Roman bricks which stands on the foundations of the deified Claudius (*divo Claudio constitutum*), there is a high-up fireplace which formed the cell of James Parnell, the boy who walked all the way from Retford to comfort, and to learn from, Fox the Older in Truth when he was imprisoned at Carlisle. Parnell was fragile, clever and brave, and was virtually murdered at Colchester by the town gaoler and his sadistic wife. He was eighteen, and the Friends' proto-martyr, their Stephen. Fox and Whitehead visited him in prison: it was all so Pauline, so as it was in the beginning, right down to the fully exacted cruelties. Parnell's body lies somewhere under the municipal flower-beds. He would have made a perfect subject for a Britten opera. The manner of his death was brought about by the usual lewd fun. Having stuck him high up in a recess in the castle wall like a sideshow, his food was placed twelve feet below him on the floor. To reach it he had to scramble down a rope naked while the gaoler's wife and her acquaintances watched. The joke went on for ten months until, ill and weak, he fell. The verdict of the court was 'suicide by fasting'. 'I have seen great things,' Parnell told the embarrassed gapers as he lay dying. They said he would have been a great writer.

Coming to Pendle from Quaker East Anglia is to cover the same ground. Fox the Older moved fast. Only two years after viewing his Galilee from the enormous hill, he had formed the Society, and it had organized the conquest for Christ of the main population centres of England. George Whitehead from Orton, Westmorland, and Richard Hubberthorne from Yealand were commissioned to carry the new riteless, quiet communication to Norwich, the third city in the land, and to our county. Where, I have often wondered, did they meet our George Fox? It must have been disconcerting for them to find another, independently arrived at similar conviction, in East Anglia. It had long been notoriously open religious ground anyway, reform blowing through it decades before Henry and Catherine's divorce. 'Do different' was ever our cussed motto. Boehme the visionary shoemaker taught that it was necessary for opposing ideas to clash if you wanted to spark off the real illumination. No row, no light. Thus the Valiant Sixty spread out across Britain to stand outside where 'the painted beast had a painted house' – i.e. in the churchyards – to force the clergy into a hard-knocking debate. The latter were bewildered as much as resentful. It was cold outside, complained the rector of Fenny Drayton. The congregations switched easily to being cheerful bloodthirsty mobs. Both parson and Friendly challenger shared a word-perfectness where the Bible was concerned, their mouths full of the glorious new translations, and much did indeed take fire, especially in naturally cantankerous Suffolk and Norfolk. The whole area was historically questioning and devoutly schismatic. It had also been, prior to the seventeenth century, very rich but was now, as Christian groups of all kinds refused to conform to what they saw as an official state church, rapidly becoming very poor. The cloth trade had gone north and west to where the fulling rivers ran faster. Nailed to a chimney which would have been smoking away at that moment, and which now holds aloft my TV aerial, I have a framed cry of regional despair. It is addressed to King Charles I by the clothiers of Suffolk and tells him that pressing fears have befallen his loving subjects because 'our cloathes for the most part, for the space of eighteen months remain upon our hands, our stocks lying dead therein, and we can maintain our trading no longer. The cryes for food of many thousands of poor, who depend on this trade, do continually press us, not without threats, and some beginning of mutinies . . .' King Charles said that 'they did well to petition Him, and He thought they did it not before they had just cause'. But it was 1642, and he was engulfed in a more desperate crisis than a local trade recession. Had there been some seer to prophesy it, the establishment of the Society of Friends on our acres would before too long do them a power of economic and social good. Gurneys, Barclays, Frys, Colmans, Martineaus and numerous other Quaker and Unitarian capitalists and philosophers would be taking charge of this, and of that extended horizon of eastern England known as the New World.

My boyhood intimation of three centuries of native-heath dissent was of something scenically low-lying, with places of worship on the barn and farmhouse level, as opposed to that which went on in the late medieval wool churches (usually in

Low terms), whose lovely towers rose as high as they could above the fields. As children we knew few Quakers but those we did were discreetly grand. Their meeting-houses stood in quiet lanes off the main road and had notice-boards with Peace Pledge Union posters pinned to them. When accused – of all things! – of embroiling the nation in blood, George Fox told the King's Bench court, 'I have never learned any war postures.' As a boy I attended a number of Peace Pledge Union meetings but all I can remember about them now is the atmosphere and texture and scent of the meeting-house itself, the plainness and quiet so positive that they could have been scrubbed into the wood. I was in the choir in the wool church, or rather a collegiate church built by a local man who had become the Archbishop of Canterbury in 1375, and which contained, in a glazed niche in the vestry, his severed head. This varnished skull made sufficient backing to the glass for us to use it as a mirror when we robed. We unlocked the little shutter which protected it and concentrated on our own reflected faces without emotion as we combed our hair. Archbishop Sudbury, born only a few yards away, keeper of the papal palace, Bishop of London, examiner of Wycliffe, scourge of John Ball and crowner of Richard II, as well as Chancellor of England, stared hollowly back. It had taken an Essex man eight goes of a rusty sword to decapitate the Archbishop when the Wat Tylerite mob dragged him to Tower Hill for execution. A romantic, unsafe, radical-cum-conservative priest, he was nothing to us but a wide-eyed bone. A carpenter had carved his talbot's (whippet) head under a miserere seat in the choir and it had become the official emblem on the municipal arms. Dog's head and uncelebrated martyr's head, they were level in our boyish parochial regard. I was actually more intrigued then by the agony implied by 'miserere seat', tipping these medieval stalls up and wondering just how they inflicted their holy pain, as lolling on the little ledge beneath proved to be most comfortable. But then so were the legendarily austere benches in the meeting-house. It was because our ancestors understood the basic support required for the praying human frame. A skyscape flashed through the old uneven glass of both buildings, pale heavens, tapping branches and free birds. The lower panes of the meeting-house windows were frosted and those of the church, the ones which faced me in the chancel,

Norwich: the Old Meeting House

In 1642 William Bridge, who had been expelled by the Church of England for his Puritanism, founded the city's Congregational Church, whose members built this delicately proportioned place of worship half a century later. Its confident pilastered and pantiled statement is that of a religious group which has emerged from harassment and illegality.

Almost next to it is Thomas Ivory's Octagon Chapel, built in 1756, and so elegant that Wesley wondered how 'the old coarse Gospel should find admission here'.

George Fox was in Norwich in 1659, when it was a very different tale. The mayor 'granted out a warrant to arrest me'. However, he 'became pretty moderate' when Fox explained how the Friends worshipped, and the worst trouble came from the Anglican priests. The Quakers' chief difficulty, in Norwich and elsewhere, was to prove to the authorities that they weren't Ranters. Richard Hubberthorne and George Whitehead were little more than boys when they left Westmorland to establish Quakerism in the south-east. Norwich was to become one of its most distinguished and influential centres, rich, intellectual and powerful.

that is, were plastered up and filled with painted apostles. The model for St John had been a Victorian rector's son, they said. His head was straight from some Cambridge playing-field, where it must have been worshipped. When all the gas-mantels were alight in this church they created a susurration which made me imagine that all the people who had ever entered it were on the move, the murdered Archbishop as well. The silences of the meeting-house could be touched. George Fox, when still in Westmorland, once used a haystack for a pulpit and then said not a word. His congregation was riveted. It had heard nothing like it.

Pendle and its consequences ran through East Anglia less like some fresh mainstream sweeping all before it than as probing rivulets. For example, we had at home a shelf of those stubby calf-bound little 'pocket-books' to which early-nineteenth-century young ladies sent their 'effusions', as they themselves called their poems. They were published by George Fulcher, a

Norwich: the Old Meeting House, interior (opposite)

considerable effusionist in his own right, and the biographer of Gainsborough. Fulcher's tombstone was just round the corner from the Archbishop's head and although he had died in 1855 I counted him among my childhood familiars. In order to keep some kind of literary reputation where his Pocket-Books were concerned, as well as effusions, he published poems by Hood, Hemans and – Bernard Barton, the Quaker poet. Barton was our link with·the literary heart; Byron, Lamb, Southey, indeed everybody wrote to his clapboarded cottage in Woodbridge with respect and affection, even if not with actual enthusiasm for the torrent of verse which poured from it. His daughter Lucy married Edward FitzGerald – a nine-months disaster of, in its own way, Tchaikovskian proportions. Barton was a bank clerk whom the Friends attempted to liberate (much as the Woolfs and their friends attempted to liberate Eliot from his bank) by raising £1,200 for him to live on, a tidy sum then. But he went on working at the bank until days before his death in 1849. His odd son-in-law-to-be, FitzGerald, attended his corpse to its grave by the side of the Friends' Meeting House in Turn Lane, Woodbridge, once my favourite of all of East Anglia's Quaker temples and built while both George Foxes were still living, but now a smart house. The illuminating fact about the non-brilliant Barton, and quite unseen by me due to the thick process of localization which overtakes so many individuals, obscuring their true origins, was that he came from Carlisle, from the land of 'great convincement [where] the plants of God grew and flourished, the heavenly rain descending and God's glory shining upon them', as George Fox, the Older in Truth, said.

Barton, Lucy FitzGerald, Churchyard the artist and George Crabbe the poet's son, a rum lot, roamed the field paths around my house, French's Folly, the same lanes and tracks where our George Fox meditated on Boehme. How did the German shoe-maker's discoveries arrive at Charsfield and, at the same moment, in the limestone land between the Lune and the Ribble? Neither Fox mentions reading *The Signature of all Things* or *The Way to Christ*. Neither, at the moment when they themselves were convinced, had heard of each other's Pendle or Charsfield. Neither was remotely interested in landscape other than seeing it as the temporary territory of souls. But Boehme saw it as evidence that its Creator lived.

8

Desert Wisdom from Norwich

Deserts are now often regarded as ecological errors requiring correction. It is a view of them which would have astonished the early Church, for which they were the ultimate places for hearing the voice of God. The desert flower, spiritually speaking, was the hardest to pluck but the prize of all prizes. It thrived in silence and it was this special silence of the wilderness which drew men to it, not its hardships and inhospitality. They, however rough, were mere traveller's difficulties as he, the created one, pressed on until, exactly how it was impossible to say for there was no language for such a union, merged with his Creator. People went to deserts because they were voids into which God spoke. Silence, too, is ultimate prayer and those who sought it in deserts felt that they were breathing in and exhaling prayer, that they were nearest to the physical aspect of this world which provided a suitable dwelling for its Maker. 'The silence of the mind is the true religious mind,' said Krishnamurti, 'and the silence of the gods is the silence of the earth. The meditative mind flows in this silence, and love is the way of this mind.' The tradition of deserts being where the divine voice can be listened to is among the most ancient and world-encompassing. Both the Judaic and Christian faiths were struck, as it were, in desert sand, and eremitism, or desert-dwelling, was the way of life of Christ's own cousin John. The eremite, (h)ermite or hermit, was a solitary person who attempted to develop his spiritual nature until, like a spacecraft, it escaped the pull of this earth and took off on a journey to God which transcended description. 'The English mystics,' wrote Gerald Bullett, 'are those men and women who have enjoyed contact and communion with something more real than is given in everyday human experience, an utterly indubitable quickening power ...' Once in the desert, they besought its message. 'Elected silence, sing to me,' pleaded Gerard Manley Hopkins. St John of the Cross wrote of *'la soledad sonora'* – of the vibrant sounds which informed solitude. Throughout his ministry Christ continually escaped to secret waste lands to be alone. Once, his desert-listening was shatteringly rewarded with the voice of his enemy, not his beloved Father. Such terrors were to be there for many of his desert-dwelling followers and Martin Luther understood them so well that he warned off Christians from what he regarded as fiend-infested desolate regions. 'The devils are in woods, in waters, in wildernesses, and in dark pooly places, ready to hunt and prejudice people.'

Post-medieval writers are very mixed in their feelings about solitude and its benefits. For them deserts were a treacherous nothingness and solitude itself either a breakdown between an individual and society or, worse, a punishment. Although the

behaviour of the young contemplatives known as the Essenes in Jesus's time should have made desert-dwelling a fairly understandable activity, we know from the Jews' reaction to St John the Baptist, the great proto-eremite, that it had not. St John insisted that he was nothing more than a voice crying aloud in the wilderness, 'Make way for the Lord' – a herald, no more. His abnormality was to make a loud noise in a landscape where silence was usually practised. Jesus defended this strange kind of eremiticism. If John was mad, as they were calling him (he was near-naked and living on next to nothing), then why had they also been drawn to the desert, and in their droves? 'What was the spectacle that drew you to the wilderness? A reed-bed swept by the wind?' You went, he accused them, to *see* a prophet! The verb in the desert context is startling. They went to stare and not to listen, which is the only reason for resorting to deserts. Later on Christ warned his followers against false prophets who would use deserts to amplify their messages. 'If they tell you, "He is in the wilderness," do not go out; or if they say, "He is there in the inner room" [the hermit's cell], do not believe it.'

It could be said that the early Church was eremitical or desert-dwelling through and through, not only because of the Desert Fathers, who literally lived in wild regions, but because for centuries the Church did its most important work, prayer and evangelization, from monasteries which had been carefully sited for solitude. Many of the towns in which they now find themselves simply grew up from the settlement which had to provision them, provide labour for their farms or put up their guests. But gradually those who sought the mystic desert flower discovered a way of doing so, either in the community itself or at the very centre of ordinary human activity. After the Reformation even this desert-listening kind of vocation at the heart of things became incomprehensible and the path of solitude and silence became a worrying and questionable one. The wilderness itself ceased to be an empty, untamed terrain and became anywhere where men carried on their God-ignoring activities. The novelist James Hanley allows a character to say, 'You talk about walking in the wilderness, but what else *is* the world but that, and besides, aren't we all walking in one wilderness or another, since only we can make them?' Hanley was obviously thinking of the opening sentence of Bunyan's *Pilgrim's Progress* in which

The reedbeds of the River Yare

The tall-stemmed *Phragmites communis*, out of whose desolation came so much usefulness – music (bassoon, pipe, organ, chanter), architecture (plaster base, roofing), craftsmen's tools (the East Anglian weavers used it to separate the warp) and food (fish and wildfowl). Reeds also symbolized human vulnerability. Man had risen above the rest of the natural order, but stalkily, and without God's protection he could be easily bruised. 'Man is no more than a reed, the weakest in nature. But he is a thinking reed,' said Pascal. Marshlands possessed a special intellectual stimulation for some mystics, perhaps because they are the least silent of 'deserts'.

Christian says, 'As I walked through the wilderness of this world . . .'

Gradually, desert-dwelling as a way of coming close to the heart-centre of God, as a method of listening to him and catching glimpses of his face, was seen to be a discipline which could be practised in a busy city as advantageously as in an empty tract of waste land. Cities were every bit as parched, stony, dry and howling places as the wildernesses which sprawled between them. Villages too. By the fourteenth century it became almost a civic norm to attract religious solitaries to a town. The hermit was given a cell but was allowed to leave it and walk about, the 'recluse' could not. He or she totally withdrew from the world and was not seen. The anchorites and anchoresses (from the Greek *anachores* = I withdraw) were recluses who lived in rooms attached to churches according to the Ancrene Rule. They could not leave their anchorages but, having a window on to the world as well as one on to the altar, they combined their intensive prayer life with that of community advisor, and in many cases were the wisest of psychologists, welfare officers and confidants.

How and why Norwich became the eremitical centre of Britain remains mysterious in itself. Certainly as a city of metropolitan standing by the Middle Ages, the evidence of whose cultural, religious and political splendour can be seen to this day, and near enough to Europe's northern ports to receive every fresh idea and discovery, it could well have attracted the kind of intellectual men and women for whom reclusion presented an ideal existence. But the slowly emerging fact seems to be that there was something special about this tear-shaped eastern capital in its many-towered flint walls lying on the south bank of the Wensum which, paradoxically, drew together hundreds of solitaries, making it at one time as peopled a 'desert' as certain actual deserts were in the fourth century, when hermits lived in them in crowds. Norwich's role in this mystic journey would have been little more than a few scratchings in the local records office were it not for the fact that one of its many recluses, an anchoress named Julian after the little church to which her anchorhold was attached, wrote a book, the very first book, indeed, to be written in English by a woman. It is called *Revelations of Divine Love* and because it has come down to us in two contemporary

Norwich Cathedral: boss (Charles Hall)

Angelic woodlander or one of the old green gods staring through the foliage at the daily passage in the east walk cloister? Carved in stone during the early fourteenth century, along with hundreds of similarly exquisite bosses, the young Julian could have met this spiritually ambivalent gaze.

'After this I saw the whole Godhead concentrated as it were in a single point, and thereby I learnt that he is in all things. I looked attentively, seeing and understanding with quiet fear. I was thinking, "What is sin?"'

versions it is thought that the author wrote a short first account of the visions or 'showings' that are the subject soon after they happened, and then, twenty or so years later, a longer version which reflected the spiritual and intellectual growth which had occurred as a result of them, and also as a result of her highly developed prayer-life as a recluse. There is no proof that her fellow solitaries, or anyone else in Norwich or elsewhere either read it or even knew of its existence during her lifetime. Margery Kempe, the first Englishwoman to write her autobiography, and who came to Julian for advice, and who spent 'many days' with her, makes no mention of it. It would be correct to say that Margery Kempe had her astonishing autobiography written down by a scribe, as she herself was illiterate, but such is its individuality, vigour and raciness that it cannot be said to be 'ghosted' in the modern sense. She was a solid well-to-do matron from Bishop's (King's) Lynn with a passion for God and travel who, after bearing fourteen children, made a pact with her husband that they should have no more sex, and began to travel the world. Her adventures on the way to Canterbury,

Jerusalem, Compostella and Rome, her troubled pursuit of holiness, and most overwhelmingly her candid portrait of herself as a noisy, tiresome female lacking in restraint, makes the *Book of Margery Kempe* one of the most revealing of all personal documentations of the late Middle Ages. In effect, Margery was the antithesis of Julian, yet the careers of both women witness to a degree of feminine freedom and power which can also be counted as fruits of the desert. Margery's description of her coming to Julian for advice over 'many days', written in what might be called the self-despising third person, which was Margery's way of humility, is the only one we have of the great mystic. It is one of those treasured eyewitness statements which fall into the 'and did you once see Shelley plain' categories.

Holkham Beach and distant Blakeney Point, Norfolk

It was a seascape like this which hung in the memory of Dame Julian and which formed the periphery of her desert. But for her friend Dame Margery of Lynn it was the embarkation ground for Jerusalem. The Cistercians lived here, a tough, practical brotherhood. In the eighteenth century 'Coke of Norfolk' transformed the immediately inland fields into one of the legendary successes of the Agricultural Revolution.

Then she was bidden by Our Lord to go to an anchoress in the same city, named Dame Jelyan, and so she did and showed her the grace that God put into her soul, of compunction, contrition, sweetness and devotion, compassion with holy meditation and high contemplation, and fully many holy speeches and dalliance that Our Lord spoke to her soul; and many wonderful revelations, which she showed to the anchoress to find out if there were any deceit in them, for the anchoress was expert in such things, and good counsel could give. The anchoress, hearing the marvellous goodness of Our Lord, highly thanked God with all her heart for his visitation, counselling this creature to be obedient to the will of Our Lord and to fulfil with all her might whatever he put into her soul ... 'I pray God, (said Julian) grant you perseverance. Set all your trust in God and fear not the language of the world, for the more despite, shame and reproof that you have in the world [Margery's explosive behaviour and her loud weeping during worship in a Norwich church had brought her much abuse and criticism, as her often challenging original theological views had brought her near to accusations of heresy], the more is your merit in the sight of God. Patience is necessary for you, for in that shall ye keep your soul.

The two women, Julian over seventy and Margery born the very year of Julian's 'showings', in 1373, would have stood on either side of the parlour window, learned ladies in their way, their profoundly different desert routes having brought them far along the path leading to the same goal. In her thumbnail sketch, Margery dictates a sentence from Julian which might be a quote from her *Revelations of Divine Love*. Margery has said in effect

that the Holy Spirit sometimes inspires her to react unlovingly towards church services and those taking part in them, to which Julian replies, 'The Holy Spirit moveth ne'er a thing against love, for if he did, he would be contrary to his own self for he is all love.'

The most striking contrast between Julian and Margery was that brought on their outlooks by a minimal and maximum sight, respectively, of the physical world. Margery had seen what few women of her time had seen, virtually the entire world as it was known to the medieval Christian – with her own restless Norfolk eyes! Julian had seen, perhaps, no more than a single city from the east and, after her enclosure, that same city from the south. Yet Margery the world-traveller came to her because she knew that the cell had provided Julian with a view of God that far surpassed anything she had seen in spite of all her experiences of Europe and the Middle East.

On 8 May 1373, the third Sunday after Easter, at four in the morning – the timing has a precision which seems at odds with a medieval century – the future 'Recluse atte Norwyche' had among other revelations a 'showing', as she preferred to call it, of God and his Son as a lord and his gardener. Julian was then thirty and would have been known to those surrounding what was very nearly her death-bed by her real name, which is now lost. Julian she came to be because the Benedictine Community at Carrow gave her leave to anchor herself to a little thatched church within its jurisdiction and dedicated to Julian, the first Bishop of Mans, patron saint of hospitality, and to St Edward. The church stands just above the Wensum ford which since Roman times had provided entrance to Norwich, and was convenient for anyone hoping to be well received in it. From her world-window, Julian would have seen a constant procession of travellers seeking such divine favours as they climbed the hill to the church, also the new, crisp, flint walls and towers of the city, the new spire on the cathedral, crowded King's Street running into it, and the wild marshes and heathland beyond the river. It was there, in the desert, or on an uncared-for 'earth', as she called it, that her lord and his gardener expressed their 'two-fold truth'.

It is only scholastically human that when a six-hundred-year-old literary masterpiece is rediscovered that it should be combed for information other than that to do with its subject. One doesn't have to read very far into Julian's *Revelations of Divine Love* not to realize that its author, who lived a long life in this world, saw everything in it with a delight and comprehension which are unparalleled in devotional literature. So might there not be in its pages, unconsciously crept in below the figurative landscape of prayer, just a handful of plain views of fourteenth-century Norfolk? There are, but only a few, and they catch the musing eye like the shadows cast by trees in an old photograph. Everybody who is momentarily captured by this kind of reality finds himself breaking Julian's God-bound narrative to stare at the actual mile or two of medieval scenery which is passing. These now famous distractions include an allusion to 'the seaground, with its hills and dales green seeming as it were most begrowing with wrake [seaweed] and gravel', a reference to the celebrated shrine of St John of Beverley in the East Riding, which has made some historians wonder if she was a Yorkshirewoman, particularly as the *Revelations* contain certain northern phrases, touchingly homely things such as the blood from the crown of thorns spreading out across Christ's forehead 'like the scales of a herring', also, in its abundance, falling 'like the drops of water that fall from the eaves after a heavy shower' and, in an overwhelmingly realistic picture of the crucifixion, 'his hanging in the air, like some cloth hung out to dry'. The great mass of eleventh- to fourteenth-century buildings of Norwich, and their decorative furnishings, which Julian would have seen before she was enclosed and which she would have heard about long after the door had been shut on the world, the pattern of the city still virtually the same as the pattern of it which she held in mind, are absent.

As well as being full of mystics and solitaries of all kinds, Norwich was filled too with unprecedented disasters. The Lollard suppression, the Black Death, the Hundred Years' War and the Peasants' Revolt fall across its highly developed religious life like the plagues of Egypt. Julian saw its six thousand population reduced by a third – she who had written 'Since I was still young I thought it a great pity to die', but was yet able to write 'all shall be well'. Held at the centre of things by her vocation, Julian's felt words gain in authority when it is realized that she was able to say them when so much surrounding her was

The River Blyth at Southwold, Suffolk

The ancient country through which the river flows is known as the Blythings. Upstream to the north are the 'Saints', six villages all called South Elmham, but with different dedications to distinguish them, which they often fail to do. At South Elmham St Cross, in a little wood, there is a strange unfinished seventh-century church whose final construction may have been prevented by Danish raiders. Above the river at Blythburgh stands one of England's most exquisite parish churches, Holy Trinity, which William Morris used as an example of how medieval architecture should be repaired during his campaign against Victorian church 'restoration'. This is the land of St Felix.

seething in violence, epidemics and annihilation. 'The ultimate philosophy of mysticism, as I understand it,' wrote Gerald Bullett, 'makes the world in which we find ourselves not less but more real: not a figment of fancy, not a solipsist dream, but an indubitable and significant experience in which we all share.' Julian's genius was her ability to show others how to share the highest reality that there is. Most mystics can do little more than point to a path. She found words to describe every inch of the sacred territory which prayer had opened up to her. She remained in one spot and wrote the most tremendous of travel books.

Naturally she would depict God and his Son (the lord and his gardener) where she had come closest to them, in the desert, or on 'the bare, deserted *earth*', as she called it. There God sits until each individual finds him, when he makes 'man's soul to be his own city and his home'. Aware as she is that what was revealed during her sixteen 'showings' is, like the nature of God himself, inexpressible, Julian has no option but to resort to metaphor and to her own consummate use of English. 'Concrete imagery is the life of language; that which by its nature eludes exact expression can only be suggested, or hinted at, by resort to symbolism,' says Gerald Bullett. 'Something is lost as well as gained by the process; but it is an inevitable one, and we can no more be surprised that the mystic expresses himself in terms of his own religious tradition than that he uses his own language ... Mysticism is essentially empirical, not theoretical. Any theories built upon it can be, and should be, judged in the light of pure reason.' Julian's journey to God through Christ is that of a mystic of her day, but her ability to record it is such a dazzling one that its effect has been to make it a journey for all time. *Revelations of Divine Love* has become, six hundred years later, one of the most alluring of all modern spiritual progresses. Who, caught up in its optimism, rationality and verve, would not take his soul into the wilderness of a city for the Love dwelling there?

Julian and her contemporary desert-guides, Walter Hilton, Richard Rolle and the anonymous author of *The Cloud of Unknowing*, were one in their wish not to keep the delights of their spiritual path-findings to themselves. Quite the reverse – their books are charts which are purposely designed to lead anyone who reads them along the road to God. Julian, in her analogy of God and his Son to a rural lord and his obedient gardener, tells her readers, in effect, not to worry. She has a teaching, she says, which is 'like the beginning of the ABC'. Although she, like the other mystic guidebook authors, is writing for fellow solitaries, there is nothing cabalistic about her *Revelations of Divine Love*. It exists to channel the love of Christ into the universe. In the gardener revelation she explains about deserts and cities in the spiritual sense in which she experiences them. But before she arrives at this scene of Christ's matchless cultivation of love in a barren place, she provides the reader with her celebrated image of a hazelnut as God's perfectly finished, perfectly love-encompassed creation. It was the second thing she saw during the long sequence of her showings on that May morning as death receded from her, and when all her pain and weakness suddenly disappeared and 'I was as fit and well as I had ever been'. The first showing had been of the cruelly garlanded head of the dying Jesus, and of the Virgin looking like an ordinary simple girl, literally 'the handmaid of the Lord', instead of the Mother of God. After describing it Julian moves into one of the most inspired written concepts of the divine love since St Paul. Nothing is lost or distractingly added if we fleetingly glimpse the spinneys and copses just beyond the walls of Norwich as we read it. Julian is only following her Master in her supremely effective use of plants as metaphors.

And he showed me more, a little thing, the size of a hazelnut, on the palm of my hand, round like a ball. I looked at it thoughtfully and wondered, 'What is this?' And the answer came, 'It is all that is made.' I marvelled that it continued to exist and did not suddenly disintegrate; it was so small. And again my mind supplied the answer, 'It exists, both now and forever, because God loves it.' In short, everything owes its existence to the love of God. In this little thing I saw three truths, the first is that God made it; the second is that God loves it; and the third is that God sustains it ... We have got to realize the littleness of creation and to see it for the nothing that it is before we can love and possess God who is uncreated.

However reticent Julian is on the beauties and wonders of what has been created, it is impossible to read her without recognizing that her joy, vitality, her sanity and spiritual energy were partly a response to the physical world. Like most recluses, she would have treasured its minutiae, the latticed sunshine, the tendrils of bindweed finding their way into the cell, the ways of her cat, the contrasting scents of the winter and summer fields blowing across the city, the single view of the outside which, due to the seasons and her own trained gaze, did indeed become 'all that is made'.

When, in the fourteenth showing of God's love towards what he has made, Julian sees him as a lord who delights in the earthly treasure which he owns, it becomes clear that she is not at all the type of mystic who suppresses the splendours of this life for the life to come. As 'all that is made' was made out of love, and as love is infinite, the whole of Creation, according to her sensible thinking, was threaded through with what was deathless and eternal. Else, why should God have shown himself to her in the guise of a conscientious landowner who sent his only servant off to 'do work that was the hardest and most exhausting possible'? The servant was to be

a gardener, digging and banking, toiling and sweating, turning and trenching the ground, watering the plants the while. And by keeping at this work he would make sweet streams to flow, fine abundant fruits to grow [... and show her that the treasure of the earth] had its being in the wonderful depth of his eternal love. But its worth to him depended on the servant's careful preparation of it, and his setting it before him, personally. All around the master was nothing but wilderness.

Gradually, via agonizing labour, the servant and his master are to be discovered neither in deserts nor in nature but at rest and peace in their own '*city*', cities, not the countryside, however well-cultivated, being where one would expect to find all that was worthy, all that was powerful and sublime. A thousand years before Julian, St Augustine had seen the Church as 'The City of God', and St John had seen heaven as a new Jerusalem. Unlike those three other hermit geniuses of her day, the author of the incomparable *Cloud of Unknowing*, Richard Rolle and Walter Hilton, whose desert-dwelling seems to have been entirely developed in rural surroundings, Julian's appears to have been the far more difficult task of listening to God in a city which, during her lifetime, was the very reverse of 'rest and peace'. How, for example, did she manage to exclude the spiritual hubbub set up by all those other desert-dwellers cooped up in Norwich's new walls? But how most of all did that amazing comprehension of love which she discovered, and (almost as amazing) found a language for, not become distracted and distorted by what was occurring all around her? How was she able to say that 'Sin is behovely [necessary] but all shall be well', when her city, fashioned in so many architectural ways according to heavenly principles, was putrescent with the deaths of the plague-stricken, rebels against the feudal system, spiritual inquirers, not unlike herself, who came to grief with orthodoxy, and those engaged in what must have struck everybody as an everlasting war? It is salutary for the modern pilgrim to the site of Julian's cell to realize that today's Norwich, with all its traffic and a population swollen from six to a hundred and nineteen thousand, is probably quieter now than when she lived in it. And ironic to discover that St Julian's, the tiny church to which she clung for her quiet life, itself ended up in the uproar of a direct hit by a German bomb in 1942. Fragments of the stones she saw have been incorporated in the new St Julian's. But the building itself, in East Anglian terms, could never have been much and, like Bemerton and Little Gidding, and like the Baptist himself, one should visit it to listen, not to look. Julian grew old in the cell here, just one of a succession of listening women who dwelt by the chancel wall, and whose existence would now be as remote and elusive as theirs are had she not written or talked down her book.

The history of *Revelations of Divine Love* is not unlike the history of one of those ancient seeds which lie around for centuries in dry corners until some propitious combination of circumstances makes them germinate. And not only this, but its philosophical origins, too, had taken their time before managing to arrive at such an enchanting flowering. Where did Julian's astounding ideas come from? What is the point of her declaring that her visions were shown to 'a simple and uneducated creature' when she is clearly neither? Because of the conventions of her times, say some. Yet she clearly has a right to take her place with the supreme writers of her age, including Chaucer and Langland.

Apart from the Vulgate, Julian's main influence was the writings of a mystic whom she and all her contemporaries believed to be the Dionysius whom St Paul converted at Athens, but who was actually a sixth-century Syrian monk whose name is now lost. Neither of these feeders of her imagination was able to restrain her originality. She deflates the widely held notion of her day that pursuing God was the specialized activity of a few good people. 'There is nothing very special about seeking. It is a thing that every soul can do with God's grace ... So I saw him and sought him; I had him and wanted him. It seems to me that this is and should be an experience common to us all.' God

Norwich: the city's fortifications

It took 37,000 tons of stone to build a wall round Norwich between 1297 and 1334. The major defences were those guarding the river entrance to the city just below St Julian's church. All the towers were gleaming new black flint when the author of *Revelations of Divine Love* took up residence there. She saw through them to where, in Robert Graves's poem,

Christ of his gentleness,
Thirsting and hungering
Walked in the wilderness;
Soft words of grace he spoke
Unto lost desert-folk
That listened wondering.

is not only our Father but our Mother. Because we are for ever being born of him, Jesus too is our ever-loving Mother. 'This fine and lovely word *Mother* is so sweet and so much its own that it cannot properly be used of any but him.' Towards the end of her book she sums up the common experience of Adam-Everyman, as she calls him, or each human being. It is her Compline.

Our faith is a light, coming to us naturally from him who is our everlasting Day, our Father, and our God. By this light Christ, our

Dame Julian's little home attached to the church wall had vanished centuries before the 1942 bombing. The restorations of 1953 allowed the architect A.J. Chaplin to build this cell on its known site. Had it not been for Julian's swiftly accelerating twentieth-century importance it is doubtful if the bombed church would have been rebuilt, as Norwich suffers from an *embarras de richesses* of medieval ecclesiastical architecture. A Norman doorway rescued from the similarly bombed church of St Michael at Thorn in Ber Street opens into the cell. The wooden platform on the left shows the original floor level. Here dwelt for many years one of Christianity's finest visionaries and writers.

Mother, and the Holy Spirit, our Good Lord, lead us through these passing years. The light is measured to our individual needs as we face our night. Because of the light we live: because of the night we suffer and grieve. Through the grief we earn reward and thanks from God! With the help of mercy and grace, we know and trust our light quite deliberately, and with it we go forward intelligently and firmly . . .

Later she adds, wittily, 'In God's sight we do not fall; in our own we do not stand.'

Mother Julian is an upsetting and dangerous writer. It could never have been her intention to destabilize orthodox Christianity, yet she does. She draws her readers away from the comforts of accepted religious practices by which she herself must have been sustained to a great extent, and leaves them somewhat stranded in a brightness which at first puts them at a loss. While being a marvellous gazetteer to the spiritual rewards of the desert, every individual who succumbs to her guidance is finally left with a, 'Where do I go from her?' For reading about a journey is not the same as having made it. Mother Julian's readers are taken to where a sun-like love, which permeates every fraction of the universe, pours down on them, and are then expected to journey on in this glorious climate. Somebody said that the words '*Theodidacta, profunda, ecstatica*' should be carved on her tomb. Taught of God, profound, ecstatic. But where is her tomb? Is it beneath the little car-park? Is it long-settled bomb-dust from 1942? Is it at Carrow Priory with those of many other clever ladies? Wherever it is, or was, for her it would have been of no consequence. There is something distinctly anti-relic about her and she might well have appreciated those Arabian customs which decree that even the bodies of kings should lie in unmarked sand. As Britain's increasingly powerful desert-trained religious voice, Mother Julian speaks only from where life is. Her mysticism incorporates all things physical and all things spiritual. 'I had, in part, received a touch of God – and it was fundamentally natural. For the foundation of our reason is in God, who is the substance of everything natural . . . We have our life and our being in nature . . .'

The use of the empty landscape as a divine sounding-board is a religious discipline which rather disturbs us now. We ask, how can we be sure that what might be heard there is part of the ultimate reality, and not just our own preferences – or our madness? 'I wonder if it is really possible to be absolutely truthful when you are alone,' wrote Isak Dinesen in her story, 'The Roads Round Pisa'. 'Truth, like time, is an idea rising from, and dependent upon, human intercourse. What is the truth about a mountain in Africa, that has no name and not even a footpath across it?' A similar question was posed by Charles Reade in his *The Cloister and the Hearth,* in which human love has to enter the eremitical place before it can contain anything positive. And in Oliver Goldsmith's ballad, 'The Hermit', Edwin the recluse is as dead until Angelina brings him back to life with her love. All three writers fail to see the desert, whether it is a wilderness or a cell, as a place where the seeker *dwells.* That is the key-word. John Donne, although writing about sexual love, had a better understanding when he wrote,

> *For love, all love of other sights controls,*
> *And makes one little room, an everywhere.*

The benefits of solitude have always been the least tried

benefits, and known only to the few. 'Solitude is for me a fount of healing which makes life worth living,' said Jung in a letter to a friend. 'Talking is often a torment for me and I need many days to recover from the futility of words.' The recovery of the grounds of solitude, both religious and ecological (Mother Julian would not have allowed such separate categories) has been among the most beneficial advances of recent years. People like Kenneth Leech, the race relations officer for the General Synod of the Church of England, are able to write about the desert experience in a way which would have been considered curious, to say the least, a generation or two ago. Reminding us that the gentle suburban route is not going to get us very far, spiritually speaking, Leech insists that the road of faith is still a desert road full of risks and hostility, self-stripping, slow progress, intense clarity, drastic purification and self-discovery. He adds,

Solitude is not a luxury, a form of spiritual escapism. It is a necessity if our action and our commitment to justice is to be pure and authentic. Radical action follows from radical contemplation. Solitude is necessary to preserve us from superficial activism, from exhaustion, from fanaticism. To watch with the eyes of the Dove, to seek discernment, is a vital prerequisite of Christian action. We act if only we have seen, and the desert is the place of sharpened perception ... We need to stress the need in our modern urban deserts for houses of prayer. Today the desert has come back to the city. It is in the city that we see the marks of sterility, of dryness, of desperate isolation. Never has the city more urgently needed its contemplatives ... it is a place of conflict and spiritual resistance. When the church became established the early contemplatives sought the wastes of the desert in order to maintain the purity and revolutionary wisdom of the Gospel within a compromised church. Now, as the Constantinian era draws to its close, the contemplatives are returning to the cities. Nothing is more urgent today than the recovery of the desert contemplative and prophetic traditions ... it is on the union of these two that the future of western Christianity to a great extent depends.

As the Jews found Yahweh in the howling wastes through which they had to journey before reaching Canaan, their earthly paradise, so Mother Julian and many unknowable others saw and heard Christ in the howling wastes of medieval disease, war and social injustice. Thomas Merton, a twentieth-century desert-dweller, wrote, 'Our evils are common, and the solutions to them can only be common. But we are not ready to undertake the common task because we are not ourselves. Consequently, the first duty of every man is to return to his own "right mind" in order that society itself may be sane.' Mother Julian believed that she was nothing more than an ordinary creature at prayer, but even those who now find such activity mystifying would have to admit, as they read her book, that her sanity was on another level altogether to what we know of the sanity of those who ran the affairs of her day. It was out of a desert-found level-headedness that her vision, theology, poetry and timeless relevance sprang. Hers is a perennial bloom, as useful and delightful for our generation as her own.

On the whole, there has been a general human flinching from solitude, from untrodden, untouched landscape. In his diary Thomas Hardy wrote, 'An object or mark raised or made by man on a scene is worth ten times any such formed by unconscious Nature. Hence clouds, mists, and mountains are unimportant beside the wear on a threshold, or the print of a hand.' Alexander Selkirk, too, who had spent five long years alone on the island of Juan Fernandez, and whose trials there inspired Defoe's *Robinson Crusoe*, preferred urban hazards any day.

> *Oh, solitude, where are the charms*
> *That sages have seen in thy face?*
> *Better dwell in the midst of alarms,*
> *Than reign in this horrible place.*

Yet Crusoe's solitude proved to be so thrilling that Defoe had to write two more novels on the same theme, the final one being *The Serious Reflections ... of Robinson, with his Vision of the Angelick World*, in which the desert was to produce assets which would have astounded Selkirk. It was the subject of this last Crusoe novel which captured the imagination of the contemporary French writer Michel Tournier in his wonderful story, *Friday, or the Other Island* which analyses the effects of being alone. Tournier's Crusoe is a young Quaker from the Fens who is shipwrecked on the island of Speranza in 1759. His first instinct is to civilize his desert. For the next century and a half men would 'bring civilization' to the empty wilds of the world, if they could. It was a daunting obligation for a man on his own, as Tournier's Robinson Crusoe soon discovered. 'Each man has his slippery slope. Mine leads to the mire. That is where Speranza drives me when she grows evil and shows me her animal face. The mire is my defeat, my vice. My victory is the moral order I must impose on Speranza against her natural order, which is but another name for total disorder ... Solitude is not a change-less state imposed on me by the wreck of the *Virginia*. It is a corrosive influence ... there is only one viewpoint, my own, deprived of all context.' Eventually, after strongly rejecting his island-desert's natural order, including the natural order of Fri-day, when he turns up, the eighteenth-century civilization in which Crusoe is encased cracks open, like veneer in a hot room, and he is exposed to love, love of the sun, of himself and ultimately of Another. So much so that he declines to leave his island, the empty ground which was to provide an unobstructed view of who and what he was beneath the cultural trappings, when the rescue ship calls. Ironically, it is Friday, the wild man, who takes advantage of this and who leaps aboard.

Evelyn Underhill and the modern students of Christian mysticism emphasize its practical appeal for all kinds of people, learned and simple, for hundreds of years. Many of them chose sanctity as a career, much as we might choose teaching or med-icine. Or maybe one of the creative arts might be a better analogy, something for which one had begun to show a gift, but which required a lot of training, application and an ability to work on one's own. Youngsters like St Francis and Richard Rolle, 'ran away to God, as other lads run away to sea, sure that their only happiness lay in total self-giving to the one great adventure in life', wrote Evelyn Underhill. In this sense Julian might be said to have exhibited the most ambitious longings when she begged God to give her, at the very beginning of her sanctity career, those revelations which were usually hoped for only after a lifetime's prayer. Her petitions were audacious, the longings of a saint in a hurry. They were granted on the day she should have died, instead of which she had to live in order to write her book about them which, in turn, and most strangely, was to be a book for the twentieth century. One could say of her book what St John of the Cross said of himself in his apology for being a solitary.

Drinkstone, Suffolk

The post-mill on the high land between Bury St Edmunds and Stowmarket, built in 1689. Derelict windmills emphasize stilled activity. Once they were as commonplace in every village as the inn, and the old county maps are sprinkled all over with their sails. The Clover family, which ground corn in this one in the late eighteenth century, are Suffolk millers to this day. Each windmill was the village meteorological station. Each too, like ships, was feminine. There was a sail language by which millers could speak to each other over corn-filled distances. But it was the grindstones which provided the dread religious imagery, the relentless separating of the desired from the undesirable. 'God's mill grinds slow; but sure,' wrote George Herbert. Once among the most sociable spots of the community, windmills are now part of its industrial wilderness.

Twickenham–Teddington: February floods

The later landscape of Thomas Traherne's brief, happy life. Described as 'a master of the Affirmative Way, which pursues perfection through delight in a created world', Traherne was totally unknown until his manuscripts were discovered on a second-hand book barrow in Farringdon Road, London, in 1903. Since then he has rapidly advanced into the heart of a very English form of mysticism in which an ecstatically appreciated countryside carries the believer to a deeper understanding of God. Traherne died at Teddington when he was thirty-six. He lived in the High Street, where he was both chaplain to Sir Orlando Bridgeman and 'minister' of the parish church. Gazing on flowers, the river, trees, the subtle seasons, Traherne said, 'Never was any thing in this world loved too much.' His masterpiece is a sequence of poetic devotions called *The Centuries*, in which he demolishes the conventions of guilt and gloom in religion as heresies, and advocates joy.

For Nature teacheth nothing but the truth.
I'm sure mine did in my virgin youth.
The very day my spirit did inspire,
The world's fair beauty set my soul on fire.

Traherne's family came from Lugwardine, Herefordshire, a place named after Lug, the great Celtic god of light.

So now if from this day
I am not found among the haunts of men,
Say that I went astray
Love-stricken from my way,
That I was lost, but have been found again.

He sees the religious solitary as a bride, a dove, waiting in her profound aloneness for her lover Christ. But the very waiting enchants the landscape, making it distractingly lovely, and Christ, in language rather like that of Prospero, has to command it not to dominate his dove, this being that is winging back to him.

In solitude she bided
And in the solitude her nest she made:
In solitude he guided
His loved-one through the shade
Whose solitude the wound of love has made.

This last stanza from a poem of St John of the Cross, who lived nearly two hundred years after Mother Julian, could be her biography. St John's desert was part a prison in Toledo and part the wooded landscape around Baeza, beautiful river country which so excited him that he did something which none of the English mystics until Traherne would have thought of doing, he allowed the scenery itself to be Christ.

My Love's the mountain range,
The valleys each with solitary grove,
The islands far and strange,
The streams with sounds that change,
The whistling of the lovesick winds that rove.

Traherne found a divinity which went beyond the English countryside almost impossible to conceive. The Herefordshire and Middlesex landscapes intoxicated him and invalidated all ambition very much in the same way as when others were overcome by God and wanted nothing more but to be able to worship him. If Traherne had a theological problem, it was to have found himself born into paradise, and not to have to wait until he died into it. Angels and other citizens of heaven wander through his Welsh borders and his home counties, unable to tell the difference. Traherne himself certainly had no intention of allowing this blissful earth-time to be frittered away by the usual calls on it.

> When I came into the Country, and being seated among silent Trees [he was very talkative and one of the reasons he sought solitude was to escape from his own loquacity], had all my Time in my own Hands, I resolved to Spend it all, whatever it cost me, in search of Happiness, and to Satiat that burning Thirst which Nature had Enkindled in me from my Youth. In which I was so resolut, that I chose rather to live upon 10 pounds a yeer, and to go in Lether Clothes, and to feed upon Bread and Water, so that I might hav all my time clearly to my self; then to keep many thousands per Annums in an Estate of Life where my Time would be devoured in Care and Labor. (*Centuries*, III, 46)

Unlike Mother Julian, Richard Rolle and the other earlier English mystics, Traherne is a landscape-ecstatic, adoring the 'desert' itself. But, alas, one has only the briefest stay in it. It is 'like a Gentlemans house to one that is Travelling; it is a long time before you com into it, you pass it in an Instant, and leave it for ever. The Omnipresence and Eternity of God are your Fellows and Companions ...' Teddington and Credenhill, his tiny parish near Hereford, are both everything and nothing – just the 'Beautiful Frontispiece of Eternitie, the Temple of God, the Palace of his children'.

Traherne is saying that we have the right to enjoy this world while it is briefly ours. Why, he says, 'I remember the Time when the Dust of the streets were as precious Gold to my Infant Eys, and now they are more precious to the Ey of Reason.' How sweet it is, he says, as one rides and eats and talks, that one is not only the heir to the natural scene but also 'the Friend of GOD!' Eventually, like all mystics, he proceeds to sights which even he is unable to clarify. To do so is the very essence of the desert journey. When we read even the miraculously lucid Mother Julian, we have to recognize that what she has described falls short of what she had seen. St John of the Cross spoke for her and all mystics when he wrote:

> *The farther that I climbed the height*
> *The less I seemed to understand*
> *The cloud so tenebrous and grand*
> *That there illuminates the night.*

9

Singing the Scene

When (and if) the longest-lasting residual popular element of Britain's religion has to be named, it won't be the Bible or this or that liturgy, or some sacrament-turned-folk-rite, such as a christening or a 'church' wedding, but the hymn. In churches and chapels up and down the land it has become the most enjoyed part of the service and certain hymns are now the summaries of such convincing beliefs and images as an individual is likely to hold in any depth. If the success of televised hymn-singing was analysed, we would see that it derives from staring into a great range of faces made privately devout while engaged in public song. From the beginning men have sung to, and of, their gods, and the splendid anthology known as the Book of Psalms is the oldest collection of such God-addressed songs still in general use all over the world. The Jews, one of the most poetic and musicianly of nations, may have held on to their identity via a strict adherence to the Mosaic law, but it was the Book of Psalms which released their soul to the Gentiles. And along with these holy songs was carried a detailed description of the Palestinian landscape which partly inspired them. Jewish 'psalm' (Greek for the twitching of a harp-string) and Christian 'hymn' (Greek for a song in praise of gods and heroes) merged in a single territory which has become an easily recognized homeland for Christians everywhere. Once a Christian, for the dweller of Leicestershire and Ruislip – or Wollongong or Rangoon for that matter – it became easy and natural to wander amongst the hills and pools of Judaea.

Agnostic William Hazlitt tenderly describes his old father, a Unitarian minister, becoming happily lost in his own special mixture of Judaea and Shropshire.

After being tossed about from congregation to congregation ... he had been relegated to an obscure village, where he was to spend the last thirty years of his life, far from the only converse that he loved, the talk about disputed texts of Scripture, and the cause of civil and religious liberty. Here he passed his days, repining but resigned, in the study of the Bible, and the perusal of the Commentators - huge folios, not easily got through, one of which would outlast a winter! Here were ... glimpses, glimmering notions of the patriarchal wanderings, with palm-trees hovering in the horizon, and processions of camels at the distance of three thousand years ... questions as to the date of creation, predictions of the end of all things, the great lapses of time, the strange mutations of the globe were unfolded with the voluminous leaf, as it turned over; and though the soul might slumber with an hieroglyphic veil of inscrutable mysteries drawn over it, yet it was in a slumber ill-exchanged for all the sharpened realities of sense, wit, fancy or reason. My father's life was comparatively a dream; but it was a dream of infinity and eternity, of death, the resurrection, and a judgment to come!

For most of us it is not the Bible-explainers but the hymn-writers who now weave together this atlas of Holy Land and England. They have a way of presenting dogma undogmatically, and of being able to leap from culture to culture and from age to age, often quite effortlessly - if one omits the inspired toil of the translators. Good hymns hang around for ever, even if, like many of those which were rescued from centuries of neglect by Victorian hymnists of genius such as John Mason Neale, they vanish from mind for a period. The fact was that they perfectly existed and so were capable of making a complete return when reintroduced. What they also did, of course, was to both complicate and enrich the existing hymn-landscape by bringing to it all those earthly-heavenly scenes which the Early Fathers, and poets such as the medieval Peter Abelard, had unified.

'What is a hymn?' St Augustine was asked. His stylish reply is still generally accepted as the ultimate definition.

A hymn is the praise of God by singing. A hymn is a song embodying the praise of God. If there be merely praise but not praise of God it is not a hymn. If there be praise, and praise of God, but not sung, it is not a hymn. For it to be a hymn, it is needful, therefore, for it to have three things - praise, praise of God, and these sung.

A fourth requirement has been added, which is that a hymn is

Misericord, Lavenham, Suffolk

Misericords, those carved brackets under the hinged choir-seats upon which it was permissible to lean during the 'standing' part of the service, are a treasury of early church music. The woodcarvers seem to have been given their imaginative *carte blanche* in this area and they drew fantastically from sacred, mythical and secular sources alike.

The players on the Lavenham misericord owe something to a bestiary and, in the case of the mermaid, something to a popular local legend that these creatures lived in the local ponds. Mermaids descended from the sirens whose wondrous singing would have lured Ulysses and his fellow voyagers to destruction had he not first filled his crew's ears with wax and then had himself tied to the mast. When there was no response to their song the sirens died. Ralph of Coggeshall wrote of a merman which the Orford fishermen caught and sent to church to become a Christian, but he managed to escape. In Matthew Arnold's poem a merman, deserted by his human wife for Christ, hears her 'Singing most joyfully' for the King of Heaven, not for 'the kings of the sea'.

the singing of praise of God by a congregation of people. And here its spell lies. It is no coincidence that the times of the great awakenings of a periodically dozing-off Church produced fresh and often superb hymns. Ambrose, Luther, Charles Wesley, and John Mason Neale understood how to create the collective affirmation of their centuries by means of the hymn. They altered and re-presented old hymns, ancient country songs even, as well as inventing new ones. They fashioned a veritable indestructible pattern of tune and language, knowing that for most people their hymns would be the least complicated path to religious experience. Others rhymed the Psalms, occasionally modishly in landscape terms. Israel's shepherd-poets are found looking up at Ben Nevis or, when Joseph Addison rewrote Psalm 23, contemplating a painting by Claude.

> *When in the sultry glebe I faint,*
> *Or on the thirsty mountain pant,*
> *To fertile vales and dewy meads*
> *My weary wandering steps he leads,*
> *Where peaceful rivers, soft and slow,*
> *Amid the verdant landscape flow.*

Contrast this with George Herbert's,

> *He leads me to the tender grass,*
> *Where I both feed and rest;*
> *Then to the streams that gently pass:*
> *In both I have the best.*

Yet hymns which reflect even the fashionable scenic standards of their day do not in most cases become unfashionable. When they become irrelevant it is not because they are composed in some bygone florid style but because time has proved them hollow and unworthy to stand against so much that remains packed with meaning. Milton's 'Let us, with a gladsome mind', written when he was fifteen, contains descriptions of the heavens which make them sound like the elegant backdrop of a court masque, yet when they are sung within the context of his transcript of the 136th Psalm, with its repeat, 'For his mercies ay endure, Ever faithful, ever sure,' after each brief verse, their very artificiality, or conceit, is what preserves them. What we have in the *English Hymnal* is no more than a comet's-tail glimmer of this boy-poet's treatment of the psalm, but had a modern congregation to sing his entire glittering paraphrase, including the following, so accustomed is it to take every type of hymn in its stride, it would do so quite naturally. Hymns are heavily dated yet during the singing of them they become timeless, their archaisms no obstacle.

> *That by his wisdom did create*
> *The painted Heav'ns so full of state.*
>
> *That did the solid Earth ordain*
> *To rise above the watry plain.*
>
> *That by his all-commanding might,*
> *Did fill the new-made world with light.*
>
> *And caus'd the Golden-tresséd Sun,*
> *All day long his cours to run.*
>
> *The hornéd Moon to shine by night,*
> *Amongst her spangled sisters bright.*
>
> *For his mercies,* etc.

Just as John Constable insisted that what occurred in the sky provided the keynote to the land, so in theological terms the natural heavens provided the hymnists with a dramatic range of cosmic and meteorological images. Hymns are very starry, weatherbeaten, sunburnt, airy, cloudy constructions and, above all, light-filled. Most British hymns correspond with British

Harvest festival at St Peter and St Paul's Church, Alpheton, Suffolk

The village lies between the cornfields made famous by Adrian Bell in his novels *Corduroy, Silver Ley* and *The Cherry Tree*, written in the 1930s, and those celebrated by Robert Bloomfield in *The Farmer's Boy*, 1800. Bloomfield also wrote a poem called 'The Horkey' describing the old 'harvest home' when the last corn was literally brought to the farmer's house to preserve its spirit through the winter. These pagan habits vanished in the nineteenth century when the present exceedingly popular harvest festivals began to take place in the parish churches, and fruit, flowers and cereals were piled all around, and a large loaf laid on the altar.

Hymns were urgently required for these new services, now only second to Christmas in folk estimation. The most famous of these, 'We plough the fields, and scatter', began as an eighteenth-century song in a rural sketch and was only Christianized in translation. The rest of the harvest hymns reflect the ancient pre-industrialized agriculture. Henry Alford wrote 'Come, ye thankful people, come' in 1844 when he was vicar of Wymeswold, Leicestershire, John Hampden Gurney wrote 'Fair waved the golden corn' in 1851 for children in his London parish who were unlikely ever to have seen such a sight, and W. Chatterton Dix his 'To Thee, O Lord, our hearts we raise' in Bristol in 1864. Except in church, never was the 'sacred summer land of harvest' less felt, less seen – even by country people – than it is today. The corn at Alpheton hangs on a pulpit made by the village carpenter during the time of Milton, who wrote,

All things living he doth feed,
His full hand supplies their need.

weather conditions and are strong on the seasonal changes. Their writers have plunged the Gospel in our climate, in our noons and midnights, as well as in many old weather hazards which no longer affect us to any great extent. But before they arrived at a particular country and its climate, there was the question of the globe itself, and it is always surprising when it comes to lines like 'While earth rolls onwards into light', from John Ellerton's, 'The day thou gavest, Lord, is ended' how profound these global references still are. Ellerton's hymn, with its richly elegiac perpetual wave of a tune, was written for a missionary society in 1870. For a hymn addressed to a Britain at the height of its imperial power, its last verse must have come as something of a shock to many worshippers.

> *So be it, Lord; thy throne shall never,*
> *Like earth's proud empires, pass away . . .*

It was the Empire as much as the recognition of a universal God which brought references to a spinning globe into the British hymn. It was comforting for thousands of scattered families to realize that while some rested and some woke many weeks of ship's journey apart, the Church itself remained unsleeping. Many other hymn-writers were concerned with this universal view. Neale, translating a hymn by St John of Damascus, requests 'all that is made', as Dame Julian puts it, to sing in praise of the Resurrection.

> *Now let the heavens be joyful,*
> *And earth her song begin,*
> *The round world keep high triumph,*
> *And all that is therein.*

Expansionist policies expanded Britain's hymn-scenes. If the sun never set on its national interests, it could not set on its Christianity either. Missionary clergy introduced exotic scenery which became a sanctified version of the richly descriptive tales from Africa and India, often illustrated with water-colours and line drawings, which both children and adults loved to read right up until the Second World War, and which disturbed the green land in which England's God traditionally dwelt. This global stretching of what was felt to be England's own hymn imagery was short-lived and Rudyard Kipling himself can be said to have hymned it out of sight in his melancholy 'Recessional' –

> *Far-called, our navies melt away;*
> *On dune and headland sinks the fire:*
> *Lo, all our pomp of yesterday*
> *Is one with Nineveh and Tyre!*

Singing the 'Afric's sunny fountains' and 'Java's spicy breezes' hymns makes one instantly aware that although they were composed in order to redirect Victorian gaze from the land of God's favour to the lands of error, they embody most of all Britain's concern for her scattered nationals, the great host of often youthful soldiers, sailors, administrators and missionaries required to live far from the scenes they dreamed of. However, duty called and as the young Richard Heber, Bishop of Calcutta, put it,

> *Can we, whose souls are lighted*
> *With wisdom from on high,*
> *Can we to men benighted*
> *The lamp of life deny?*

What was very much more startling, although never considered remotely odd at the time, was the ability of Chinese, African and Indian Christian converts to accept an ancient hymnology from Europe and the Middle East containing no references at all to their own landscape. Yet this is what happened. The acceptance became possible because, except for such puzzling things as snow in certain instances, or a Heaven symbolically founded upon architectural ideals unknown to a black tribesman, hymns had a way of maintaining central truths by dealing principally in the universal basics of landscape. Their fields, mountains, rivers, pastures, seas and cities, although originally described to suit the imagination of dwellers on the banks of the Great Ouse or a town in County Wicklow, were able to suit a congregation's own territory the world over. All the same, it remains both mysterious and moving to listen to a Peking church singing hymns that were written for Buckinghamshire or Cornish villagers two hundred years previously.

The foundations of this common entrance to Christianity's hymn-country are, of course, the Psalms. Christ's stories and teachings are steeped in them. So was Everyman's native scene once he had got hold of them in the vernacular. He worked and played, fought and prayed on a local map through which the contours of David's Palestine clearly obtruded. His burn was also Siloam's rill, his Pennine Hebron. Before the Reformation the Book of Psalms was the one book of the Bible to which the laity had unrestrained access and were allowed, and even encouraged, to interpret personally. After the Reformation, few other hymns being permitted, people not only sang the Psalter but walked in it, so to speak. Owen Chadwick says that the version of the Psalter known as Sternhold and Hopkins taught the people of England, and of early reformed Scotland, more about the Christian religion than any other book outside the

New Testament. Thomas Sternhold's and John Hopkins's metrical psalter was published in 1562 by John Day, the great printer from Suffolk whose beautiful Saxon type was one of the splendours of the Elizabethan age. The hymns prefixed 'old' – the 'Old Hundredth', the 'Old 124th', etc. – in today's collections come from this psalter, which for generations was the fount of England's sacred song. Day's Psalter lasted right up until the end of the seventeenth century, when the 'New Version' of rhymed psalms by Nahum Tate (who wrote the libretto for Purcell's *Dido and Aeneas*) and Nicholas Brady, the poet-rector of Stratford-on-Avon, succeeded it. Thomas Hardy's poems and novels reveal how, by the mid nineteenth century, the psalms in their latest shape had become part of the background music of his time. Recalling Evensong in the village church when he was eighteen, a girl by his side, he wrote,

> *On afternoons of drowsy calm*
> *We stood in the panelled pew,*
> *Singing one-voiced a Tate-and-Brady psalm*
> *To the tune of 'Cambridge New'.*
>
> *We watched the elms, we watched the rooks,*
> *The clouds upon the breeze,*
> *Between the whiles of glancing at our books,*
> *And swaying like the trees.*
>
> *So mindless were those outpourings! –*
> *Though I am not aware*
> *That I have gained by subtle thought on things*
> *Since we stood psalming there.*

Over sixty years later, in a strange church, Hardy was to encounter a beloved metrical psalm re-fashioned by Edwin Monk, one of the chief figures of the Anglican musical revival which accompanied the Oxford Movement, and at first resented the changes which he made. Then came acceptance:

> *So, your quired oracles beat till they make me tremble*
> *As I discern your mien in the old attire,*
> *Here in these turmoiled years of belligerent fire*
>   *Living still on – and onward, maybe,*
>   *Till Doom's great day be!*

The Parish Church, Puddletown, Dorset

Puddletown – Piddletown for centuries, until Victorian delicacy altered it – was Thomas Hardy's home town, and the 'Weatherbury' of his Wessex. In his day it had a population of 1,200 which included many of his relatives and the girls he never forgot. Both he and his father occasionally played the violin in the church band and this building was filled with the hymn-singing which haunted him for life. His most complete picture of Puddletown and its farming environment appears in *Far from the Madding Crowd*. One of the men who went to make up the character of Jude lived in Puddletown. Bathsheba and her lovers knew its streets. Tess once travelled through it. On one of her small journeys, momentarily very happy, she sang the 'Benedicite'.

There was a wild side to Puddletown churchgoing, laconically summed up in

Into Church
Out of Church
Into Cat,
Out of Cat,
Into Piddle.

The 'Cat' was the Old Catt Inn and the Piddle the river which received its slops. Tumbling straight from pew to pub, with the singing still going on in one's head, is an experience which has a long history.

When Hardy writes of the psalms, branches, wind and sunlight beat against the church windows, and on the psalter itself in the churchyard. Their language and music escapes from an interior where the living worship, to an exterior where the dead dance. After his first wife's death, after years of mutual bitterness, she withdrawn to the top of Max Gate, he to his study, he even wondered if the 'Old Hundred and Fourth', with its tune by Thomas Ravenscroft (who composed 'Three Blind Mice') might not have brought them together.

> *Why did we never sing it,*
>   *Why never so incline*
> *On Sundays or on weekdays,*
> *Even when soft wafts would wing it*
>   *From your far floor to mine?*
>
> *Shall we that tune, then, never*
>   *Stand voicing side by side*
> *On Sundays or on weekdays?*
> *Or shall we, when for ever*
>   *In Sheol [Hell] we abide,*
>
> *Sing it in desolation . . .*

This psalm-hymn is the famous 'O worship the King' which promises God's 'frail children of dust' a protection that pours through their temporal environment. It is a surging appreciation of a free and natural existence which soars away beyond the scope of Emma and Thomas Hardy's stubborn situation, and they knew it. But 'why did we never sing it', why did they never put a stop to their great uncaring, and make a beginning in that caring which breathed in the air, which shone in the light, which streamed from their local hills and which each, she as a conventional religious woman of her day, and he as the ablest of all writers who have attempted to reveal man's connection with place, knew might well be found beyond gloomy Max Gate? Why? Because Hardy, while in no doubt about the failings of his marriage, had every doubt about the beneficence of nature. All that he might have done in his and his wife's 'desolation' would have been to break the silence with an old tune. In another poem, a woman organist, sacked from the chapel for leading an immoral life, plays the 'Old Hundredth',

'Saint Stephen's', 'Mount Zion', 'New Sabbath', 'Miles-Lane', 'Holy Rest', 'Arabia' and 'Eaton', and realizes that she adores hymn-tunes 'Above all embraces of body', and poisons herself while playing Ken's evening hymn (music by Tallis), in which sleep and death, bed and grave, wind drowsily in and out of each other until they assume a common ordinariness. Hardy is the great melodramatic interpreter of hymn-emotion. Unable to believe in the consecrated scenery which crowds their verses – rocks, rivers, cliffs, trees, etc., for him, had no role in the conveyance of God's love to humanity – he was yet able to dwell with unique effect on the extraordinarily emotive power of hymn-singing itself. Strangely in the circumstance of his agnosticism, the landscape of his novels, like that of the hymns, is frequently 'Judeanized', with overwhelming effect. His characters are often half in the West Country and half in the land of the Books of Ruth, Samuel and the Kings – the latter being his favourite of all the Bible books.

A landscape, the psalmist maintained, was where 'the kings of the earth gather and go by together'. It was stately and filled with strong cities for which men wept when exiled from them and yet, contradictorily, it was also 'no staying place'. It was full of towers and mountains, plants and creatures, all to be admired, and yet it was a mistake for men to think in terms of 'their dwelling-places enduring from one generation to another, and to call the lands after their own names', for each of them would be 'gnawed by death'. All the same, this world was as divine as the next one because God had made it and owned it – 'The earth is the Lord's and all that therein is.' It was there to enjoy; not to enjoy it, or to spoil or destroy it, was sacrilegious.

In the Psalms landscape is utilitarian and poetic at the same time. It preoccupies the senses, intoxicates the imagination and feeds the stomach; its folds are full of sheep, its valleys are so full of corn that they sing; it is marvellously wooded. Animals have their kingdom in it. 'The fir-trees are a dwelling for the stork. The high hills are a refuge for the wild goats, and so are the stony rocks for the conies ... There go the ships and there is that Leviathan whom he had made to take his pastime therein.' Nobody really knows what a Leviathan is or where the word came from. Miles Coverdale, whose superb translation was to bring the Psalmist's native scenes into every Englishman's

reckoning, intended it to represent the ultimate in marine creatures – 'Canst thou draw out leviathan with an hook?' asks Job,
recollecting the vastness of his whale. God comes down into
this wild and tamed landscape 'like rain into a fleece of wool'.
Families thrive in it – 'Thy wife shall be as a fruitful vine
upon the walls of thine house' – and a carving of a vine was
the most popular subject to run along the main beam, inside or
out, of a Tudor house. But the Psalmist's home views do not
gloss over the earth's terrors and miseries, and there are the
horrible pits, mire, clay, hailstones, dark waters, thick clouds
and, worst of all, 'deeps'. Psalm 130, *'De Profundis'*, is the hymn
of a man who is out of his depth, who is treading silt, whose
life is rapidly ebbing. 'My soul fleeth unto the Lord, before the
morning watch, I say, before the morning watch.' We often die
in the small hours. The pastoral climate of the Psalms is so
dominating that one forgets that their authors were never far
from the sea. One of them aligns 'the raging of the sea with the
madness of the people', in a devastating picture of social unrest.
Always they refer to the moon and stars as 'lights'. Centuries
later the Letter of James would speak of every good gift coming
'down from the Father of lights' who, unlike the moon, has 'no
variableness, neither shadow of turning.' It was James who wrote
the words of warning used in the service of Compline, which
means the completion of the day's prayer – 'Be sober, be vigi-
lant, because your adversary the devil, as a roaring lion, walketh
about, seeking whom he may devour.' This lion nightmare has
in this century been given a fresh emphasis in T.F. Powys's
novel *Mr Weston's Good Wine* and in Russell Hoban's novel *The
Lion of Boaz-Jachin and Jachin-Boaz*. The latter is about the youthful son of a map-maker who bequeaths him 'a master map that
would show him where to find whatever he might wish to look
for'. Jachin-Boaz wishes to look for a lion who happens, unbe-
known to him, to be walking about, seeking whom he may
devour. It is a brilliant, fated double-search in which the
master-map provides directions very much like those which
generations of men followed in the Book of Psalms – and
eventually in their hymnbooks.

From the first century on, poets and musicians began to sup-
plement the Psalms with hymns addressed to Christ, but it was
not until the late fourth century that the Church's master

hymn-writer appeared – St Ambrose. It was Ambrose who in-sisted that the whole congregation should sing, and not just priests and choirs, and soloists with good voices. His glorious hymns laid down the pattern of Britain's holy song right up to the Reformation when, being in Latin, they dropped out of use. Known as the Father of Church Song, and credited, along with St Augustine, with the co-authorship of the '*Te Deum*' itself, the Western Church's most splendid non-Biblical hymn, Ambrose's genius was forced to lie in abeyance until the 1840s when a Sussex clergyman, John Mason Neale, was to bring his hymns back into common use by means of a masterly translation.

The Ambrose-Neale hymns are among the ultimate 'creation' songs. They ignore that notion of the earth which sees it as a blessed harvest scene with the occasional dangerous bog and briar, and present it as a time-held sphere in whose light and dark revolutions men and the Trinity are ceaselessly involved. Their imagery has a blinding colour-laden brightness like birds' wings. In them, Ambrose-Neale begs Christ to bestow his grace 'on our senses here below', and the Holy Spirit to 'inflame with perfect love each sense'. So far as the natural world exists in them, it is purely one of night and morning. Christ and his followers, the latter temporarily trapped in Time, wheel across an earth which is featureless except for the short and long sha-dows of the natural day. And yet these great and ancient hymns were not written for saints and ecstatics but for the ordinary worshipper, the agriculturalists and city-dwellers of the late Roman Empire, people with their feet on the ground even if their eyes were on heaven. Victorian Tractarians taught the Am-brose-Neale hymns to the rough hordes of the factory towns, where Christ for some became a preserver of their sanity in a quite literal, and even in a medical and scientific way. 'Come, thou Redeemer of the Earth' they sang in the sulphurous slums, and 'Creator of the earth and sky' and 'O Trinity of Blessed Light'. The rich sang the same in Kensington. Hardy, in his Journal, wrote:

A service at St Mary Abbots ... The pale crucified figure rises up from a parterre of London bonnets and artificial hair-coils, as viewed from the back where I am ... When the congregation rises there is a rustling of silks like that of the Devil's wings in Paradise Lost ... They pray in the Litany as if under enchantment. Their real life is spinning on beneath this apparent one of calm, like the District Railway-trains underground just by – throbbing, rushing, hot, concerned with next week, last week ...

Bishop Ambrose of Milan exceeds all other hymn-writers in his use of the metaphor of brightness but there were later poets who came very near to him in this luminous sphere, particularly the fourteenth-century German monk Thomas à Kempis in his 'Light's Abode, celestial Salem' and the seventeenth-century Welsh medic Henry Vaughan, who reasoned,

> *Men might look and live as glow-worms shine,*
> *And face the moon:*
> *Wise Nicodemus saw such light*
> *As made him know his God by night.*

Ambrose's hymns are like brands hurtling through the centuries, igniting whoever comes close to them. In religious terms they immolate all that is trivial and irrelevant. In his Vulgate version of the Old Testament, how often his eye must have rested on the command, *'Fiat lux'* – let there be light. From his Italian see, via his hymns, he was able to show to the north what Shelley called 'the white radiance of eternity', a way of seeing which was to affect the look of the land as well as men's glimpses of heaven for ages to come. G.S. Fraser, writing of T.S. Eliot, says that 'images especially from his boyhood memories of New England, granite shores, pine trees, sea mists, gulls, the noise of the sea and its salt smell, recur frequently. It was as if Christian belief had re-baptized nature for him.' Hymn-priests like Ambrose (and his genius-translator John Mason Neale) do indeed re-baptize nature. The sixth-century Fortunatus, recovering from a long spell of near-blindness, tells the world in his Easter morning processional hymn that 'Light on the third day returns' and that it must delight in 'the fair beauty of earth, from the death of the winter arising' – resurrection inside the church and also outside in the fields and woods.

But the Christian epitome of residential perfection was not the village but the city. Cities were good. They expressed man's highest social achievement. It was a privilege to be a citizen of one of them. Christ himself was approached as the prince of a city state – that lover of Bethany! Humanity travelling to his city called it Jerusalem, although in the old hymns it often

The Shepherd of Duddo (Northumberland)

'*There is very little that is romantic about sheep, though for some reason they enter both literature and painting in an idyllic manner not bestowed to an equal extent upon other stock, while it will be some time before the shepherd loses his poetic place ... He is still conceived of in a haze, for few people know what he actually does ... And he is seldom seen searching for a dear lost sheep and rejoicing over it when found more than over the ninety-nine others that did not go astray; he is more often discovered searching their bodies for maggots ...*'

John Stewart Collis
The Worm Forgives the Plough

Not for ever in green pastures
 Do we ask our way to be;
But the steep and rugged pathway
 May we tread rejoicingly.

Not for ever by still waters
 Would we idly rest and stay;
But would smite the living fountains
 From the rocks along our way.

Mrs L. M. Willis (1864)

sounds like a perfected version of Athens, Rome, Florence or even London. Every good town provided its inhabitants, and those who farmed within sight of it, with all the 'Jerusalem' imagery they needed. Heaven was each man's nearby earthly town made flawless. It was constructed from the best building materials which nature could supply and ornamented with its rarest gems. Inside, it was buoyant, restless, ecstatic. It was crowded and loud with song. Its social structure, like that below, was hierarchic, as Raphael's paintings and the tremendous west window of King's College, Cambridge, show, but with a secure lodging for every redeemed soul for ever. Order and harmony reign. 'Jerusalem is a city that is at unity with itself,' says Psalm 122, and although the author of the Letter to the Hebrews reminded Christ's first followers that 'here we have no continuing city, but we seek one to come', architecturally the first soon laid down the requirements for the second. The longing of the early Christians for the city of God which the most ancient hymns reflect bears little resemblance to the morbid heaven-anticipated sentiments of the mid nineteenth century, although the many popular hymns of this latter period which so hanker after death and 'rest' do force one to remember the dreadful conditions in which countless toilers lived, and from which death was – as they frankly admitted – a 'release'. And so thus to journey on to where a homely God sat waiting in a perpetually spring-like English meadow, and to spotless clothes and timeless singing, and to have their favourite earthly scenes translated into metaphysics, or what Sabine Baring-Gould called, 'The land of pure delight'.

St John, sentenced to slave in the Patmos saltmines and writing coded encouragement to the little churches which St Paul had founded in Asia Minor, told them of a dream he had had of a *new* Jerusalem. It was square in shape and so exquisite in its immaterialism that John could only describe it by using the names of earth's rarest minerals, or mined substances. From then on this jewel-box of a heaven has presented a strongly contrasting image to the hymn-writers to that conveyed by Christ himself who, when pressed, refused to picture his kingdom as a perfected version of an Eastern city-state. To the dying thief, he did not say, 'Today you will be with me in the City of God', but in 'Paradise', or God's safe garden.

But the most influential aspect of St John's heaven where the hymn-writers are concerned is its light. In the Greek it has a *clean* river flowing through it, and trees of life growing on the river banks, and a source of illumination which lay quite outside that of the natural element. 'And there shall be no night there; and they need no candle, neither light of the sun, the Lord God giveth them light.' It was this light, more than the most inspired of other allegorical means, that the poets and musicians of the Christian centuries knew had to be captured in a hymn for it to survive. All the same, the most beautiful and loved of the world's cities remained the most popular metaphor of life in the world to come, and the finest buildings, the walls of Chester, the towers of Ely, the palaces of London and Edinburgh and a man's own home with its sermonizing doors, windows and rooms for being awake or asleep in, tended to direct his thoughts less to total enlightenment than towards some ultra-citizenship and domesticity. Cities, cathedrals, churches, houses and gates exist for us to be inside them, and the long list of 'Jerusalem' hymns are full of pleas for entrance, as well as of staggering descriptions of what the soul will find within. Up until the Reformation England possessed seventeen cathedrals, both Romanesque and Gothic (terms unknown to their builders) and their stunning interiors, as well as their soaring external stone in the landscape, pointed the medieval mind to heaven. After the Reformation, the hymn-writers obliged the new Jerusalem to take in all kinds of rural acres, and by the eighteenth century Samuel Johnson could write,

> *City of God, how broad and far*
> *Outspread thy walls sublime!*
> *The true thy chartered freemen are*
> *Of every age and clime*

moving easily from this good civic scene to one of rustic bliss in which villagers toil idealistically, like those in Stubbs's painting 'The Reapers', as they united in 'One working band, one harvest-song'.

But the heaven of the earlier hymn-writers was not always massively architectural. The Parisian Peter Abelard, born when Durham, Peterborough and St Alban's cathedrals were being created as sublime confiners of sacred space, directs the singer to his 'dear native land' – to that continuity of the immortal element in nature 'Which having been must ever be', as Wordsworth put it. The word 'mansion', used by Tyndale in his translation of St John's Gospel, instead of 'abode', furthered the popular notion of heaven as a magnificent house with separate rooms for each of the redeemed. What Christ was promising his followers was an abiding place, adding, 'I am the way' to it. St Augustine's concept of 'The City of God' was that of a communal state of being, divinely administered and perfectly activated by love. But these inspired definitions have never been enough for a religion which, almost from the beginning, felt the need to express itself in buildings, and generally speaking our hymns reflect a soul journeying from 'thy courts below' (the parish churches) to 'thy courts above', as Henry Light paraphrased the 84th Psalm. The author of this psalm is most insistent that he must have his *home* with God and reminds him that even the sparrow has a house. The poet doesn't demand anything more than a shelter and says that he would rather be a doorkeeper in God's house than live in style where God was absent. William Blake correctly understood the Christian requirement to work towards building a 'city of God' wherever one happened to be, and his 'Jerusalem' challenges the defilement of Milton's England by modern industrialists. This, still the most powerful of all conservationist hymns, is the first of a poem-sequence based on John Milton's idea of a man's being the centre or hub of all things wherever he lives, or whoever he happens to be.

> . . . *every Space that a Man views round his dwelling-place,*
> *Standing on his own roof, or in his garden . . .*
> *Such Space is his Universe:*
> *And on its verge the Sun rises & sets, the Clouds bow*
> *To meet the flat Earth & the Sea in such an order'd Space:*
> *The Starry heavens reach no further, but here bend and set*
> *On all sides, & the two Poles turn on their valves of gold;*
> *And if he move his dwelling-place, his heavens also move*
> *Wher'er he goes . . .*

These natural limits of what each can see from the place where we happen to live, Blake is saying, must also contain our vision, otherwise we shall ruin them. Jerusalem and an England profaned by its materialism, alike, have to be given back 'into the

Little Langdale, Westmorland

The country through which George Fox sent the Friends' doctrine to be fixed to market-crosses. A valley path leading between hills and mountains, and skirting a stream, locked in solitude, is the essence of hymn landscape. For Isaiah the poet a valley was a humble place which, due to its intrinsic virtue, would one day be exalted. But the heights, due to their dominance, would be brought low, whilst the crooked ways would be made straight and the rough places plain. Mary's song extolling the glory of the Lord transfers this reversal of fortunes to mankind. The mighty have been put down from their seat and the humble and meek (free from self-will and pride) have been exalted.

Farming communities in hilly territory, separated from each other by spidery sheep-tracks and cartways, dwelt in a doubly religious scene, the one of a divinely protected homeliness and labour, the other of elemental creation. With the sublime being of the *Veni Creator Spiritus* in residence on the mountain-tops, the heights could only remain a proud throne and the valleys a lowly but 'singing' natural home for men. Huge shadows and moods play across such country. 'Love is of the valley,' wrote Tennyson, 'come thou down / And find him.'

arms of God'. These 'Milton' poems of his are mystical nature-study lessons for a society which is abandoning the profits from its fields for the profits from its factories. In them, Blake tells his countrymen that God has sent to 'two servants, Whitefield and Wesley', to warn them against the half-life which they are experiencing, and he appeals to their common sense. Are they 'idiots or madmen' to allow such things to happen to their environment? Charles Wesley spent most his life riding the length and breadth of this strangely changing scene, and re-teaching the Gospel via thousands of hymns which he wrote himself. It is ironic that by the polishing of a single rural line in Wesley's most famous Christian hymn, 'Hark! the herald-angels sing', Whitefield (it is thought) unwittingly destroyed the few words which summed up what was actually happening all over Georgian Britain as Wesley and his followers restored its faith.

'Hark! how all the welkin rings, glory to the King of Kings,' Wesley had written, inspired by vast congregational hymn-singings at toil-amphitheatres such as Gwennap Pit in Cornwall. The 'welkin' was that arch of sky which Blake describes as forming each man's 'universe', and to make it 'ring' had long been the way to celebrate it. Right up until the present century harvesters made the cut fields echo with their shouts. 'Hark, how all the welkin rings' has been happily restored in the modern *English Hymnal*.

Wesley's hymns were often taught by 'throwing' their lines, one by one, to the congregation, a method used later by music-hall artists – Gracie Fields did it with 'Sally' – except that what Wesley's audiences caught was a rich mixture of contemplative and social Christianity so exultantly set to music that it made them both prayerful and activist. In 'Hail the day that sees him rise', he makes Christ 'love the earth he leaves', and although, for a poet who spent the greater part of his life on a British journey, there are minimal references to its scenery in so vast a hymn opus, there is equally no repudiation of it. In 'Love Divine, all loves excelling' men are 'changed from glory into glory', which was a sharp reminder to those who degraded their fellows that in doing so they were defiling a sacred creation. His *Journal* too is almost devoid of landscape descriptions. Weather, rough roads, careful place-names, that is about all. For the most prodigious of all hymn-writers, Charles Wesley's Britain was mapped out in a series of wild crowds which had to be first tamed, and then exhilarated, by a religious language which became most potent and beautiful when sung. 'The multitude roars on every side', he wrote, as he channelled the roar into what was once nervously called 'Methodisty' singing. When in Bristol he was told of a child's dream. A little girl dreamed that she had gone for a walk with Christ.

While we were walking, he said, 'Sing.' I said, 'What shall I sing?' And he said, 'Sing praises unto the King of the place.'

Wesley's favourite preaching and hymn-teaching place was Gwennap Pit, near Redruth. He said it was by far the finest natural amphitheatre in the kingdom. Old mine workings had collapsed, causing a meadow to fall in shallowly in the form of a vast grassy saucer, and this accidental concavity produced

Gwennap Pit, Redruth, Cornwall (Francis Frith Collection)

The whole of the Wesley family were considerable musicians and for over a century they were in the van of the movement which made both congregational and choir singing a major element in worship. John Wesley's evangelizing contemporary, Whitefield, had led thousands of singing converts along the Gloucestershire lanes, to the horror of the authorities. Wesley 'managed' his rapt multitudes by crowding them into natural declivities, or sometimes into huge disused industrial buildings, such as the old gun foundry in Finsbury. He was embarrassed by open-air preaching at first but after finding that the Sermon on the Mount provided 'a pretty remarkable precedent' he stopped worrying about respectability and set out on what was to be a lifetime's searching for what he called his 'building materials' – i.e. the ordinary people, so long neglected by the Church. He was a little man with the vivid face of an artist. He spoke eloquently, though never for more than twenty minutes, and he made Britain sing.

In Cornwall his mission to the tinners, a terribly abused industrial group, eventually transformed the entire West Country. 'We reached Gwennap a little before six, and found the plain covered from end to end: it was supposed that there were ten thousand people . . . I could not conclude until it was so dark (it was a September evening) we could scarce see one another; and there was on all sides the deepest attention; none speaking, stirring, or scarce looking aside. Surely

here, in a temple not made with hands, was God "worshipped in the beauty of holiness"!'

Gwennap Pit became a conservatory of song. Soon, Methodists all over the land were being called by their Cornish nickname, 'the Canorum', from the Cornish *canor*, singer.

the acoustic advantages of a Greek theatre. He preached there seventeen times in all, to immense congregations. In 1773,

The people both filled the pit and covered the ground round about to a considerable distance. So that supposing the place to be four score yards square, there must be about two-and-thirty thousand people; the largest assembly I ever preached to. Yet I found all could hear, even to the skirts of the congregation. Perhaps the first time a man of seventy has been heard by thirty thousand persons at once.

Two years later he watched the packed Gwennap Pit singing the hymns he had written, the tinners and their families, and Cornishmen of all classes united and transported by music. It was, he wrote in his *Journal*,

the most magnificent spectacle to be seen on this side of heaven. No music on earth is comparable to the sound of many thousand voices ... I think this is my *ne plus ultra*. I shall scarcely see a larger congregation till we meet in the air.

Gwennap Pit was eventually lined with thirteen circles of turf seats and in the 1830s borrowed by the Chartists for their meetings. Wesley's control of the music there, and the tinners'

The organ, Roseworthy Methodist Chapel, West Cornwall

Charles Wesley's legacy to Cornwall had to be housed in hundreds of granite and slate chapels, and these especially fitted out for Methodist hymnody. Many of his hymns had been composed and sung in wild weather on hillsides, when he and his 'world' parish were soaked to the skin, and with 'hurling, fighting and drinking, and all manner of wickedness' raging around him. His brother John actually published – in America – the first Church of England hymnbook, and by 1738 they had, between them, persuaded Anglican Methodists at Oxford of the importance of hymn-singing in worship and evangelization. Thus began the much praised (and much mocked) 'Methody' song. It now permeates modern Christendom.

The invention of the harmonium by a Danish doctor, who was also fascinated by acoustics, and its eventual mass production, chiefly in Boston, turned countless chapels into vast or minute concert halls and had a lasting effect on community singing. Originally called 'orgue expressif', these plaintive reed organs have accompanied the rhythmic roar of packed congregations for over a century but are now being replaced by inferior electronic sounds.

rapturous response to it, must have been like that of the conductor and the promenaders in the Albert Hall. Rich strains, rather than echoes, of the Gwennap tradition of hymn-singing can still be heard in chapels, on Cornish harbour walls, and from pubs, and on every Whit Monday the great Pit itself rocks to 'O for a Thousand Tongues' and other favourites. Cornish singing has been compared with that of the Welsh, but it is wilder, less florid. Wesley, it has to be remembered, preached several times on the level at Gwennap before high winds drove him to take shelter in its commodious Pit.

In the evening I preached at Gwenap. I stood on the wall, in the calm, still evening, with the setting sun behind me, and an almost innumerable multitude before, behind, and on either hand. Many likewise sat on the little hills ... but they could all hear distinctly while I read, 'The disciple is not above his Master.'

Because Wesley's *Journal* contains only a functional view of landscape it would be a mistake to believe that such an out-of-doors poet saw nothing else. There was just no time to write it down.

The best hymn-writers see this world as a passing scene, but one not to be missed where its natural sights are concerned. Hymns such as John Keble's 'Lord, in thy name thy servants plead', in which a Cotswold village says its Rogation prayers, or Christina Rossetti's 'In the bleak mid-winter', which so perfectly brings together a bitter English country day and the coming of Christ's Kingdom, and there are hundreds more of them, are earthy but not earth-bound. That is the secret of their popularity. The psalms excepted, the proto-earth-delighting hymns are the 'Benedicite', which is part of the Book of Daniel from the Septuagint, and St Francis's 'Canticle of the Sun'. From these there has descended many a nation's religious appreciation of its particular landscape. 'Two worlds are ours,' reminded Keble, a mystic one and that 'plain as the sea and sky'. Curiously for the world at large, the predominance of the hymns found in the most used collections, *Hymns Ancient and Modern* and the *English Hymnal*, even if their words generalize British scenery, are most evocatively tied to distinct geographical locations by the custom of giving their tunes the names of places. Thus, the familiar gazetteer of song. Vaughan Williams said that the hymns of Christendom show more clearly than anything else that a unity of spirit actually exists in the Church, and so indeed it does in this form. But it is pleasant to find 'Forest Green' ('O Little Town of Bethlehem'), 'Stockport' ('Christians, awake!'), 'Saffron Walden' ('His are the thousand sparkling rills'), 'Aylesbury' ('Breathe on me, breath of God'), 'Chislehurst' ('Hail the day that sees him rise'), 'Little Cornard' ('Hills of the north, rejoice'), Parry's 'Bournemouth', Holst's 'Sheen', S.S. Wesley's 'Colchester' and Purcell's 'Westminster Abbey' – and so many more – bringing together in the deepest association Britain's religious song and map. 'In Christian song,' says the Preface to *The English Hymnal*, 'Churches have forgotten their quarrels and men have lost their limitations, because they have reached the higher ground where the soul is content to affirm and adore.'

'O the power of church-music!' wrote John Donne, somehow without conceit as he listened to his own cathedral choir singing his own hymn, 'Wilt thou forgive'.

St Patrick, the Scot who converted Ireland, wrote a stupendous hymn in which he 'binds' to himself, first the love of Christ, and then the 'virtues' of nature – all that he would have seen in Scotland as a boy, around Tours, where he studied as a young man, and, most memorably, in the wild scenery of Sligo, Armagh and Antrim. Translated first by Dr Petrie from an ancient Irish manuscript in the Library of Trinity College, Dublin, in 1839, it was actually released once more into the Christian world half a century later by the indefatigable Mrs Alexander. Known as 'St Patrick's Breastplate', its theme is the advice of St Paul to the Ephesians, when he told them to 'put on the whole armour of God'. An important part of Patrick's spiritual armour was 'the stable earth, the deep salt sea', wind, sun, stars, 'the old eternal rocks'. Legend had it that it was with such a landscape-creator God as his protection that he annually set off to argue it out with the violently recalcitrant pagan king at Tara. The latter worshipped nature, and the wonders of Meath would have provided him and the saint with a common ground for adoration. Incorporating the green divinities into Christianity was less a wile by the early missionaries than a recognition that these divinities too were witnesses to the gospel of love. But it was often tough for those who, naturally, and like the king at Tara, found it impossible to conceive of anything more life-giving than the sun.

Hymn scenes have ranged all the way from the cosmic to the village ditch, and their compass is best expressed in Erasmus Darwin's long and strange poem, 'The Economy of Vegetation', some lines from which suggest such contemporary dilemmas as black holes and nuclear destruction, and what next? Calling the stars the 'Flowers of the sky', Darwin tells them,

> *ye too to age must yield,*
> *Frail as your silken sisters of the field!*
> *Star after star from Heaven's high arch shall rush,*
> *Suns sink on suns, and systems systems crush,*
> *Headlong, extinct, to one dark centre fall,*
> *And Death and Night and Chaos mingle all!*
> *– Till o'er the wreck, emerging from the storm,*
> *Immortal* NATURE *lifts her changeful form,*
> *Mounts from her funeral pyre on wings of flame,*
> *And soars and shines, another and the same.*

It was in this atmosphere of what might be called primal searchings by science and the Church that a twenty-eight-year-old clergyman, too sickly, he felt, for ordinary parish duties, accepted the Trollopian position of warden to an almshouse at East Grinstead and, having already set in motion forces which were to re-sanctify Britain's then often sordid parish churches, set out to release into them a magnificent hymnology which had also been forgotten for centuries. The year 1848, when Neale settled in East Grinstead, was to be the *annus mirabilis* of the English hymnbook, and if any one spot is to be held in hymnal veneration, let it be there. At East Grinstead John Mason Neale set out to return to the Church its earliest, best song, hymns by the Greek and Latin masters which had been silenced at the Reformation. He incurred the wrath of his own Catholic party, which was against any hymn being sung in the vernacular, and was himself in turn uncharitable, to put it mildly, towards almost every other hymnody, damning Isaac Watts (his *bête noire*), Wesley ('Among the Wesleyans it is well known that the Hymnbook has almost usurped the place of the Bible'), Cowper ('Probably the worst original collection of hymns ever put forth is the Olney Book'), and all the translations of the ancient hymns which other Tractarians, as well as himself, were anxious to put back into use. Among an almost blanket condemnation of the hymns then being sung in church, Neale singles out Toplady's 'Rock of Ages' for qualified praise. It was, he said, 'undoubtedly the best original hymn in the English language, provided it be taken as a penitential devotion, and not as the ordinary and proper expression of a Christian's everyday prayers'. It was a curious choice for Neale to make. Toplady was a fervent, narrow Calvinist, an English clergyman converted in an Irish barn and, as a later critic said, no poet or inspired singer. Yet this particular hymn of his swept the world.

Neale's holy song was inspired by his insistence on a continuum, a ceaseless flow of the best. The Latin poet Adam of St Victor was his ideal, but there were many more who excited him:

It is a magnificent thing to pass along the far-reaching vistas of hymns – from the sublime self-containedness of St Ambrose to the more fervid inspiration of St Gregory, the exquisite typology of Venantius Fortunatus, the lovely painting of St Peter Damiani, the crystal-like simplicity of St Notker, the scriptural calm of Godescalus, the subjective loveliness of St Bernard, till all culminate in the full blaze of glory which surrounds Adam of St Victor, the greatest of all.

Soon after freeing the old Latin hymns from their time-lock, Neale introduced into England the magnificent hymnology of the Eastern Church so perfectly that an Orthodox monk has, only recently, attributed to him 'a Greek soul'. Neale's masterpieces are 'Creator of the stars of night', 'Come, thou Redeemer of the earth' (St Ambrose), 'A great and mighty wonder' (St Germanus), Bede's 'The hymn for conquering Martyrs raise', 'O Blest Creator of the Light', the hymns of Prudentius, the Greek 'Christian dost thou see them', the sublime, 'The Royal banners forward go' (Fortunatus), 'Ye Choirs of New Jerusalem' (St Fulbert) and 'The Day of Resurrection' (St John Damascene). Not quite so good though lasting, were his own original hymns. His 'Good King Wenceslas' was first sung in the streets of East Grinstead by the carol parties which he loved to get up. He died there in 1866 on the Feast of the Transfiguration, aged forty-eight, a translating genius who was able to let modern Anglicans discover access to the hymn-filled courts and temples of the early Christian world.

Frequently through history the clergy have restrained congre-

Leebotwood Parish Church, Shropshire

Leebotwood stands by the main road from Ludlow to Shrewsbury, and between the Long Mynd and Wenlock Edge. It is one of the village churches of George Herbert's childhood landscape, and of the borrowed country of A. E. Housman's maturity. Nearby is Wroxeter, the Roman Uriconium. Housman wrote an agnostic 'Easter Hymn' which begins,

If in that Syrian garden, ages slain,
You sleep, and know not you are
*   dead in vain,*
Nor even in dreams behold how dark
*   and bright*
Ascends in smoke and fire by day
*   and night*
The hate you died to quench and
*   could but fan,*
Sleep well and see no morning, son
*   of man.*

The Leebotwood congregation have been singing William Bright's eucharistic hymn, 'And now, O Father, mindful of the love', written in 1875.

gational hymn-singing and even now there are many priests who know little about it as an act of collective worship for which there still remains a hunger. Among all the outpourings of religious analysis it would be hard to find an intelligent and inspired account of what occurs to the individual worshipper of Christ as he takes up the tune and words of a fine and loved

Wrynose Pass, Cumbria

In November days,
When vapours, rolling down the valleys, made
A lonely scene more lonesome; among woods
At noon; and 'mid the calm of summer nights,
When, by the margin of the trembling lake,
Beneath the gloomy hills, I homeward went
In solitude, such intercourse was mine:
'Twas mine among the fields both day and night,
And by the waters all the summer long.

From 'Influence of Natural Objects in calling forth
and strengthening the Imagination of Boyhood
and Early Youth' by William Wordsworth

Nox et tenebrae et nubila

Ye clouds and darkness, hosts of night,
That breed confusion and affright,
Begone! o'erhead the dawn shines clear,
The light breaks in and Christ is here.

Earth's gloom flees broken and dispersed,
By the sun's piercing shafts coerced:
The day-star's eyes rain influence bright,
And colours glimmer back to sight.

Prudentius, b. A D 348, translated by
Robert Pope

hymn. This singing of encapsulated spiritual thought of every age provides for the ordinary Christian the best historical understanding of his faith that he is ever likely to receive. Hymns, like secular songs, are firmly dated but, because they deal with the eternal, the best of them cannot become obsolete. They are religion's most enduring popular art. They were composed on walks, in studies, gardens, on ships, in chancels, under mountains – everywhere – but if Britain had to choose its own hymn-site extraordinary, as it were, a single location where the hymn was totally understood and re-created as both a liturgical essential and a delight, then it might well be East Grinstead. John Mason Neale recovered the finest of long-lost hymns of the Western and Eastern Churches there. His grave lies at the south-east corner of St Swithun's churchyard. St Margaret's Convent, which he founded, designed by George Street, stands to the north-west of the almshouses of which he was warden. His Church treated him very badly in his lifetime, the Bishop of Chichester, Dr Gilbert, inhibiting him from holding services 'in a certain unconsecrated building known as Sackville Chapel'. For fifteen years the bishop's ban remained. The poet-scholar who was to single-handedly so enrich Anglicanism was a Puseyite, and that was that. Neale was a fighter and a row developed which, given Neale's poverty, benign family life (four children), genius and integrity, was pure Trollope. Yet through this archetypal Victorian scene, architecture, polemics and all, soared the communal praise of the youthful Church, its springtime language and notes, dustless and pleasure-filled. Neale maintained that he did no more than go to the 'great treasury', as he called it, and return to those to whom it belonged what he discovered there. But it was more than that.

Bibliography

Anderson, M.D., *History and Imagery in British Churches*, Murray, 1971.

Augustine, St, *Confessions*, trans. R. S. Pine-Coffin, Penguin, 1971.

Beaumont, W., and Taylor, A., *Wormingford*, Vineyard Press, 1983.

Bernanos, George, *The Diary of a Country Priest*, trans. Pamela Morris, Fontana, 1960.

Bigmore, Peter, *The Bedfordshire and Huntingdonshire Landscape*, Hodder & Stoughton, 1979.

Book of Common Prayer.

Bottrall, Margaret, *George Herbert*, Murray, 1954.

Bright, Allan H., *New Light on 'Piers Plowman'*, OUP, 1928.

Brittain, Vera, *In the Steps of John Bunyan*, Rich & Cowan, 1945.

Browning, Elizabeth Barrett, *Poems*, Warne, 1892.

Bullett, Gerald, *The English Mystics*, Michael Joseph, 1950.

Bunyan, John, *Grace Abounding*, intr. G. B. Harrison, Dent, 1979.
   The Pilgrim's Progress, ed. R. Sharrock, Penguin, 1965.

Carlyle, Thomas, *Sartor Resartus*, Chapman & Hall, 1888.

Chadwick, Owen, *The Reformation*, Penguin, 1964.

Charles, Amy M., *A Life of George Herbert*, Cornell University Press, 1977.

Clifton-Taylor, Alec, *The Cathedrals of England*, Thames & Hudson, 1979.

Cloud of Unknowing, The, and Other Works, trans. Clifton Wolters, Penguin, 1978.

Coghill, Nevill, *Langland: Piers Plowman*, Longman, 1964.

Colman, Thomas W., *English Mystics of the Fourteenth Century*, Epworth, 1938.

Constable, John, *Correspondence*, ed. R. B. Beckett, Boydell, 1976.

Cook, Olive, and Hutton, Graham, *English Parish Churches*, Thames & Hudson, 1976.

Cory, William, *Letters and Journals*, ed. Francis Warre Cornish, OUP, 1897.

Cottrell, Leonard, *The Roman Forts of the Saxon Shore*, HMSO, 1967.

Crabbe, George, *The Parish Register*, Murray, 1838.

Daniell, J. J., *The Life of George Herbert*, SPCK, 1902.

De Brisay, Kay, *The Red Hills of Essex*, Colchester Archaeological Group, 1975.

Dickens, A. G., *The English Reformation*, Batsford, 1964.

Dictionary of National Biography, OUP, 1975.

Ecclestone, Alan, *Yes to God*, Darton, Longman & Todd, 1975.

Edwards, David L., *Christian England*, Collins, 1983.

Eliot, T. S., *The Complete Poems and Plays*, Faber, 1969.

English Hymnal, The, OUP, 1957.

Fox, George, *The Journal*, ed. Norman Penney, Dent, 1924.

Foxe, John, *Book of Martyrs*, 1563.

Golding, William, *Darkness Visible*, Faber, 1979.

Goodenough, S., *The Country Parson*, David & Charles, 1983.

Grieve, Hilda, *The Great Tide*, Essex County Council, 1959.

Hardy, F. E., *The Early Life of Thomas Hardy*, Macmillan, 1928.

Hardy, Thomas, *The Collected Poems*, Macmillan, 1952.

Hargreaves, C., and Greenshields, M., *Catalogue of the Bunyan Meeting, Library and Museum, Bedford*, Bunyan Meeting, 1955.

Hart, A. Tindal, *The Man in the Pew, 1558-1660*, Baker, 1966.

Hazlitt, William, *Selected Writings*, ed. Ronald Blythe, Penguin, 1970.

Heaney, Seamus, *Wintering Out*, Faber, 1972.

Herbert, George, *Works*, ed. F. E. Hutchinson, OUP, 1978.
   The English Poems of George Herbert, ed. C. A. Patrides, Dent, 1974.

Hoban, Russell, *Riddley Walker*, Cape, 1980.

Hoskins, W. G., *The Making of the English Landscape*, Penguin, 1970.

Hymns Ancient and Modern, William Clowes.

Julian, John, *Dictionary of Hymnology*, Murray, 1907.

Julian of Norwich, *Revelations of Divine Love*, tr. Clifton Wolters, Penguin, 1982.

Keyes, Sidney, *Collected Poems*, Routledge, 1945.

Langland, William, *Piers the Ploughman*, translated into modern English by J. F. Goodridge, Penguin, 1959.

Leech, Kenneth, 'Nourishing an Urban Desert', *The Times*, March 1983.

Lough, A. G., *The Influence of John Mason Neale*, SPCK, 1962.

Loukes, Harold, *The Quaker Contribution*, SCM, 1965.

Mandelstam, Osip, *Selected Poems*, trans. C. Brown and W. S. Merwin, Penguin, 1973.

Masefield, John, *The Everlasting Mercy*, Sidgwick & Jackson, 1911.

Newell, E. J., *The History of the Welsh Church to the Dissolution*, Elliot Stock, 1895.

Pelphrey, Brant, *Love was his Meaning: the Theology and Mysticism of Julian of Norwich*, Salzburg Studies in English Literature, 1982.

Pevsner, Nikolaus, The Buildings of England series, Penguin.

Pownall, David, *Between Ribble and Lune*, Gollancz, 1980.

Rolle, Richard, *The Fire of Love*, trans. Clifton Wolters, Penguin, 1972.

St John of the Cross, *Poems*, trans. Roy Campbell, Harvill Press, 1951.

Sayer, Frank, *Julian and her Norwich*, Sayer, 1973.

Thomas, Keith, *Religion and the Decline of Magic*, Weidenfeld & Nicolson, 1971.

Tibbutt, H. G., *Bunyan Meeting, Bedford, 1650–1950*, Bunyan Meeting, 1951.

What They Said about John Bunyan, Bedford County Council, 1952.

Tournier, Michel, *Friday, or the Other Island*, Penguin, 1969.

Traherne, Thomas, *Poems, Centuries and Three Thanksgivings*, ed. Anne Ridler, OUP, 1966.

The Way to Blessedness, ed. Margaret Bottrell, Faith Press, 1962.

Turner, James, *The Shrouds of Glory: Six Studies in Martyrdom*, Cassell, 1958.

Vipont, Elfrida, *George Fox and the Valiant Sixty*, Hamish Hamilton, 1975.

Waddell, Helen, *The Wandering Scholars*, Constable, 1952.

Walton, Izaak, *The Life of George Herbert*, Pickering, 1848.

Warner, Marina, *Joan of Arc: the Image of Female Heroism*, Weidenfeld & Nicolson, 1981.

Watkin, E. I., *On Julian of Norwich and in Defence of Margery Kempe*, University of Exeter, 1979.

Young, Percy M., *Alice Elgar*, Dobson, 1978.

Index